Observations on
International
Tourism
Communications

**FIRST WORLD CONFERENCE
ON TOURISM COMMUNICATIONS**
Madrid, Spain, 29-30 January 2004

**PRIMERA CONFERENCIA MUNDIAL
SOBRE LAS COMUNICACIONES EN EL TURISMO**
Madrid (España), 29 y 30 de Enero de 2004

**PREMIÈRE CONFÉRENCE MONDIALE
SUR LA COMMUNICATION DANS LE DOMAINE DU TOURISME**
Madrid (Espagne), 29 et 30 Janvier 2004

TOURCOM

OBSERVATIONS ON INTERNATIONAL TOURISM COMMUNICATIONS
Report from the First World Conference on Tourism Communications

ISBN: 92-844-0711-7

Publicado en mayo 2004 por la Organización Mundial del Turismo
Published in May 2004 by the World Tourism Organization
Publiée en mai 2004 par l'Organisation mondiale du tourisme

WTO - OMT
Capitán Haya, 42 - 28020 Madrid (España)

www.world-tourism.org

• • •

ÍNDICE / CONTENTS / TABLE DES MATIÈRES

ACKNOWLEDGEMENTS

This report is the product of the WTO Press and Communication Department, based on the First World Conference on Tourism Communications (TOURCOM), held in Madrid, Spain, on 29–30 January 2004. Production of this publication has been supervised by WTO Chief of Press and Communications, Rok V. Klančnik. The speeches were compiled and layout done by Olivia Doxsee. Proofreading by Bernadette Hurley, transcription from French and proofreading (Spanish and French) by Dolores de Rafael. The cover, TOURCOM logo and the programme brochure were designed by Graforama, Madrid.

The members of the TOURCOM Organizing Committee were Rok V. Klančnik (Chairman), Alla Peressolova (Assistant Chairman), Olivia Doxsee, Bernadette Hurley, Anne-Marie Hince (Internet) and Elena Borrego. Collaborators of TOURCOM were Deborah Luhrman and David Ing.

TOURCOM Organizing Committee wishes to give special thanks to the State Secretariat of Commerce and Tourism of Spain, specifically **Javier Piñanes Leal** of **TURESPAÑA**, **Ana Larrañaga Larrañaga** of **FITUR** (International Tourism Trade Fair), to **Covadonga Quijano Ruiz Diaz** of the **Madrid Tourist Board** (Patronato de Turismo de Madrid), and to the sponsors of the Conference – Sergat Spain, Hong Kong Tourist Board, ITE Travel Exhibitions, Reed Travel Exhibitions, Iberia (official carrier), Poder Volar, CNN (general media sponsor); and International Hotels & Restaurant Association (IH&RA), Dream Company a/s, World Federation of Journalists and Travel Writers (FIJET), European Travel Press (ETP), Voyager, National Geographic Traveler, Richard Lewis Communications, Travel Channel and Condé Nast Traveler and other media for their support.

Thanks also go to interpreters for a marvellous job, to all of the speakers for their important contribution and to more than 830 delegates from 126 countries for their participation.

Finally, the TOURCOM Organizing Committee wishes to express special gratitude to **Francesco Frangialli**, **Secretary-General** and **Dawid de Villiers**, **Deputy Secretary-General** of the World Tourism Organization for their guidance, support and trust.

Rok V. Klančnik
Chief of Organizing Committee

Madrid, May 2004

INTRODUCTION

FRANCESCO FRANGIALLI
Secretary-General

The First World Conference on Tourism Communications – TOURCOM (Madrid, Spain, 29-30 January, 2004) followed three years of crisis which underscored the importance of the relationship between tourism and the news media.

For the first time, a conference was specifically held for professionals from the tourism industry's public and private sectors to meet the media to discuss how efficient tourism communications can help the growth of one of the world's largest industries and pave the way for a brighter future for tourism. TOURCOM served as a sharing point for the latest know-how in communications and promotional campaigns.

After a series of terrorist attacks on tourism, the war in Iraq and SARS, crisis communications were high on the agenda of the Conference. Among the issues discussed at TOURCOM were general communications topics and other challenging issues, such as the role of the media in tourism, NTA/NTO communications budgets, successful promotion campaigns, branding of destinations, public relations vs. advertising, promotion vs. sales, new and digital media, cross-cultural communications and responsible tourism communications.

The event was not just a two-day series of panels. It was meant to spark off ever-increasing professional activity and a process of constant improvement in tourism communications worldwide. WTO used TOURCOM to launch its global communications campaign *"Tourism Enriches"*, designed to raise awareness of the positive economic impacts of tourism on individuals, families, communities and the world at large. In addition, one of the outcomes of the Conference was the TOURCOM Network of Communications Experts with representatives from the media and the public and private sectors of the tourism industry. The Network will serve as a high-level consulting body to the WTO and will help set the agenda for tourism communications in the future.

TOURCOM called on the media to play a responsible role in covering events which can have a strong impact on the livelihood of travel destinations and their local populations.

This difficult period burdened by economic recession, wars and terrorism, "infodemics" like the one related to SARS, has made tourism destinations and businesses more aware, than ever, of the need for effective communications programmes. Advances in communications technology, round-the-clock news coverage, globalization of the news media and a proliferation of new media outlets offering alternative viewpoints are developments that are rapidly changing the communications field—forcing all of us to update our strategies and skills.

It was in the very same setting some years ago, also at a conference held in conjunction with Spanish travel fair FITUR, that WTO introduced a new concept in tourism development called public-private sector partnership which has since become one of the pillars of the Organization.

With TOURCOM, WTO would like to expand this concept to include a third partner: the media. It is clear that tourism thrives on transparent, honest and effective communication. The media is an essential partner in this and so are the communications professionals who work in the tourism industry.

The impressive participation figures for TOURCOM – some 830 delegates from 126 countries - emphasized the great interest in communications and confirmed that media relations, public information, crisis communications became inevitable in the process of tourism development. Thirty-four speakers from seventeen countries, representing national tourism administrations and organizations, the private sector, and the media, participated in the TOURCOM Conference at the IFEMA grounds in Madrid.

They all left the Conference with a clear message: professional communications among all stakeholders in tourism, media relations, improved promotion and crisis management capacity are all in service of the development of international tourism, which is the most promising economic branch and, for many, a way of life, a path towards enhanced international cooperation and peace.

TOURCOM was a milestone in international tourism communications, but also – only a beginning of implementing a challenging task.

PROGRAMA

Miércoles, 28 de enero de 2004

15.00 – 18.00   Inscripción de los participantes

Jueves, 29 de enero de 2004

08.30 – 10.00   Inscripción de los participantes

09.00   Ceremonia inaugural
Palabras de bienvenida de los representantes de las autoridades españolas

Apertura oficial de la Conferencia y lanzamiento de la campaña mundial sobre las comunicaciones en el turismo con el lema "El turismo es riqueza"

Sr. Francesco FRANGIALLI, Secretario General de la Organización Mundial del Turismo

10.00 – 11.30   **Grupo de reflexión I - LA IMPORTANCIA DE LAS COMUNICACIONES EN EL TURISMO**

Introducción y moderadora
Sra. Debbie HINDLE, Directora General, BGB Associates, Londres (Reino Unido)

La naturaleza del periodismo de viajes
Sra. Becky Anderson, presentadora de CNN Business International, Londres (Reino Unido)

El poder de las comunicaciones en el turismo y la importancia de la inversión en actividades promocionales
Sr. Thierry BAUDIER, Director General, Maison de la France

Lo que hoy importa. Tendencias de 2004: prosperidad de los viajes en un mundo incierto
Sr. Thomas WALLACE, editor, Condé Nast Traveler, Nueva York (USA)

Liberalización con rostro humano del turismo: cómo eliminar las barreras al comercio justo en el sector turístico
Sr. Geoffrey LIPMAN, Asesor Especial sobre Comercio de Servicios Turísticos, OMT

Turno de preguntas

11.30 – 12.00   Café

12.00 – 13.30   **Grupo de reflexión II - EL TURISMO COMO FUERZA ECONÓMICA**

Introducción y moderador
Sr. Marc MEISTER, Director Gerente, Sergat España SL, Barcelona (España)

Jueves, 29 de enero de 2004 (cont.)

"Spain Marks" – Presentación de la campaña promocional
Sr. Javier PIÑANES LEAL, Director General, Turespaña, Madrid (España)

La política en el turismo: cómo cerrar la brecha de las comunicaciones entre los sectores público y privado
Sr. Christopher BROWN, Presidente y Director General, Tourism Task Force, Sydney (Australia)

El poder de la televisión en las comunicaciones sobre turismo
Sr. Gary WARDROPE, Director Comercial, the Travel Channel, Londres (Reino Unido)

Transferencia del conocimiento en turismo
Prof. Donald HAWKINS, Presidente de la Cátedra Eisenhower en Turismo, Universidad George Washington, Presidente de Consejo de Educación de la OMT

Turno de preguntas

13.30 – 15.00	Almuerzo

14.00 – 15.00   **Taller - "LOS MEDIOS SE REÚNEN CON LA OMT"**
Moderado por el Sr. Rok KLANCNIK, Jefe de Comunicaciones de la OMT

15.00 – 16.30   **Grupo de reflexión III - CUANDO LAS CULTURAS COLISIONAN**

Introducción y moderador
Sr. Mariano LÓPEZ, Decano, Cámara de Periodistas y Comunicadores de Turismo, Madrid (España)

La comunicación de la diversidad cultural en el turismo internacional
Sr. Richard D. LEWIS, Director General, Richard Lewis Communications, Londres (Reino Unido)

¿Hacia la "sociedad de los sueños"?
Sr. Rolf JENSEN, Director de Imaginación, Dream Company SA, Copenhague (Dinamarca)

Las comunicaciones: un valor estratégico para el desarrollo del turismo en países que viven el fin de un conflicto
Sr. Scott WAYNE, Director, SW Associates, Washington DC (USA)

Turno de preguntas

16.30   Café

16.30 – 18.00   **Grupo de reflexión IV - LAS COMUNICACIONES AL SERVICIO DEL CÓDIGO ÉTICO MUNDIAL PARA EL TURISMO**

Jueves, 29 de enero de 2004 (cont.)

Introducción y moderador
Sr. Dawid DE VILLIERS, Secretario General Adjunto de la OMT

El Código Ético de la OMT y las comunicaciones en el turismo
Sr. Diego CORDOVEZ, Presidente del Comité Mundial de Ética del Turismo y ex Secretario General Adjunto de las Naciones Unidas

El turismo como instrumento de desarrollo y atenuación de la pobreza
Sr. Anil Kumarsingh GAYAN, Ministro del Turismo y Ocio de Mauricio

El turismo sostenible en las comunicaciones: cómo llegar al geoturista
Sr. Jonathan TOURTELLOT, Director de Turismo Sostenible, National Geographic Society, editor de geoturismo, National Geographic Traveler, Washington DC (USA)

Turno de preguntas

Viernes, 30 de enero de 2004

09.00 – 11.00 **Debate - COMUNICACIONES DE CRISIS**
Las lecciones de Luxor, el 11-S, Djerba, Bali, Mombasa, la guerra de Iraq y el SRAS

Introducción y moderador
Sra. Deborah LUHRMAN, Consultora de la OMT, antes Jefa de Comunicaciones de la OMT

Participantes:
- Sr. Dexter KOEHL, Vicepresidente, Comunicaciones, TIA, Washington DC (USA)
- Sra. Sandra LEE, Secretaria Permanente de Desarrollo Económico, Hong Kong (China)
- Sr. Osmane AÏDI, Presidente Honorario de la International Hotel & Restaurant Association y Presidente de la Unión Inter-Árabe de Hotelería y Turismo

Las comunicaciones en la gestión de crisis: ¿a quién debería realmente dirigirme?
Sr. Steve DUNNE, Brighter Management Group, Londres (Reino Unido)

Las advertencias a los viajeros y las noticias negativas: una mirada a los principales actores y a las relaciones en la teoría y en la práctica
Sr. Christian NIELSEN, European Services Network (ESN), autor de Tourism and the Media, Bruselas (Bélgica)

Las comunicaciones de crisis y el futuro del sector aéreo
Sr. William GAILLARD, Director de Comunicaciones, Asociación de Transporte Aéreo Internacional (IATA)

Turno de preguntas

11.00 – 11.30 Café

Viernes, 30 de enero de 2004 (cont.)

11.00 – 13.00   **EL MERCADO DE LOS MEDIOS DE COMUNICACIÓN**

Las ANT se reunirán con la prensa y presentarán noticias sobre sus destinos. El acto se organizará en forma de taller, y cada destino tendrá una mesa donde sus representantes podrán reunirse con periodistas de viajes. Temas: noticias, oferta turística, viajes de prensa, etc.

13.00 – 14.30   Almuerzo

14.30 – 16.30   **Grupo de reflexión V - UNA PLATAFORMA DE LAS COMUNICACIONES EN EL TURISMO PARA EL FUTURO**

Introducción y moderador
Sr. Mustapha ELALAOUI, Presidente y Director General de Strategic Communications

Información, comunicación y turismo en la Unión Europea
Sr. Mathieu HOEBRIGS, Administrador Principal – Turismo, Comisión Europea

Creación de marcas turísticas: retos contemporáneos para las naciones, las regiones y las ciudades
Sr. Richard TIBBOTT, Presidente de Locum Destinations, Haywards Heath (Reino Unido)

De la "alta tecnología" al "trato personal": la importancia de la comunicación directa, las reuniones y las exposiciones
Sra. Stanislava BLAGOEVA-DUSCHELL, Presidenta de ETTFA, Directora de Operaciones del Grupo ITE, Directora de las ferias MITT y UITT, Londres (Reino Unido)

Las comunicaciones electrónicas en el turismo: el papel de Internet, retos y oportunidades para el turismo
Sr. Thomas STEINMETZ, Editor, eTurbo News, Hawai (USA)

Turno de preguntas

16.30   Café

16.30 – 17.00   **Observaciones finales**

La transformación de la OMT en organismo especializado de las Naciones Unidas - Reconocimiento del papel del turismo en la comunidad internacional
Sr. Rafeeuddin AHMED, Representante Especial de la OMT ante las Naciones Unidas

Conclusiones de la Conferencia
Sr. Martin BRACKENBURY, Presidente de la International Federation of Tour Operators (IFTO)

PROGRAMME

15.00 – 18.00   Registration of participants

08.30 – 10.00   Registration of participants

09.00   Opening ceremony
Greetings from the representatives of the Spanish Authorities

Official opening of the Conference and launching of the global tourism communications campaign under the slogan "Tourism Enriches"

Mr. Francesco FRANGIALLI, WTO Secretary-General

10.00 – 11.30   **Panel I - THE IMPORTANCE OF TOURISM COMMUNICATIONS**

Introduction and moderator
Ms. Debbie HINDLE, Director-General, BGB Associates, London, United Kingdom

The nature of travel journalism
Ms. Becky ANDERSON, Anchor, CNN Business International, London, United Kingdom

The power of tourism communication, the importance of investment in promotion activities
Mr. Thierry BAUDIER, Director General, Maison de la France

What matters now: trends 2004, affluent travel in an uncertain world
Mr. Thomas WALLACE, Editor, Condé Nast Traveler, New York (USA)

Liberalization with a Human Face – breaking down the barriers to fair tourism trade
Mr. Geoffrey LIPMAN, Special Advisor on Tourism Trade and Services, WTO

Questions and Answers

11.30 - 12.00   Coffee break

12.00 – 13.30   **Panel II - TOURISM AS AN ECONOMIC FORCE**

Introduction and moderator
Mr. Marc MEISTER, Managing Director, Sergat Spain, Barcelona, Spain

Thursday, 29 January 2004 (cont.)

"Spain marks" - Presentation of the promotional campaign
Mr. Javier PIÑANES LEAL, Director-General, Turespaña, Madrid, Spain

Politics of tourism - bridging the public/private sector communications gap
Mr. Christopher BROWN, CEO, Tourism Task Force, Sydney, Australia

The power of TV in tourism communications
Mr. Gary WARDROPE, Commercial Director, Travel Channel, London, United Kingdom

Transferring knowledge in tourism
Prof. Donald HAWKINS, Eisenhower Chair of Tourism, The George Washington University, Chairman of the WTO Education Council

Questions and answers

13.30 – 15.00   Lunch

14.00 – 15.00   **"THE MEDIA MEET WTO" workshop**

Moderated by Mr. Rok KLANCNIK, WTO Chief of Communications

15.00 – 16.30   **Panel III – WHEN CULTURES COLLIDE**

Introduction and moderator
Mr. Mariano LÓPEZ, Dean, Chamber of Tourism Journalists and Communicators, Madrid , Spain

Communicating cultural diversity in international tourism
Mr. Richard D. LEWIS, CEO, Richard Lewis Communications, Warnford, London, United Kingdom

On the way towards the Dream Society?
Mr. Rolf JENSEN, Chief Imagination Officer, Dream Company A.S., Copenhagen, Denmark

Communications: a strategic tool for tourism development in post-conflict countries
Mr. Scott WAYNE, Principal, SW Associates, Washington D.C. (USA)

Questions and answers

16.30   Coffee break

16.30 – 18.00   **Panel IV - TOURISM CONCERN - SUSTAINABLE TOURISM COMMUNICATIONS AND THE GLOBAL CODE OF ETHICS**

Introduction and moderator
Dr. Dawid DE VILLIERS, WTO Deputy Secretary-General

Thursday, 29 January 2004 (cont.)

The WTO Code of Ethics and tourism communications
Mr. Diego CORDOVEZ, proposed Chairman of the World Committee on Tourism Ethics and former Deputy Secretary-General of the United Nations

Communicating tourism as an instrument of development
Mr. Anil KUMARSINGH GAYAN, Minister of Tourism and Leisure, Mauritius

Communicating sustainable tourism: reaching the geotourist
Mr. Jonathan TOURTELLOT, Director of Sustainable Tourism, National Geographic Society - Geotourism Editor, National Geographic Traveler, Washington D.C. (USA)

Questions and answers

Friday, 30 January

09.00 – 11.00   **Debate - CRISIS COMMUNICATIONS**
Learning from Luxor, 11-S, Djerba, Bali, Mombassa, Iraq, SARS

Introduction and moderator
Ms. Deborah LUHRMAN, WTO Consultant, former WTO Chief of Communications

Participants:
- Mr. Dexter KOEHL, Vice-President, Communications, TIA, Washingon D.C. (USA)
- Ms. Sandra LEE, Permanent Secretary for Economic Development and Labour, Hong Kong, China
- Dr. Osmane AÏDI, Honorary Chairman of International Hotel & Restaurant Association and President of Inter Arab Hotel Industry Association

Crisis management communications – who should I really be talking to?
Mr. Steve DUNNE, Managing Director, Brighter Management Group, London, United Kingdom

Travel advisories and negative news: a look at the main actors and the relationships in theory and in practice
Mr. Christian NIELSEN, ESN – European Services Network, Author of Tourism and the Media, Brussels, Belgium

Crisis communications and the future of the airline industry
Mr. William GAILLARD, Director of Communications, International Air Transport Association (IATA)

Questions and answers

11.00 – 11.30   Coffee break

11.00 – 13.00   **MEDIA MARKETPLACE**

15

Friday, 30 January (cont.)

NTAs will meet the press and present news from their destinations. The event will be organized in the form of a workshop, where every destination will have a table at which its representatives can meet travel journalists. To be discussed: news, tourist offer, press trips, etc.

13.00 – 14.30   Lunch

14.30 – 16.30   **Panel V - TOURISM COMMUNICATION PLATFORM FOR THE FUTURE**

Introduction and moderator
Mr. Mustapha ELALAOUI, President & CEO – Strategic Communications Group

Information, Communication and Tourism in the European Union
Mr. Mathieu HOEBRIGS, Principal Administrator - Tourism, European Commission

Tourism branding - Contemporary challenges for nations, regions and cities
Mr. Richard TIBBOTT, Chairman Locum Destinations, Haywards Heath, United Kingdom

From "high-tech" to "high-touch" – importance of direct communications, meetings and exhibition industry
Ms. Stanislava BLAGOEVA-DUSCHELL, President of ETTFA, Operations Director of Group ITE, Director MITT and UITT, London, United Kingdom

E-communication in tourism – the role of the Internet, challenges and opportunities for tourism
Mr. Thomas STEINMETZ, Publisher, eTurbo News, Hawaii (USA)

Questions and answers

16.30   Coffee break

16.30 – 17.00   **Final remarks**

WTO transformation into a United Nations specialized agency – recognition of the role of tourism in the international community
Mr. Rafeeuddin AHMED, Special Representative of WTO to the United Nations

Conclusions
Mr. Martin BRACKENBURY, President, International Federation of Tour Operators (IFTO)

PROGRAMME

Mercredi 28 janvier

15 h 00 – 18 h 00   Inscription des participants

Jeudi 29 janvier

08 h 30 – 10 h 00   Inscription des participants

09 h 00   Cérémonie d'ouverture
Discours de bienvenue des représentants des autorités espagnoles

Ouverture officielle de la conférence et lancement de la campagne mondiale de communication sur le tourisme avec pour thème « Le tourisme, source d'enrichissement »

M. Francesco FRANGIALLI, Secrétaire général de l'OMT

10 h 00 – 11 h 30   **Table ronde I – L'IMPORTANCE DE LA COMMUNICATION DANS LE DOMAINE DU TOURISME**

Introduction et animatrice
Mme Debbie HINDLE, Directrice générale, BGB Associates, Londres (Royaume-Uni)

La nature du journalisme de tourisme
Mme Becky ANDERSON, Présentatrice de l'émission Business International de CNN, Londres (Royaume-Uni)

Le pouvoir de la communication dans le domaine du tourisme et l'importance des investissements dans les activités de promotion
M. Thierry BAUDIER, Directeur général, Maison de la France

Ce qui compte maintenant : les tendances en 2004 et un tourisme de société d'abondance dans un monde incertain
M. Thomas WALLACE, Directeur, Condé Nast Traveler, New York (USA)

La libéralisation à visage humain du tourisme – L'élimination des obstacles au commerce équitable des services touristiques
M. Geoffrey LIPMAN, Conseiller spécial chargé du commerce des services touristiques, OMT

Questions et réponses

11 h 30 – 12 h 00   Pause café

12 h 00 – 13 h 00   **Table ronde II – LE TOURISME COMME FORCE ÉCONOMIQUE**

Jeudi 29 janvier (suite)

Introduction et animateur
M. Marc MEISTER, Président-Directeur général, Segat Spain, Barcelone (Espagne)

"Spain Marks" – Présentation de la campagne promotionnelle
M. Javier PIÑANES LEAL, Directeur général, Turespaña (Espagne)

La politique touristique – Les remèdes au déficit de communication entre les secteurs public et privé
M. Christopher BROWN, Président-Directeur général, Tourism Task Force (TTF), Sydney (Australie)

Le pouvoir de la télévision en matière de communication dans le domaine du tourisme
M. Garry WARDROPE, Directeur commercial, The Travel Channel, Londres (Royaume-Uni)

Transfert des connaissances touristiques
Prof. Donald HAWKINS, Chaire de Tourisme Eisenhower, Université George Washington, Président du Conseil de l'Éducation de l'OMT

Questions et réponses

13 h 30 – 15 h 00   Déjeuner

14 h 00 – 15 h 00   **Atelier « LA PRESSE RENCONTRE L'OMT »**

Animateur : M. Rok KLAN_NIK, Chef de la section Communication de l'OMT

15 h 00 – 16 h 30   **Table ronde III – LE HEURT DES CULTURES**

Introduction et animateur
M. Mariano LÓPEZ, Doyen, Chambre espagnole des journalistes et des communicateurs (Espagne)

La communication sur la diversité culturelle dans le tourisme international
M. Richard D. LEWIS, Président-Directeur général, Richard Lewis Communications, Londres, Warnford (Royaume-Uni)

Vers la société du rêve ?
M. Rolf JENSEN, Chef du service Imagination, Dream Company, A.S., Copenhague (Danemark)

La communication, instrument stratégique de mise en valeur touristique des pays après un conflit
M. Scott WAYNE, Directeur, SW Associates, Washington (USA)

Jeudi 29 janvier (suite)

Questions et réponses

16 h 30 Pause café

16 h 30 – 18 h 00 **Table ronde IV – LA COMMUNICATION ET LE CODE MONDIAL D'ÉTHIQUE DU TOURISME**

Introduction et animateur
M. Dawid DE VILLIERS, Secrétaire général adjoint de l'OMT

Le Code mondial d'éthique de l'OMT et la communication dans le domaine du tourisme
M. Diego CORDOVEZ, Président du Comité mondial d'éthique du tourisme et ancien Secrétaire général adjoint des Nations Unies

Le tourisme, instrument de développement et de réduction de la pauvreté
M. Anil Kumarsingh GAYAN, Ministre du tourisme et des loisirs de Maurice

La communication sur le tourisme durable et sa cible, le géotouriste
M. Jonathan TOURTELLOT, Directeur du tourisme durable, National Geographic Society, et Directeur chargé du géotourisme, National Geographic Traveler, Washington (USA)

Questions et réponses

Vendredi 30 janvier

09 h 00 – 11 h 00 **Débat – LA COMMUNICATION EN TEMPS DE CRISE**
Les enseignements de Louksor, du 11 septembre 2001, de Djerba, de Bali, de Mombasa, de la guerre d'Iraq et du SRAS

Introduction et animatrice
Mme Deborah LUHRMAN, Consultante de l'OMT, ancienne Chef de la section Communication de l'OMT

Participants
- M. Dexter KOEHL, Vice-Président chargé de la communication, TIA, Washington (USA)
- Mme Sandra LEE, Secrétaire permanente chargée du développement économique, Hong Kong (Chine)
- M. Osmane AÏDI, Président honoraire de l'Association internationale de l'hôtellerie et de la restauration (IH&RA) et Président de l'Union inter-arabe de l'hôtellerie et du tourisme

La communication pour gérer une crise : à qui faut-il s'adresser ?
M. Steve DUNNE, Brighter Management Group, Londres (Royaume-Uni)

Vendredi 30 janvier (suite)

Les conseils aux voyageurs et les nouvelles négatives : regard sur les principaux acteurs et sur leurs relations en théorie et en pratique

M. Christian NIELSEN, European Services Network (ESN), auteur de Tourism and the Media, Bruxelles (Belgique)

La communication en temps de crise et l'avenir des transporteurs aériens

M. William GAILLARD, Directeur de la communication, Association du transport aérien international (IATA)

Questions et réponses

11 h 00 – 11 h 30   Pause café

11 h 00 – 13 h 00   **LE MARCHÉ DES MÉDIAS**

Les ANT rencontreront la presse et lui fourniront des nouvelles sur leur destination. Dans le cadre de cet atelier, chaque destination disposera d'une table autour de laquelle ses représentants pourront se réunir avec les journalistes spécialisés dans les voyages. Thèmes à débattre : les nouvelles, l'offre touristique, les voyages de presse, etc.

13 h 00 – 14 h 30   Déjeuner

14 h 30 – 16 h 30   **Table ronde V – L'AVENIR DE LA COMMUNICATION DANS LE DOMAINE DU TOURISME**

Introduction et animateur
M. Mustapha ELALAOUI, Président-Directeur général, Strategic Communications Group, Dubai (Émirats Arabes Unis)

Informations, communications et tourisme dans l'Union européenne

M. Mathieu HOEBRIGS, Administrateur principal, Tourisme, Commission européenne

La stratégie de marque : enjeux actuels pour les pays, les régions et les villes

M. Richard TIBBOTT, Président, Locum Destinations UK, Haywards Heath (Royaume-Uni)

De la technique de pointe à la personnalisation : importance de la communication directe, des réunions et des salons

Mme Stanislava BLAGOEVA-DUSCHELL, Présidente de l'ETTFA, Directrice d'exploitation du groupe ITE, Directrice du MITT et de l'UITT, Londres (Royaume-Uni)

La communication électronique dans le secteur du tourisme : rôle d'Internet, défis et possibilités pour le tourisme

M. Thomas STEINWETZ, Éditeur, eTurbo News, Hawaï (USA)

Questions et réponses

Vendredi 30 janvier (suite)

16 h 30   Pause café

16 h 30 – 17 h 00   **Remarques finales**

La transformation de l'OMT en institution spécialisée des Nations Unies – Reconnaissance du rôle du tourisme dans la communauté internationale
M. Rafeeuddin AHMED, Représentant spécial de l'OMT auprès des Nations Unies

Conclusions
M. Martin BRACKENBURY, Président de la Fédération internationale des tour-opérateurs (IFTO)

EXECUTIVE SUMMARY

ROK V. KLANČNIK
Chief - WTO Press and Communications

If you want to build a ship, don't drum up the men to gather wood, divide the work and give orders. Instead, teach them to yearn for the vast and endless sea.

-Antoine de Saint-Exupery

BACKGROUND

A wave of global changes in the tourism industry began in the final years of the last century and has overwhelmed us in the new millennium. New markets have emerged, some of them huge. The collapse of centrally planned economies gave rise to market economies, mergers, acquisitions and alliances—all bringing powerful new players to the game. The expansion of post-modern information technology has accelerated all these processes.

It was inevitable that tourism would be affected by these developments.

In the past, there was a certain *"laissez faire, laissez passer"*[1] tendency in tourism and tourism communications, at least as long growth was unstoppable, because "one simply does not mend what is not broken". Some governments even found out that they were unnecessary in this remarkable period of tourism growth. Several ministries of tourism ceased to exist or were incorporated into other ministries. National tourist boards were established, with a mere promotional and research and development role.

At the dawn of the 21st century, new macro-economic rules emerged with a need for economic restructuring. These challenges were compounded by new political and security issues and even unexpected health problems.

---

[1] From a French economist Vincent de Gournay, who in the 18th Century wrote: "Laissez faire les hommes et laissez passer les marchandises", "let the people work and let the merchandise go".

See Figure 1:[2]

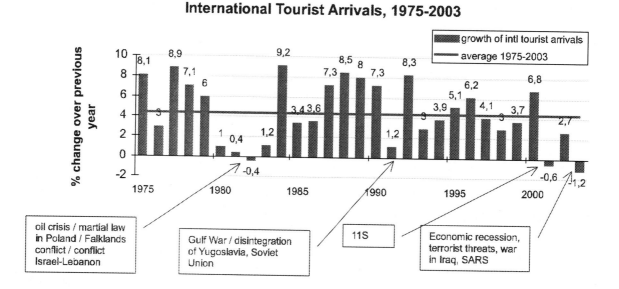

International Tourist Arrivals, 1975-2003

These challenges resulted in a series of crises in international tourism, even worse than those in the beginning of the 80s, marked by the oil crisis and martial law in Poland, or those in the early 90s, with disintegration of the Soviet Union and Yugoslavia. Even more worrisome: overall tourism growth in 2003 was the worst ever, down even more than in 2001, when the whole world was shocked by the 11S attack on the United States.

TOURISM IS ALL ABOUT COMMUNICATIONS

One cannot underestimate the interdependence of tourism communications and the international political, economic and social environment.

Most of the "official tourism communicators" - national tourism organizations (NTO) - were established just recently – in the 90s – thus, they had to perform and learn at the same time. It was also not long ago that everyone realized that travel, as a part of tourism, was a much more serious issue than just spending holidays on the beach. When some ten years ago, the then WTO Chief of Communications Deborah Luhrman, wanted to make a list of all public relations (PR) managers in national tourism organizations (NTO), she found out that only very few organizations had this kind of official.[3]

The situation in 2004 is different. Chiefs, directors and heads of communications, corporate communications, public affairs etc., in both the public and private sectors - have become indispensable high-level officers (even CIOs: Chief Information Officers), usually reporting directly to the chief executive. Their duty is no longer only to write press releases, but also to act as strategic advisors on the positioning of the organization or company. They are also responsible for media management, reputation management, web editing, negotiating, corporate branding, crisis communications, agenda-setting, raising awareness, cross-cultural communications and the communication of ethical issues.

---

[2] Source: WTO Market Intelligence and Promotion Techniques Department

[3] Deborah Luhrman – chairing the crisis communications round table at the First World Conference on Tourism Communications (TOURCOM, 29-30 January 2004, Madrid, Spain)

This happened first in the industries that are vitally profit-oriented, but tourism – where return of investment takes much more time, and the non-profit tourism organizations – could not avoid this inevitable process.

In short, it is all about communications. The process of tourism can simply not be realized without a global "noise", in which senders are communicating encoded messages through the media, decoded by the receivers, who send back their feedback and create their own messages.

Figure 2: Simple chart of basic communication[4]

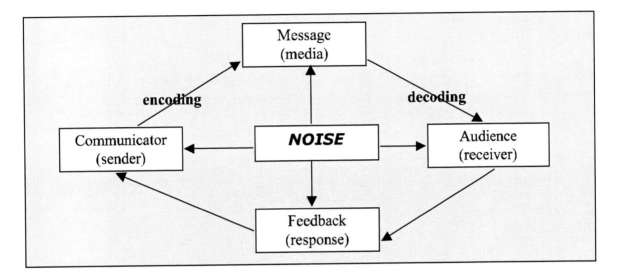

WHERE ARE WE COMING FROM?

First, we have to understand the basics. As WTO Secretary-General Francesco Frangialli wrote "The laws of science do not appear to apply to tourism. Twenty-five million international arrivals in 1950, 165 million in 1970, 703 million in 2002 and 1.5 billion forecast for 2020: tourism's growth, even if it seems to be slowing down somewhat, is not approaching any asymptote. There is no evidence of saturation of demand, at least on a global level; and the adage dear to financial traders, 'no trees rise to the sky', has not so far been borne out by the facts in this sector."[5]

Tourism is spreading far and wide; in other words it is becoming globalized. In 1950 the top fifteen destinations in the world accounted for 87 per cent of foreign visitor arrivals, in 1970 for no more than 75 per cent and in 2000 for only 62 per cent. When there is too much pressure on a region, tourists travel to another, neighbouring or comparable, region.

What drives this growth? Is tourism a natural force mushrooming on its own? Is it "pure love", pursuing dreams, escape, sympathy or a strategically planned business?

"Besides man's insatiable curiosity about the world in which he lives, three developments caused international tourism to explode and then become widespread: the increase in purchasing power and

---

4 Source: Reilly 1990 and Kotler, Bowen & Makens, 1999
5 Francesco Frangialli – A vision and three worksites, 2001

in discretionary income, in particular, of middle- and working-class households in the developed world; access to the private motor car and cheap air transport; and the expansion of free time, regulated and developed in many countries by social legislation in favour of employees," according to Mr. Frangialli.

MAGIC PYRAMID?

Is this a "magic pyramid", consisting of tourism organizations (public sector and certain representative organizations and associations), the private sector (companies), destinations and the media (which are mainly private, however, their mission allows them a special status)? The world is never perfect, but *magic*, yes, sometimes it can be. Good functioning of this pyramid means that the "noise" gets articulated through efficient, professional, comprehensive communications among all stakeholders and can boost the movement of millions of people, thousands of flights daily, as well as economic, cultural and social wealth. But at the same time it can also accentuate the dangers of possible unfair globalization practices like leakages, negative environmental impacts and unwelcome cultural uniformity.

Figure 3: Pyramid of tourism communications[6]

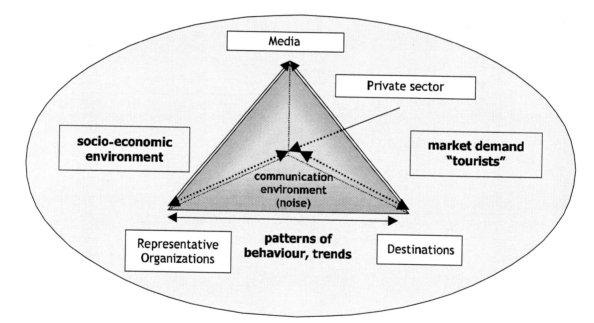

Tourism organizations—World Tourism Organization, representation organizations at regional level, national tourism administrations and destination management organizations—are the first to understand these points and should provide leadership and guidance. Too often in the past they believed that building awareness should be linked to public relations, on the other hand, some product or sales managers thought that communications was merely a waste of money. And money is always a scarce commodity.

Both supply and demand have increased substantially in the tourism market. Consequently, media attention on this, the world's fastest growing industry, has also intensified. With the ever-growing

---

[6] Klancnik, TOURCOM Executive summary, 2004

importance of tourism as a "smokeless" industry, new emerging markets and destinations, and last but not least, **the transformation of the World Tourism Organization into a United Nations specialized agency**[7], the importance of communications began to be recognized and at the same time media interest in the tourism industry increased rapidly forcing these organizations to realize the need for specialized personnel in this area.

Not an easy task. As Phillip Kotler stressed years ago: "Market changes faster than marketing", and the same is valid for tourism communications.

THE NATURE OF TOURISM COMMUNICATORS

In the 90s several governments transferred a great deal of the decision-making process to the hands of the ever-stronger private sector. They were abolishing tourism ministries and creating national tourist boards, with responsibility for promoting destinations, market research and product development. In some places, these steps were premature and resulted in a lack of guidance and institutionalized international cooperation, standards, criteria and practices.

Tourism organizations have now, more than ever, a balancing act in this new relationship among stakeholders: on one hand, to promote travel and tourism, ensure fairness and responsibility among them and, on the other hand, prevent negative impacts of tourism on the natural habitat, cultural authenticity and leakages, which are an outflow of profits from destinations. Today, we can see a huge change from the carefree tourism industry that rode the seemingly unstoppable growth trend that prevailed in the 1990s, to a tourism industry that is aware of the inevitable quest for sustainability and responsibility in its development. The latter, however, is not a process *sui generis* in tourism: with increasing environmental awareness among consumers, even traditional manufacturers—for instance, the oil and automobile industries—have performed better after they started to promote their new environmental and social-responsibility. Another example: companies in the cosmetics industry that have declared an "environmental friendly", no "animal testing" or even "dolphin-friendly" policy (among the first one being the Body Shop) as a part of their branding have started to mushroom.

As mentioned, tourism communication activities expanded from simple public relations and media relations to a range of new tasks in service to organizations or companies, executives and departments. New fields were added, to name only a few:

- corporate and destination branding;
- cross-cultural communication;
- stakeholder relations;
- negotiations;
- crisis management and communication;
- new media management and communication; and
- shift from traditional advertising to strategic PR.

---

[7] 23 December 2003

Traditionally, professional communicators in tourism were informing the media about news of tourism products or simply about marketing programmes that they were carrying out, and performance achieved. Now they must touch issues in sustainable tourism development, ethics, and crisis communications. They must master the *jargon* of the various stakeholders in tourism: politicians, financiers, and the public, while constantly updating their knowledge of how and what the competition is doing.

Some of the activities mentioned overlap the traditional activities of marketing departments, which more than ever started to focus on research and development. Practices differ, sometimes marketing and communications are two different departments, sometimes only one, but they are always two interdependent fields, that must work in close cooperation.

As far as destinations are concerned, there appears to be three different groups, having different communications needs:

1. The positive group of destinations looking for marketing and PR opportunities through various channels – the media (TV, Press, PR, Internet) – intermediary marketing opportunities – tour operators / travel agents and other representation companies.

2. The group concerned with damage limitation following a crisis, image reversal and recovery. There is, of course, interaction between these two groups.

3. The group of destinations that are invisible to consumers so that they are not included in the possible set of choices that a potential customer will make. This group wants to know how to be included in the first positive group.[8]

THE NATURE OF JOURNALISM

> *Journalism is merely history's first draft.*
> *- Geoffrey C. Ward*

Some critics – mainly from the camp of the news journalists – claim that "travel journalism is corrupt". They argue that press trips, sponsored flights, accommodations and *freebies* do not comply with professional *codes of ethics* of journalists. However, one cannot imagine great, colourful stories about distant countries or even entire glossy magazines without such practices. The sponsoring of press trips is legitimate, so the word "corruption" is not fair, at least when the journalists follow the basic rule of their profession, which is objective reporting.

The sources and providers of tourism information are many and varied. The media receive information from bodies such as :
- the World Tourism Organization, the World Travel and Tourism Council, European Travel Commission, Pacific Asia Travel Association, International Hotel & Restaurant Association and others;
- national tourism organizations, tourist boards, destination management organizations; and

---

[8] Martin Brackenbury – Observations on TOURCOM

- the private sector of the tourism industry, airline companies, hotels and hotel chains, tour operators, theme parks, etc.

But probably the most important source remains the journalist's own experience of a destination, as a Lufthansa passenger, for example, or as a diner at a Michelin-starred restaurant, as a guest enjoying a Sol Meliá bed in Madrid, as a backpacker in the state-of-art youth hostel *Celica* in Slovenia's capital of Ljubljana, or as a tango dancer in Buenos Aires…

Professionals in tourism communications are the first to want to push both hard facts and promotional information about destinations. What do they have in common with the journalists?

Even if they don't know it, the key to consumer confidence boils down to simple truth. Correct information on the quality–price ratio of a destination can have a bigger impact than glossy advertisements and slogans that include words like "paradise", "heart", etc. Readers do not buy empty hype. Tourists have become critical recipients of information. This approach grows with their experience and quality of life, allowing them to be selective when choosing destinations, and willing to pay more rather than be part of an anonymous tourist crowd.

The media will not always agree with the tourism communicator on what is important. They have their own priorities and they will not renounce that they are also profit-oriented companies. Very often, destinations will have to seek out interesting and unusual stories, to pitch to the media along with many competitors doing the same thing.

Russians in the early 90s would travel just about anywhere outside the borders of the former Soviet Union. After more than a decade of experience, their travel decisions are now more likely to be based on a variety of motivation factors, and price will often not be a decisive factor. These motivating factors need to be offered to them. The media—public and private TV, press and the Internet—serve as intermediary channels to reach them.

The media, too, just like the previously mentioned oil, automobile and cosmetics industries, have taken note of environmental awareness and social responsibility, as declared by representatives of the global media, who took the floor at TOURCOM.[9]

A travel journalist is not a public relations person. He or she is paid to pass on his or her own experience, even if he or she is sponsored to travel to distant places and enjoy. There is probably no other industry aside from tourism that offers such a personal experience to media representatives and even encourages it. Travel journalists are the heralds of what Danish futurist author Rolf Jensen calls the "Dream Society", which he predicts will supplant the Information Society.

Travel journalists, voluntarily—and usually with great pleasure—"sacrifice" themselves and their time, which would perhaps be otherwise dedicated to their families, to fly or drive to distant places and report on them. But there is also a different group of writers, those who focus on the news and "hard facts", reporting on the trends, consumer confidence or lack of it, troubles or success stories in the airline industry, and providing an ever-growing number of facts and figures. Both groups, which sometimes mix, are very important for the tourism industry.

---

[9] CNN, Condé Nast Traveler, National Geographic Traveler

Professional communicators of tourism organizations or the industry may ask themselves: if we stretch the truth in our promotional messages, may we also do so with the hard facts? The answer will almost certainly be: lies do not pay. It is the truth that ensures tourism growth and media sales, too.

Journalists covering hard facts address a target group that is different from that of those reporting on destinations. But mastering both fields is an advantage for both groups of journalists.

Among the most important challenges for travel and tourism journalists are :

- independence;
- accuracy;
- fairness;
- responsibility;
- politics of travel advisories;
- advertising, advertorials vs. reporting.

So from whom should the travel and tourism media be independent? Governments, sure, but also (other) providers of information, such as hotels, which are willing to take care of the journalist's overnight stay or the airline, which grants the ticket or at least a discount. The media always have a right to accurately and fairly report on the destination the way the journalist sees it — anything else, any required glorification, is considered to be advertising. There is a serious role for advertising in tourism, but a journalist must be allowed to do his or her job. No matter what we think of the "global" media, they do it right. Journalists and media sales people behind advertorials are birds of two different kinds of feather.

Another issue has to do with so-called "infodemics". This term emerged during the recent SARS epidemic, which caused more serious damage to tourism (especially in Asia and Canada) than the war in Iraq. Considering that up to 150,000 people worldwide die from influenza every year. Overblown SARS coverage and the resulting panic were simply scandalous and almost completely stopped tourism flows to Asia for a few months — all because the story was selling. It remains, hopefully, a good lesson for the future.

And yet another controversial issue is "travel advisories". While it is the responsibility of governments to protect their citizens, advisories have become a hot topic in international tourism. Who writes the travel advisories? Although it is the governments that issue them, they must be written by a concrete person. Does he or she know how much these documents can hurt not only the already impacted destination in crisis, but also its neighbours and entire regions? Do they modify or remove the advisories immediately, when the danger has passed? How should a journalist treat these documents? Independently, checking his or her own sources, should be one of the solutions.

The role of international tourism organizations and tourism media associations is crucial in the pursuit of these challenges.

FUTURE OF THE MEDIA RELATIONS IN TOURISM

One thing is certain: everyone wants to report on tourism and destinations, but very few tackle the issue of tourism communications—especially media relations in tourism.

What is the future of tourism communications?

We can only predict a few trends:
- **Technological:** both the media and destinations will take advantage of even more sophisticated technology (the Internet, broadband, WAP, interactive and digital television), while traditional print and electronic media will not go away.
- **Geographical:** tourism has already become globalized, yet more and more destinations will join the global media activity, start communicating and promoting, and try to take their piece of the tourism cake.
- **Changes in content:** the media will continue to specialize according to the different branches of travel industry and tourists' needs and motives for travel. We already have the media covering only wellness, i.e. spa tourism, or the air transport. On the other side, the daily newspapers, too, cover tourism-related issues, be it in the "business section" or in a special supplement or section.
- **Economic:** the media will develop more alternative ways to generate profits, also because advertising budgets are not increasing, in this endeavour they'll have to act more pro-actively.
- Both destinations and media will be forced by the market demand, not at all by any tourism organization, to accept the principles of the **Global Code of Ethics for Tourism**.

TOURISM AND THE MEDIA MEETING POINTS

Which are the most obvious changes and trends that will undoubtedly affect the tourism–media relationship?

Here is a list of trends in international society, that are or will be shaping tourism in the future (in random order):

- **Tourism is expanding to yet unseen corners of the globe**

According to the WTO forecast Vision 2020, by the year 2020, tourists will have conquered every part of the globe as well as engaging in low orbit space tours, and maybe moon tours. The *Tourism 2020 Vision* study forecasts that the number of international arrivals worldwide will increase to almost 1.6 billion in 2020. This is twice the volume recorded in early 2000s. The number of people travelling will continue to boom in the 21st century. Although the pace of growth will slow down to a forecast average 4 per cent a year—which signifies a doubling in some more than 15 years. There are no signs at all of an end to the rapid expansion of tourism. New destinations will emerge and tourism will grow in importance of traditionally industrial or agricultural national economies.

- **Services grow much faster than production in the global economy**

Economies worldwide are shifting from manufacturing to services. The latter are beginning to compete globally, just as manufacturing industries have done over the last 20 years. With the rise of the Internet based business, services can also expand to developing countries and enlarge their markets.

- **The global economy is growing more integrated**

Not only it is easier, with a help of new information technology, but it is also cheaper to be more integrated in this ever more competitive economic environment. Integration is seen on the political (European Union, NAFTA, Mercosur) and economic levels (mergers, acquisitions, alliances). Alliances of air carriers, acquisitions of hotel chains, mergers among tour operators, are taking place so that companies can gain a stronger position in the international tourism market, but still some 80 per cent or more of the tourism industry is considered to be independent, small and medium-size companies.

- **United Nations Millennium Development Goals**

An ambitious UN programme, launched at the World Summit on Sustainable Development in Johannesburg in 2002 aims to halve extreme poverty by 2015. The tourism industry has a clear responsibility in helping achieve this objective, through expansion to the least developed countries—but first they must embrace the principles of economic, environmental and socially responsible sustainable tourism development.

- **Advances in transportation will speed travel and shipping, both on land and in the air**

High-speed, large-capacity supersonic planes are no longer in the realm of science fiction, but will shortly become reality. With the rise of low-cost airlines, investment in infrastructure and deregulation of air traffic, travelling by plane became affordable to millions of new passengers. There are currently more than 500 million cars in the world and the number is expanding each year due to new production in developing countries. Cruise ships activities have become one of the fastest growing tourism segments, expanding from the Mediterranean and the Caribbean to the shores of Africa, Latin America and even Antarctica.

- **The Internet is growing logarithmically and globally**

The number of the Internet users is rapidly approaching 1 billion worldwide and will reach it by 2005. There are more than 50 million Internet users in China alone and in Japan, some half of the population use it regularly. The volume of emails exceeded that of "snail mail" by 10 to 1 already in 1999. Estimated world savings in business expenses thanks to business-to-business by Internet amounts to more than US $1.3 trillion, sales amounted to US$ 4 trillion and the share in e-commerce is still rising. New technologies require more sophisticated, knowledgeable workers, who are also potential tourists. The Internet is becoming an every-day practice in developing countries, too, while some of them, e.g. India, are among technology leaders. Children surf on the Internet before they have read about Gulliver's travels.

- **The world's population will double in the next 40 years**

Although the developed world is facing great problems with decreasing birth rates, the world's overall population will double in the next 40 years. The population of the developed nations will fall from 23 per cent of the world total in 1950 and about 14 per cent in 2000, to only 10 per cent in 2050. Population will grow especially in the least developed countries in Africa and Asia. Economic prospects and development could slow down this process.

- **Growing international exposure calls for greater safety and security**

Since 11 September 2001, the threat of terrorism has become one of the biggest obstacles to tourism growth. Over the course of time, travellers have accepted the fact that the world is not a safe place anymore, thus they have modified destinations or time plans for holidays and business travels.

Governments are introducing measures for safety and security especially at airports—which may not be pleasant, but are acceptable and – as it is very obvious – make people feel safer.

■ Money rich – time poor

This descriptive phrase, coined by the Henley Forecasting Centre[10], describes a key dilemma of our times—rising standards of living offset by ever-increasing time pressures. Today's strong focus on productivity continually demands more output from fewer people. Both parents often have to go out to work to maintain a standard of living that was achieved by one worker in the past.

■ Price sensitivity

This is to some extent cyclical, depending on economic conditions. However most commentators feel that the age of conspicuous consumption has passed, and that it will not return for a long time, if ever. People are much more sensitive to gaps between rich and poor, and there is a general reaction against the greedy behaviour of some "fat cats". While there will always be ultra-deluxe products catering to wealthy clients and for special occasions, value-for-money has become critical in most travel decisions. Consumers now have much better cost-comparison tools, especially the Internet—indeed it could also be argued that the euro is a great step forward in price transparency, especially if it remains close to parity with the US dollar.

CONCLUSION

Without any doubt, the media have a key role in the constant search for trust. It is the media that builds trust in the market by communicating attractive tourism offerings and disseminating statistics on the growth of all aspects of tourism. So to make friends-communications in tourism is different from communications in politics-communicators and the journalists should work together. They must share and develop the values that are key to world tourism development, mitigating or preventing negative impacts of it, and show their commitment to the basic principles of peace, cooperation, friendship in the world, as well as to social, environmental and economic responsibility.

Positive utopia? Not really. Only ideals, which can make this world a better place.

---

[10] Martin Brackenbury – Observations on TOURCOM

Official Conclusions

DAVID ING
Journalist

OPENING CEREMONY

Francisco Utrera, **Spain's Secretary of State for Commerce and Tourism**, described communications as "fundamental" for the tourism industry. In the case of Spain, where tourism represents 12% of the country's GDP, the need to create a positive image is especially important.

The country's tourism offices in the main generating markets are geared with a series of set procedures that enables them to provide information as quickly as possible in the case of a crisis, and which could serve as a model for other countries. Spain has a stable and safe image among visitors, it needs to protect, he said. The key issues when communicating are transparency and rapidity.

WTO Secretary-General Francesco Frangialli said that the Conference was particularly timely after three years of crisis. The industry is now more aware of effective communications programmes, and the advances in communications technology, including the globalisation of the media and the proliferation of new outlets, are forcing everyone to update their strategies and skills.

"Tourism is highly dependent on media reporting," he said. But excessive coverage can produce a reaction among travellers that is way out of proportion with the real situation. Mr Frangialli called on the press for 'news coverage' to be balanced and sober, and to use the conference to help identify standards based on mutual respect that will help rather than hinder the industry.

He also said there is a need for new standards in travel advisories issued by governments, which often had an excessive impact on countries or even entire regions. WTO is arranging a consultation on this subject with representatives from leading generating markets. He has launched the first communications campaign targeted at the public, decision makers in public and private sectors and the media, 'Tourism Enriches', with the message that tourism enriches individuals, families, communities and all the world.

PANEL 1: 'THE IMPORTANCE OF TOURISM COMMUNICATIONS'

Thierry Baudier, **Director-General of Maison de la France**, said that communications for an NTA are constantly changing because of new technology. The fact that customers are also changing makes communications even more important.

Apart from servicing the traditional media, MdlF has put particular emphasis on direct marketing through the Internet, which is now being increasingly used for purchasing travel products as well as information gathering. This includes wide use of on-screen newsletters geared to individual countries and separate niche markets.

Their communications strategy has also included a hospitality campaign among French citizens to make them more aware of the importance of receiving foreign visitors.

Thomas Wallace, Editor-in-chief of Conde Nast Traveler, said that e-mail polls carried out among their readership–"affluent US travellers"-show that they believe security issues will be here for a long time.

Their readers do not like the safety and security measures, but they understand why they have been introduced and are "willing to tolerate them." They are "learning to live" with the idea of risk being involved in travel. The polls also showed that the friendliness of people in a destination is now the most important factor in deciding on where to travel.

Becky Anderson, anchor-woman for CNN, said that the very nature of news is often gloomy, and that to get a message across the travel industry has to be more pro-active and rely on more than press releases.

In the case of breaking stories there is a need to provide "the most significant person" possible to comment on events. "There is nothing worse than a 'no comment'," she added.

The designated spokesperson needs to be well trained and prepared, and ready to anticipate questions that they may not be accustomed to from dealing with their own national media. To promote good news, she said there are plenty of slots to be filled on magazine feature programmes, which are open to "clever pitching". To be considered, they have to be new products.

Particularly relevant for CNN are stories that involve the environment and other socially responsible issues, and ones with a strong visual impact.

WTO Special Adviser Geoffrey Lipman said that countries have to be prepared for globalized television networks that need to fill 24-hour schedules.

He described WTO's 'Liberalization with a Human Face Campaign' and the Organization's efforts to provide leadership in linking the global economy with socio-political issues, which he suggested fitted in with the sort of coverage recommended by Ms. Anderson.

Tourism has to be seen as an "export in services sector" in trade talks to make sure that lesser developed countries (LDCs) benefit. Putting more money into the economies of developing nations such as China and India will help to lift outbound tourism from these countries. Asked what tourism represents for LDCs, he said the income from a richer country's tourists "far exceeds" financial aid from their governments and "it is likely to stay that way".

PANEL 2: 'TOURISM AS AN ECONOMIC FORCE'

Javier Piñanes, Director-General of the Spanish Tourist Board - Turespaña, said that the image of advertising campaigns keeps evolving with the changes in customer trends.

Spain's latest campaign, 'Spain Marks' is aimed at combining the feeling for various qualities such as the country's rich culture and sense of hospitality, while providing flexibility to change with events and to enable joint promotions with companies and regional boards. Although the campaign had been researched before it was launched, he acknowledged that it is "very difficult to measure the results of a campaign."

Donald Hawkins, Professor of Tourism at the George Washington University, spoke on the subject of the "foundation of communication being knowledge". He described how WTO's chain of education institutes are involved in research and co-operative products, and partnership efforts with the private sector.

Christopher Brown, CEO of Australia's Tourism Task Force, said there is a need for destinations to "spend time worrying about the message, and not just the product". Communications need to be honest, he added. In the case of the SARS epidemic, if governments had been more open with information in the first place, "they would not have had such problems later".

He also said that the industry needs to be more pro-active, to "chase the media and be honest when problems arise." In the case of a crisis, information needs to be regularly updated to meet the needs of a globalized media. The designated spokesperson should have a direct link with the chief executive.

He recommended using professionals to help in communications campaigns. "Communications is worth doing properly, and is too important to be done in an amateur way. "Every country has a tourism product to offer. The difference is the way you can beat your neighbour."

Gary Wardrope, commercial Director of the Travel Channel, spoke of the growth in inter-active television, with over half a million holidays now being booked directly in the UK. He said countries could make big cost-savings by working with this sector through advertising and sponsorship of documentaries.

PANEL 3: 'WHEN CULTURES COLLIDE'

Richard Lewis, chairman of Richard Lewis Communications, and author of the book 'When Cultures Collide', spoke of the big differences in customs and habits between peoples. With this difference in communication styles, the industry ought to look closely at whether its communications are right for the people it is trying to attract. "It is important to make them feel comfortable," he said.

Rolf Jensen, Chief Imagination Officer at the Dream Company, also an author, who wrote "The Dream Society", said that most destinations have a good tourism product.

"What counts is what makes your destination different." Pointing to the examples of creating a 'Santa Claus home' in Finland and ice-hotels in Sweden, he said that destinations that address the dreams and desires of consumers would benefit.

Scott Wayne, Principal at SW Associates, spoke of his experience in Bosnia where tourism is seen as one of the tools in the recovery of the country following the civil war.

This type of country suffered from various factors such as a bad image and often "poorly developed or presented products" – "all challenges which are communications related". To help the tourism industry, one of the first projects being carried out in Bosnia is to develop associations for travel agents and hoteliers, and the tourist board on the state level. Stressing the immense tourism potential of Bosnia and Herzegovina, he said "tourism is the key for economic development and – sometimes even more important – to achieve unity and cooperation among different ethnic groups and cultures in a country that seeks its way out of post-war problems".

PANEL 4: 'TOURISM CONCERN'

Diego Cordovez, (then candidate) for the first Chairman of the World Committee on Ethics in Tourism, said that in an increasingly inter-dependent world the WTO "Global code of Ethics for Tourism" would provide a framework to promote the responsible and sustainable growth of tourism.

Its wording included a specific call for the media to play its part in achieving this goal. The press, especially the specialized travel press, should offer honest and balanced information on events that can influence the flow of tourists.

Anil Kumarsigh Gayan, Minister of Tourism and Leisure for Mauritius, said that attacks from Bali to Mombassa had shown a clear link between terrorism and tourism. "Tourists are very sensitive creatures, and terrorists know their attacks discourage tourism."

Africa's image is "changing for the better", he added, although there are still scarce resources for helping education or efforts to halt the unnecessary supply of weapons. "There must be a determined effort by the rich countries to encourage growth in developing countries."

He said the media should be "more sensitised against the havoc it can cause" and "look carefully at the consequences" of its coverage of events. "Little things are blown out of proportion. We can't gag the media but they should be more responsible".

While communications need to be closely monitored, for many countries it is "better to have no publicity at all than negative publicity". With trends in tourism changing rapidly, he called for more public and private sector co-operation and for both to be "on the lookout for new products" to be promoted.

Jonathan Tourtellot, Director of Sustainable Tourism at the National Geographic Society, said countries should be looking beyond increasing the number of tourist arrivals. "It is important not to measure head counts but the social and economic benefits" of tourism.

He coined the phrase "geotourism" which he defines as "tourism that sustains or enhances the geographical character of a place – its environment, culture, aesthetics, heritage and well-being of its residents." This sector is too important to be treated as "a niche market" when it comes to promoting products, he said. According to Tourtellot, "geotourism" is a broader term for "ecotourism", but they are complementary, since "ecotourism" primarily raises the issue of environmental awareness.

DEBATE ON 'CRISIS COMMUNICATIONS'

Dexter Koehl, **Vice President for public relations and communications at the Travel Industry Association of America**, outlined his association's efforts to redress the immediate effects of the September 11 attacks with "a 10-week counter-offensive before the smoke had cleared".

With the media "hungry for any news", the TIA had set out to present a common message by arranging interviews and posting latest information on its website. There was also an advertising campaign, initially within the United States and later in leading generating markets, with the aim of reassuring consumers about the safety of travel.

His advice is to develop a strategy and message for dealing with crises and to "stick with it". There is a need to communicate with leading markets; and to involve the entire industry and government, especially when it comes to "leveraging resources" to support the campaign. "You have to move quickly and take control of a situation; otherwise it will take control of you."

Sandra Lee, **Permanent Secretary for Economic Development and Labour of the Hong Kong Special Administrative Region**, said that the effects of the SARS epidemic had demonstrated the three stages in a crisis – the initial reaction, consolidation once the nature of the crisis becomes clearer, and recovery.

Communication has to be honest, direct and responsible with a specific message that needs to be updated regularly. To disseminate news to the international media, information was released at the same time each day in Hong Kong during the SARS epidemic. To stimulate recovery, there is a need for partnership, with airlines and hoteliers working together to encourage visitors to return.

Hong Kong's experience had shown the need for strong leadership, "speaking with one voice", relying on professional spokespersons to give reassurance, and liaison with all groups of the community. One novel form of communicating had been the use of SMS messages being sent out by mobile phones to dispel some of the rumours surrounding SARS. She also emphasized the need to think ahead. "You need to plan recovery from the very beginning" of the crisis.

Dr. Osmane Aïdi, **Honorary President of the International Hotels & Restaurants Association**, said that the succession of crises in the Middle East had prompted special efforts to encourage intra-regional, short distance tourism.

To help promote this, they had worked with the media and the Arab Union, to encourage travel between neighbouring countries in the region, particularly since the events of September 11. "Tourism has suffered greatly," he said. In such circumstances, governments can help by introducing measures such as visa facilitation to ease travel.

Steve Dunne, **Executive Director of Brighter Group**, said that his public relations group looks to "hidden channels" other than the media to "help recover empathy and sympathy and reassure markets."

Each crisis starts with a vacuum, he said, "when it has just happened or is about to burst." When little is known, there are dangers from rumour and speculation. Once it has begun, the media concentrates on communicating the crisis. The "most challenging" stage is the recovery, in repairing an image.

He suggests working closely with opinion formers, "harnessing people of influence" such as tour operators, transport operators and hoteliers whose own business will be adversely affected. "But this has to be started before a crisis breaks," he added. Inter-active web sites can be used to keep them informed, and once the crisis is resolved fam trips should be organized to "get them involved". "An advertising campaign gives little return if the product is not being sold."

Christian Nielsen, Editor at the European Service Network, which produces publications for the European Commission, said there is a need for government travel advisories to be regularly updated to keep travellers informed.

But once a crisis is over "tourists tend to forget very quickly", he said, especially if a recovery plan is supported by special promotions. "Some tourists have selective memory if the price is right."

William Gaillard, Director for Corporate Communications at IATA, said that as air transport is the backbone of the sector, any serious incident that involves aircraft can have a "disastrous effect" on travel.

Aircraft get a "disproportionate amount of coverage" in the media because they "provide drama, although they are still the safest way of moving around." The TWA crash near New York in 1996 had proved to be a watershed in the industry. It came just before the Olympics were held in Atlanta, with news images breaking within minutes and various theories as to the cause being aired on the Internet.

IATA now has its own response and training programme for senior executives, one that is also used by oil companies and banks. One of the top priorities IATA recommends is to hold a press conference as soon as possible. But it also suggests explaining what is being done to help the families of the bereaved.

PANEL 5: TOURISM COMMUNICATION PLATFORM FOR THE FUTURE

Richard Tibbott, chairman of Locum Destinations, said that branding should be "a statement of the essence of a destination" and that the image should be very focused.

He highlighted the case of New Zealand that had moved from being seen as "dull to cool in a decade". Its image had been enhanced by the staging of the 'Lord of the Rings' films, which promote its 'scenery rich' offer.

Stanislava Blagoeva, President of the European Travel Trade Fairs Association, said that despite new technology, there is still a major role for direct communication through fairs and meetings. "Exhibitions are a communication tool. The benefits of virtual fairs will never replace real ones."

Thomas Steinmetz, CEO and publisher of eTurbo News, said his on-line travel trade newsletter now goes out to nearly 200,000 readers. While the future will see ever more opportunities for inter-active services through the Internet, he acknowledged "it will never replace television and newspapers."

Mathieu Hoebrigs, Principal Administrator for Tourism at the European Commission, explained how the information and communications systems, especially where they involve tourism, function within the European Union.

OBSERVATIONS

MARTIN BRACKENBURY
President of the International Federation of Tour Operators

At this Conference we have each of us been on a journey – a new interesting journey from which I, for one, have learned a great deal. It is time for each of us to assess where we started from, where we are now, and what might be useful considerations for the future.

The first observation is that there appear to be three different groups of countries and destinations, which have different needs:

1. The positive group of destinations looking for marketing and PR opportunities through various channels – the media (TV, Press, PR, Internet) – intermediary marketing opportunities – tour operators / travel agents and other representation companies.

2. The group concerned with damage limitations following a crisis, image reversal and recovery. There is, of course, movement between these two groups.

3. The group of destinations that are invisible to consumers so that they are not included in the possible set of choices that a potential customer will make. This group wants to know how to be included in the first positive group.

The second observation is that people (including the Secretary-General of the WTO, as he said) are looking for increased skills as communicators as well as increased knowledge of knowledge of what the media is looking for and what to do. How to plan, how to make communication strategies, how to manage in a crisis, how to make the necessary partnerships and so on.

What is clear is that the speed of change is more rapid than the changes in marketing and communication. Companies and countries are finding it difficult to keep up.

However what is emerging is a coherent set of skills, processes and organizations that will help to minimize the effect of crises on reputation, visitor members, tourism receipts and jobs.

The third observation is about journalism.

At the summit of the aspirations of countries with a free press is to have informed citizens. The countries know that news organizations are there to make money – they must entertain and retain their attractiveness if they are to have a long-term future so they have to compete for the attention of consumers.

This should not get in the way of getting the truth – through investigative journalism, by turning over stones, or by explaining contexts through observation and enquiry thus providing us with an independent understanding of the world. Unfortunately, as we know, the truth appears to depend upon where you are coming from – leading to a clash of opinions. Truth under these circumstances is often hard to discern.

We could learn more from each other if we had the opportunity not only of presentations but also of small workshops in which much more detailed exchange of views between public / private partners and the media could occur. I urge WTO Communications Section and its colleagues to consider a mixture of presentations and workshops as a format for future TOURCOM meetings.

My fourth observation is about technology.

I have been left with the conviction that the power of TV and, the PC as TV, is still at an early stage – technology on the Internet with broadband is set to become ever more important, converging to provide a range of visual information in real time that will inform and re-assure potential customers about the choices available.

The fifth observation is about Government information, particularly travel advisories. Information for citizens to be delivered in a neutral manner.

At one time travel advisories were relatively straightforward – information about some local natural disaster or conflict that need to be taken account of. Now potential tourists know that they are potential targets. Travel advisories, to protect citizens, became even more important. They are also much more difficult to write, partly because of the difficulties in assessing the actual threat and secondly because, potentially, they can act as a barrier to trade. The responsibility is on governments to take great care in the language used, the areas affected, as well as being prepared to change the advice if the nature of the threat abates.

My last observation is that tourism communication enriches – it enriches those who might travel, those that do travel, those that work in travel and tourism. The value added in expert tourism communications is enormous, it costs sometime huge sums but that investment makes a gigantic difference to tourism outcomes.

SIDE EVENTS

The **MEDIA MARKETPLACE** was for the majority of participants, mainly from destinations, a brand new experience. Each registered destination was assigned an information point, at which they were receiving international journalists, without prior notice and introducing them to news from their countries or regions. This new PR instrument was very well received by destinations, both – as a new know-how and for establishing worthwhile contacts with prominent international journalists. As some of them said - "They will know for the future, how to prepare themselves better and what the journalists really want and need, but to implement this new knowledge they need more events of this kind".

Observation from the journalists: WTO should take a lead in organizing such a media marketplace at every TOURCOM Conference or seminar and consider if it is appropriate to organize it also at large travel shows like WTM, ITB, MITT, and FITUR. This event spares a lot of time for journalists, because it focuses on media-relations only.

THE SCREENING OF PROMOTIONAL VIDEOS sparked great interest. It was positioned at an optimal place, opposite the registration desk and close to the coffee-break area. The purpose of screening was threefold:
- to share capacity in communicating destinations through attractive video footage;
- to promote destinations cooperating with TOURCOM; and
- to entertain.

CEREMONIA INAUGURAL

OPENING CEREMONY

CÉRÉMONIE D'OUVERTURE

- **FRANCISCO UTRERA MORA**
  Secretario de Estado de Comercio y Turismo de España

- **COVADONGA G. QUIJANO DÍAZ**
  Directora del Patronato de Turismo de Madrid

- **LUCAS FERMÍN**
  Director General de IFEMA

- **FRANCESCO FRANGIALLI**
  Secretary-General of the World Tourism Organization

CEREMONIA INAUGURAL

FRANCISCO UTRERA MORA

Secretario de Estado de Comercio y Turismo de España

(resumen)

Señora Directora del Patronato de Turismo de Madrid, Dª Covadonga González Quijano,

Señor Director General de IFEMA, D. Fermín Lucas

Señor Secretario General de la Organización Mundial del Turismo, Sr. Francesco Frangialli,

Distinguidos señores y señoras

La calidad de los productos y la oferta turística española incluye asimismo aspectos hoy especialmente sensibles como los relativos a la seguridad de los destinos. Ya he señalado que en la valoración de los turistas, turistas además conocedores del destino puesto que más de un 75 por ciento manifiestan haber visitado nuestro país previamente en 4 ó más ocasiones, como decimos uno de los aspectos más positivos que aparecen en las encuestas de satisfacción de estos turistas, es precisamente la seguridad que perciben en nuestro país.

Desde España se está realizando un gran esfuerzo para conseguir una buena gestión de crisis tanto en mercado emisores como en mercados de destino, y permítame que este sea la segunda de los componentes de esta breve intervención.

En los mercados emisores en relación a la seguridad, en estos mercados emisores existe una normativa interna de TURESPAÑA dirigida a nuestra red de oficinas españolas de turismo en el exterior que establece los procedimientos que deben adoptarse en caso de crisis con el objetivo básico, entre otros, de proporcionar información precisa y detallada tan rápidamente como sea posible a los medios de comunicación y a la clientela interesada. Nosotros pensamos que la esencia de la comunicación está en la transparencia de la información y en la rapidez con que esa información sea transmitida.

Por lo que se refiere a la gestión de crisis en destinos además de lo anterior, es decir, además de aplicar los mismos criterios que en la gestión de crisis en mercados emisores, se han de recordar los avances para fomentar precisamente la seguridad en los destinos, pudiendo decirse, como por ejemplo, las actuaciones emprendidas por la Asociación Española de Compañías Aéreas en Baleares con la existencia de un centro de gestión de crisis en el aeropuerto de Palma o la buena gestión realizada gracias a la excelente colaboración y coordinación de las Administraciones Públicas implicadas y del propio sector empresarial con motivo de algunas acciones terroristas que desgraciadamente se han padecido, y puntualmente y de forma cada vez más espaciada, yo me atrevo a afirmar que con una clara perspectiva a su desaparición a corto plazo, se han venido registrando en España como digo alguna de estas acciones específicamente orientadas a dañar y perjudicar el sector turístico español se han tratado de forma de comunicación con transparencia y con rapidez en la información, y se han sorteado rápida y brillantemente. Y quizá esto pueda servir como modelo de práctica a servir para la gestión eficaz de situaciones de crisis en otros países.

De hecho estamos también trabajando para generalizar a todos los destinos españoles mediante medidas apropiadas que en la actualidad se vienen estudiando con las autoridades competentes en materia de seguridad a generalizar precisamente el centro de gestión de crisis que tenemos establecido puntualmente en el aeropuerto de Palma.

Este es el camino que hemos seguido en España una tarea emprendida por el sector público y privado que seguiremos impulsando para transmitir la más fiel imagen de la equilibrada realidad de la España actual que todos cuantos nos visitan están percibiendo y que fundamentalmente hemos ayudado a construir entre todos y sobre todo, en los últimos 25 años. Imagen, permítanme reiterarlo, de un país moderno y plenamente europeo, serio, de gente trabajadora como el que más, dentro de nuestro contexto europeo, de un país estable y seguro, de un país con estándares europeos de calidad, diseño e innovación en sus empresas, de un país amigo de sus aliados y además de un país que cumple sus compromisos y que no defrauda las expectativas de quien nos visita.

Muchas gracias.

CEREMONIA INAUGURAL

COVADONGA G. QUIJANO DÍAZ
Directora del Patronato de Turismo de Madrid

Señor Secretario General de la Organización Mundial de Turismo,
Señor Secretario de Estado de Comercio y Turismo de España,
Señor Director General de IFEMA,

Distinguidos señores y señoras.

En mi calidad de Directora de Turismo de la ciudad de Madrid, quisiera en primer lugar darles la más cordial bienvenida a Madrid y a esta primera Conferencia Mundial sobre las Comunicaciones en el Turismo.

Al mismo tiempo, quisiera felicitar a la Organización Mundial de Turismo (OMT) por haber sido declarada recientemente organismo especializado de pleno derecho de las Naciones Unidas. Para nosotros es un gran honor que la OMT tenga su sede en Madrid desde 1975, y por ello nos sentimos doblemente satisfechos.

Nos encontramos en el incomparable marco de FITUR, foro de encuentro privilegiado que nos invita a la reflexión e intercambio de conocimientos; y especialmente hoy en relación con el tema de la comunicación en el turismo, de excepcional interés para todos.

El turismo es una gran industria, generadora de riqueza y empleo en todo el mundo, que se está enfrentando a grandes cambios estructurales, los cuales exigen nuevas formas que se adapten a las circunstancias de cada momento.

La innovación, la profesionalización, las nuevas tecnologías y la excelencia y mejora continua son las mejores fórmulas para conseguir el éxito. Y, en cualquier caso, la comunicación es la clave en la sociedad de la información.

El turismo de la Ciudad de Madrid representa una extraordinaria combinación de cultura, ocio y negocio. Tenemos mucho que comunicar. Madrid ha dado un paso de gigante, es una ciudad viva, dinámica, moderna e innovadora, que está teniendo un gran desarrollo económico. Este año, en especial, tenemos varios acontecimientos mediáticos importantes. En primer lugar, la inauguración de las ampliaciones de los tres museos que conforman el Paseo de Arte de Madrid.

El **Museo del Prado** ha comenzado ya la construcción de un nuevo edificio anejo, diseñado por Rafael Moneo, que ocupará una superficie total de aproximadamente 17.000 metros cuadrados y supondrá una inversión de 42,6 millones de euros. El objetivo fundamental de la ampliación es conseguir que el Prado pueda exponer los fondos que ahora no pueden ser exhibidos por falta de espacio.

El **Museo Thyssen Bornemisza** espera concluir en el primer trimestre de 2004 su ampliación, que dará cabida a la colección privada de la viuda del barón Thyssen, Carmen Cervera. La colección, con obras de los siglos XVII al XX de la pintura española y universal, ocupará 16 nuevas salas que se ubicarán en los edificios contiguos al Palacio de Villahermosa. El proyecto es obra de los arquitectos españoles Manuel Baquero y Francesc Plá.

La tercera y quizá más ambiciosa remodelación, por su inversión (68,4 millones de euros) y por la profunda modificación que supone del entorno urbano de la madrileña Glorieta de Carlos V, frente a la Estación de Atocha, corresponde al **Centro Nacional de Arte Contemporáneo Reina Sofía**. La obra, dirigida por el arquitecto francés Jean Nouvel, se espera que concluya en la primavera de 2004 y se compone de tres modernas construcciones anejas al histórico edificio de Sabatini, que permitirán aumentar en más del 50 por ciento la superficie dedicada a exposiciones.

El 22 de mayo tendremos el otro gran acontecimiento importante del año: el enlace de SAR el Príncipe Felipe con Dª Leticia Ortiz, que ya ha despertado un gran interés por parte de los medios de comunicación de todo el mundo.

Además, en este 2004 tendrán lugar otros hechos destacables: próximamente se reabrirá el Museo Lázaro Galdiano y se inaugurará el Museo de Traje; y el gran proyecto de la nueva terminal del Aeropuerto de Barajas culminará a finales del año.

Durante estos días y en este marco único que es FITUR tendremos una excelente oportunidad para acercar estos dos mundos tan apasionantes como son la comunicación y el turismo, buscando el beneficio de esta gran industria generadora de desarrollo y bienestar para la Humanidad.

Muchas gracias por estar aquí.

CEREMONIA INAUGURAL

FERMÍN LUCAS
Director General de IFEMA

Buenos días,

Muchas gracias a la Organización Mundial del Turismo, y a su Secretario General por su invitación a participar en el acto de inicio de esta importante Conferencia.

Bienvenidos a FITUR y a IFEMA, y mis deseos de que su estancia en nuestros recintos feriales sea todo lo grata y productiva posible.

Quiero aplaudir la iniciativa de la OMT de celebrar esta primera Conferencia Mundial sobre las Comunicaciones en el Turismo precisamente en FITUR, ya que viene a subrayar dos cuestiones igualmente fundamentales:

En primer lugar, la oportunidad que representa FITUR para profundizar entre los profesionales de esta industria en la importancia que ha adquirido manejar las mejores técnicas de comunicación empresarial e institucional para no solamente afrontar situaciones de crisis sino para mejorar la competitividad de los productos y destinos turísticos. Hoy en día el manejo de valores intangibles como los que están ligados a la comunicación significa adquirir una ventaja competitiva que puede ser crucial

Y, en segundo lugar, porque viene a significar el papel estratégico que FITUR tiene como mejor exponente de este escenario de competitividad creciente en el sector turístico. Efectivamente ferias de la envergadura de FITUR son en esencia ejercicios integrales de comunicación lo que permite ser testigos de la aplicación de muchas de las experiencias que a lo largo de estas dos jornadas van a ser revisadas y estudiadas.

Desde ambas consideraciones, me gustaría animar a todos ustedes a que aprovechan la celebración de esta Conferencia, en la que van a participar destacados ponentes, y les deseo, a la OMT y a todos ustedes, que sean capaces de impulsar unos sistemas de comunicación que favorezcan no sólo el crecimiento de esta actividad sino la confianza de los usuarios en esta industria.

Asimismo, me gustaría señalar la importante labor que está realizando la OMT, y particularmente su apoyo a FITUR, en cuyo marco viene tradicionalmente desarrollando diferentes iniciativas, como la que ahora da comienzo, que ayudan a convertir a esta feria en un espacio fundamental no sólo para el negocio, sino también para el análisis, el debate, la reflexión y la actualización de los conocimientos.

Muchas gracias.

OPENING CEREMONY

FRANCESCO FRANGIALLI
Secretary-General of the World Tourism Organization

Señor Secretario de Estado de Comercio y Turismo, Don Francisco Utrera Mora,
Señora Directora del Patronato de Turismo de Madrid, Doña Covadonga González Quijano,
Señor Director General de IFEMA, Don Fermín Lucas

Distinguished delegates,
Ladies and gentlemen,

It is my great pleasure to open TOURCOM — WTO's first ever world conference on tourism communications. FITUR is always an excellent opportunity to welcome WTO Members and friends to our hometown of Madrid, but interest and participation in this Conference has far exceeded our expectations—with delegates registered from 126 different nations, making it a truly global event.

I believe there are several reasons for the great interest in this topic. First of all, it is being held at just the right moment, following three years of crisis in our sector, which underscored the importance of the relationship between tourism and the news media.

Secondly, this difficult period has made tourism destinations and tourism businesses more aware than ever before of the need for effective communications programmes—like media relations, promotional activities, and branding.

Thirdly, advances in communications technology, round-the-clock news coverage, globalization of the news media, and—at the same time—a proliferation of new media outlets offering alternative viewpoints are developments that are rapidly changing the communications field—forcing all of us to update our strategies and skills.

The aim of TOURCOM then is to provide the tourism industry with new information about how to communicate better, to provide the communications professionals here with new information about how the tourism industry works and in the process stimulate creative solutions that will improve the working relationship between tourism and the media.

Ladies and gentlemen,

I believe the nature of tourism and the nature of the media have a great deal in common. One of the fundamental objectives of the media is to educate and inform readers, listeners and viewers. Because it is only through objective, timely and abundant information that a society can truly be independent, democratic and free.

The value of tourism is similar. In the WTO Code of Ethics for Tourism it states in the preamble that the "direct, non-mediatized contacts tourism engenders between men and women of different cultures and different lifestyles, represents a vital force for peace, friendship and understanding". When we travel, we get to know different cultures, we come into contact with new ideas, new values, and different religions. Tourism is clearly a process of education and of liberation.

It is no accident that in old regimes throughout the world there were many restrictions on travel, just like there were many restrictions on the media.

On the other hand, tourism by nature is highly dependent on media reporting. The vast majority of holiday decisions are made by people who have never seen the destination for themselves. They select a place to go, they buy plane tickets and reserve hotel rooms based only on what they have learned from their travel agent, from friends and above all from the media. Research has shown that the media is many times more influential in the selection of holiday spots than travel agents and even more influential than the recommendations of friends.

The series of crises that has shaken the tourism sector in recent times has made all of us more aware of this dependence than ever before.

Tourism has really taken a beating over the past few years. Beginning with the tragedy of September 11th, the war in Afghanistan and then in Iraq, several tragic attacks on tourists—in Bali, in Djerba, in Mombassa, and in Casablanca—where innocent people were deliberately targeted so that it would create maximum attention around the globe, followed by the SARS epidemic, accidents such as the Prestige oil spill here in Spain, natural disasters and at the same time a major economic downturn in key tourism generating markets....it seems we have been spared nothing!

My impression is that the impact of these different shocks on the tourism industry varied greatly depending on the way that they were reported in the news media. Look at the bombings last November in central Istanbul, for example. The Istanbul bombings were widely reported, but not as obsessively as several previous incidents in the same city, and consequently they haven't caused nearly as much disruption in the tourism industry.

Or look at the difference in the 24-hour-a-day coverage of the SARS crisis last spring—which brought travel in Asia to a standstill—compared to the low-key coverage of the new SARS cases this winter. Many tourism officials in Asia are now saying that their SARS crisis last year was not an *epidemic* at all, but rather an *infodemic*.

Traveller panic over these problems is in part irrational. It's a reaction to excessive media coverage and to a perceived safety threat that is often way out of proportion with the real situation. Seasoned travellers already know this and we can see that the general public is also becoming somewhat desensitized to crisis. For example, we can see a difference between the Gulf War in 1991 when air travel decreased dramatically throughout the entire world, and the reaction to the war in Afghanistan or Iraq—where it was mainly travel to the region that was affected.

This growing insensitivity helps destinations recover more quickly from a crisis, as public attention turns to the next big news story. But journalists still need to be aware that the way they interpret and the way they report on an event can have severe implications for tourism. On the other hand, if news coverage is balanced and sober, it can have fewer negative impacts. I hope your discussions here in TOURCOM over the next two days will focus on this point and help identify communications standards based on mutual respect that will help rather than hinder our industry.

This is exactly what's called for in the Code of Ethics. In Article 6, which spells out the responsibilities of the various stakeholders in the tourism industry, it says: "The press and particularly the specialized travel press should issue honest and balanced information on events and situations that could influence the flow of tourists; they should also provide accurate and reliable information to consumers of tourism services."

Ladies and gentlemen of the media, that is what the tourism sector requests of you.

At the same time, we're working on another initiative to encourage more accurate tourist information in the travel advisories issued by governments for their citizens. As many of you know, travel advisories are frequently criticized for not providing enough details about the exact nature or location of a safety threat. Consequently there is often a negative impact on tourism to an entire region.

While our Code of Ethics recognizes the right and the responsibility of governments to warn their citizens about potential dangers, we feel there is a need for new standards that will help protect destinations in the developing world from unnecessary loss of tourism income. To move this project forward, WTO is organizing a consultation with foreign office representatives from the major tourism generating countries next month. We are also convening a special International Conference on Travel Advisories to be held in Syria later in the Spring. We'll be sure to keep all of you informed of our progress in this area.

*   *   *

On Tuesday, WTO announced preliminary results for world tourism in 2003. They showed a decline of 1.2 per cent in international arrivals last year, this after a decline of half a per cent in 2001 and a modest gain of 2.7 percent in 2002.

The complex series of problems that have hit our sector one right after another for the past three years have brought growth of the tourism industry to a standstill. But nonetheless some 694 million people visited a foreign country last year and WTO's panel of experts believes the perspectives for 2004 are positive.

The long awaited recovery of the European economy is expected to follow the recovery already underway in the United States and Japan. And there is a strong pent up demand for travel by people who postponed holidays, or business travel or meetings due to the circumstances of the past few years.

These are the two main factors that give me optimism as 2004 gets underway. If there are no major new disasters and fear begins to abate, if security procedures now in place prove effective but not so bothersome that they extinguish the desire to travel, then I believe we can have confidence in the industry's remarkable resilience and its ability to rebound after a crisis.

Ladies and gentlemen,

While the tourism industry has suffered from greater volatility during this recent crisis period, it has also had some positive outcomes. When things are going well, tourism growth tends to get taken for granted. Unfortunately, it's only when the going gets rough that attention is focused on the tremendous benefits of tourism—in reporting about lost earnings, export income, tax receipts and employment.

A new realization of the importance of tourism communications is another positive outcome of this difficult period. One destination after another has had to deal with the impact of a crisis situation. Most tried harder than ever before to communicate with the media, with their partners in the travel industry and with potential tourists—to keep them informed about what was actually happening in the destination.

At WTO, our Tourism Recovery Committee has issued a series of crisis management guidelines that focus on communications and we held five regional seminars on this topic around the world last year.

Governments have been putting a higher priority on tourism since the crisis period began. And that same recognition of the importance of tourism has taken place at the highest level in the General Assembly of the United Nations, which unanimously agreed on December 23rd to make the World Tourism Organization its newest specialized agency. This decision puts tourism for the first time on an equal footing with other essential human activities: such as industry, agriculture, education, culture, health and labour—all sectors that already have a specialized agency within the United Nations.

It is a great moment of recognition for the tourism industry: recognition in particular of its ability to alleviate poverty through the creation of small and medium-sized tourism businesses and the creation of new jobs.

For this reason WTO is undertaking a new communications campaign with the slogan "Tourism Enriches". En francais: "Le tourisme, source d'enrichissement" y en español: "El turismo es riqueza". There is a brochure introducing the campaign in your information pack.

This is the first time WTO has aimed a campaign at the general public and the message we want to communicate is that tourism enriches society at all levels: the individual, the family, the community, and indeed the entire world. It's a simple, upbeat idea and a simple beginning, but ultimately the campaign is intended to be developed and used by the tourism ministries in our member countries as they see fit.

The success of "Tourism Enriches" also depends in part on its diffusion in the media and for this I call on the collaboration and creativity of all of you attending this Conference.

Years ago in this same auditorium during FITUR, WTO introduced a new concept in tourism development called public-private sector partnership. This idea has been widely embraced by our membership and now forms one of the pillars of the World Tourism Organization. With TOURCOM, WTO would like to expand this concept to include a third partner: the media. It's clear that tourism thrives on transparent, honest and effective communication. The media is an essential partner in this and so are the communications professionals who work in the tourism industry.

We are taking advantage of this Conference to call upon all stakeholders in the tourism industry and the media, to work more closely together and make an effort to exchange regular and truthful information that helps ensure sustainable growth of international tourism.

I wish your Conference the utmost success in strengthening this new partnership and stimulating exciting communication amongst all of you.

I hereby declare TOURCOM open.

GRUPO DE REFLEXIÓN I
La importancia de las comunicaciones en el turismo

PANEL I
The importance of tourism communications

TABLE RONDE I
L'importance de la communication dans le domaine du tourisme

- **INTRODUCCIÓN / INTRODUCTION / INTRODUCTION**
  Debbie Hindle
  Managing Director, BGB Associates

- **THE NATURE OF TRAVEL JOURNALISM**
  Becky Anderson
  Anchor, CNN – Business International

- **LA COMMUNICATION AU SERVICE DE LA PROMOTION TOURISTIQUE**
  Thierry Baudier
  Directeur général, Maison de la France

- **WHAT MATTERS NOW: TRENDS 2004, AFFLUENT TRAVEL IN AN UNCERTAIN WORLD**
  Thomas Wallace
  Editor-in-Chief, Condé Nast Traveller

- **TOURISM LIBERALIZATION WITH A HUMAN FACE – BREAKING DOWN THE BARRIERS TO FAIR TOURISM TRADE**
  Geoffrey Lipman
  Special Advisor on Tourism Trade and Services, World Tourism Organization

INTRODUCTION

DEBBIE HINDLE
Managing Director, BGB Associates

Welcome to the first session of TOURCOM, in which we look at the importance of tourism communications.

You can be sure that the people you're trying to communicate with, consider you in one of three ways:
- They consider you favourably. They've heard good things about you.
- They consider you unfavourably. Something has put them off travelling with you, or to your country.
- Third, they don't consider you at all. You're just not on their list of options.

Two out of those three things aren't great.

So, over the next two days we'll hear how we can communicate with these three audiences.
- How do we prompt the favourable group to travel?
- The unfavourable group to overcome their reservations?
- The people who don't consider us to put us on their shopping lists.

But we have to communicate in an uncertain world

We're gathered here today in a world in which it's harder than ever to plan, or predict with certainty.

In this world - nothing is as certain as change.

Or, as marketeer Philip Kotler once said: "Markets change faster than marketing"

And what changes.
We now face the impact of governments giving cautious safety and security advice to their citizens.

We've faced rapidly changing public confidence in entire regions of the world.

Tourist boards are having to work harder and smarter to communicate.

I've been struck in the past two years by seeing tourist boards work incredibly hard to find new source markets – promoting intra-regional travel, appealing to their near-neighbours.

Or to see tourist boards realise the huge potential of promoting to their own expatriates.

To see creative partnerships with commercial companies to make taxpayers' money go further.

Hoteliers and tour companies, in the meantime, are seeing a decline in the influence of major tour operators and travel agents and a rise in independent travel.

We now can't rely traditional patterns of tourism business and the entire structure of our industry is changing before our eyes.

Travel agents are becoming tour operators. Hoteliers are building stronger marketing consortium, or even becoming tour operators. Tourist boards are building stronger connections between suppliers and travellers.

So - we are gathered to consider communications at a time when the pace of change is breathtaking. We may have new audiences, new industry partners, new methods of distribution, new customers.

Markets are definitely changing faster than marketing.

Our first session this morning should help you to keep one step ahead of the trends.

It gives me great pleasure to introduce our four speakers this morning.

THE NATURE OF TRAVEL JOURNALISM

BECKY ANDERSON

Anchor, CNN - Business International

Introduction

You've heard about the trends in the travel industry for 2004 and about the market for upscale travel, so let me stick to a broader overview of what we do as broadcast journalists, how that affects the tourism industry and how you might better communicate your message to us.

Broadcast Journalists – what you need to know about us.

1. Let's use CNN International as an example. CNNI pumps out round the clock news 24/7 via some 15 satellites to some 200 million households in upwards of 210 countries around the world. So far as communicating a message to the global world is concerned, you would be hard pressed to find a better medium.

2. The 24hr TV news industry is highly competitive environment – more competitive today than it has ever been. News is marketed in many ways through many mediums – particularly with the introduction of the Internet. So the success of any programme maker depends on his/her ability to select the stories the audience wants to hear and assembling those stories into a coherent, intelligent programme or "news belt."

3. Almost inevitably, anything that threatens people's peace, prosperity or well being is news and is likely to make headlines. And that means the news is often about events which are at best sad or gloomy for a country and its people or at worst, disastrous. That is the nature of news. But whether the story is a positive, or negative one, the aim is to provide an objective picture of the news event. The reporting should always be accurate, relevant and balanced.

4. Whilst I wouldn't consider CNNI a travel and tourism broadcast medium per se, much of what we do is highly relevant to the traveller and therefore to any country's tourism industry. For example, a story about a suicide bomb in Madrid, SARS in China, avian flu in Vietnam, or even currency fluctuations that adversely affect a country's economy are all obvious and important stories for a 24hr news organisation and are all relevant to the travelling public and therefore the tourism industry.

Types of TV programmes

There are two distinct styles of programming within the 24hr TV news format.
1. Magazine programmes which are less news sensitive and give producers and reporters time to put

together in-depth feature reports on a variety of topics. (See attached Programme outlines for CNNI's feature shows).

2. The News cycle - which repeats and updates a sequence of hard news that is repeated throughout the day.

How the tourism industry can better communicate its message.

Whether the story is a breaking news event or a magazine-style feature piece, the rules remain the same.

1. **Be prepared**. With any event, be it positive or negative for a country or area, preparation on how you communicate the message is key. Anticipate an event and organise the way you might manage the message to the broadcast medium. Learn from past experience on who best to talk to and how best to effectively get your message across.

2. **Be proactive**. This is particularly important when managing a crisis. That means making your highest ranking official available for interview with as much information about the event as possible. He or she must be well versed on the issue and able to communicate both sides of any argument.

3. **Make sure you are communicating your message to the right person at the TV or radio station**. There is no point pitching ideas or calling an organisation on the off chance you are going to reach the right person. **On a breaking news story**, contact either the Input Editor, the Assignment Editor or the Day Booker on what's known in most organisations as "the Desk." **On a magazine-style show**, do your research and find out who the producer is.

4. **Anticipate the questions**. International news networks can be a lot more probing and controversial than domestic news networks. Make sure your spokesman/woman is prepared to answer the most difficult questions in an effective and intelligent way. Communicate the message in an open, honest fashion. Anyone perceived to be hiding the facts or using too much "spin" will be rooted out.

5. **Don't expect to be treated with kid gloves!** Whilst an international news organisation should never be intentionally aggressive or disrespectful with an interviewee, the line of questioning that a reporter or presenter might take could be a lot more adversarial than a domestic organisation might pursue.

6. **Pitch story ideas/events effectively**. Make sure you are talking to the right person/sending PR material to the right place. And make sure the stories are relevant and new. Journalists who have been around for some time get very bored of seeing the same tired stories year in year out.

7. **Pictures**. This is particularly important when pitching ideas for magazine shows. Provide video footage which has been professionally shot and is available in the right broadcast format (PAL for most parts of the world. NTSC for the U.S. Also make sure material is available in a digital format as most organisations are upgrading their technology). We may not use it but it's useful to have and might sell the producer on an idea for the future.

8. **Monitor TV channels and their programming**. There is nothing worse for an assignment editor or producer than being pitched to with an idea that doesn't fit a programme's remit.

Conclusion

Whether you are communicating your message to a news assignment editor on a breaking news story or to a producer on a magazine-style show, ask yourself these questions:

- Is the story important, significant or immediate?
- Does it have a proximity factor, a human interest angle and/or a novelty angle?
- And finally, is it new?

LA COMMUNICATION AU SERVICE DE LA PROMOTION TOURISTIQUE

THIERRY BAUDIER

Directeur général, Maison de la France

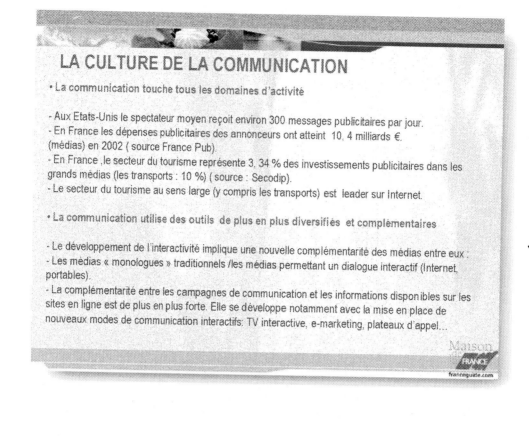

LA CULTURE DE LA COMMUNICATION

• La communication touche tous les domaines d'activité

- Aux Etats-Unis le spectateur moyen reçoit environ 300 messages publicitaires par jour.
- En France les dépenses publicitaires des annonceurs ont atteint 10, 4 milliards €. (médias) en 2002 (source France Pub).
- En France ,le secteur du tourisme représente 3, 34 % des investissements publicitaires dans les grands médias (les transports : 10 %) (source : Secodip).
- Le secteur du tourisme au sens large (y compris les transports) est leader sur Internet.

• La communication utilise des outils de plus en plus diversifiés et complémentaires

- Le développement de l'interactivité implique une nouvelle complémentarité des médias entre eux :
- Les médias « monologues » traditionnels /les médias permettant un dialogue interactif (Internet, portables).
- La complémentarité entre les campagnes de communication et les informations disponibles sur les sites en ligne est de plus en plus forte. Elle se développe notamment avec la mise en place de nouveaux modes de communication interactifs: TV interactive, e-marketing, plateaux d'appel…

Maison FRANCE
franceguide.com

LA COMMUNICATION : une évolution permanente

L'évolution de la communication pour un ONT se caractérise par la combinaison :

⊙Et d'une communication interactive , sur mesure et personnalis ée basée sur les opérations de marketing direct et l'utilisation d'internet

⊙D'une communication « classique « basée sur la projection d 'une image de la destination et/ou de ses produits,utilisant principalement les médias traditionnels

Maison FRANCE
franceguide.com

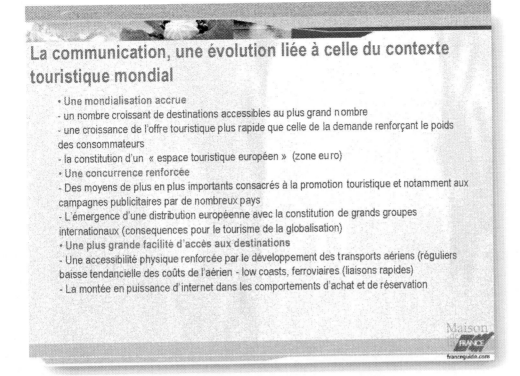

La communication, une évolution liée à celle du contexte touristique mondial

- Une mondialisation accrue
- un nombre croissant de destinations accessibles au plus grand nombre
- une croissance de l'offre touristique plus rapide que celle de la demande renforçant le poids des consommateurs
- la constitution d'un « espace touristique européen » (zone euro)
- Une concurrence renforcée
- Des moyens de plus en plus importants consacrés à la promotion touristique et notamment aux campagnes publicitaires par de nombreux pays
- L'émergence d'une distribution européenne avec la constitution de grands groupes internationaux (consequences pour le tourisme de la globalisation)
- Une plus grande facilité d'accès aux destinations
- Une accessibilité physique renforcée par le développement des transports aériens (réguliers baisse tendancielle des coûts de l'aérien - low coasts, ferroviaires (liaisons rapides)
- La montée en puissance d'internet dans les comportements d'achat et de réservation

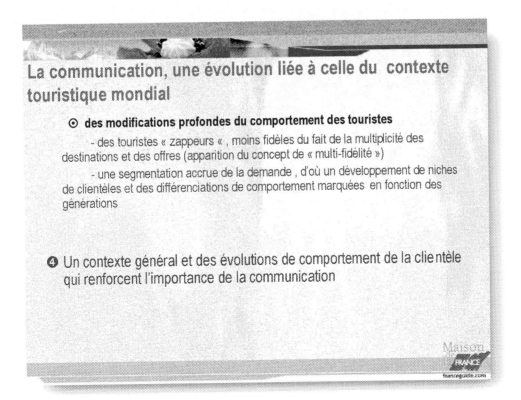

La communication, une évolution liée à celle du contexte touristique mondial

⊙ **des modifications profondes du comportement des touristes**

- des touristes « zappeurs « , moins fidèles du fait de la multiplicité des destinations et des offres (apparition du concept de « multi-fidélité »)
- une segmentation accrue de la demande , d'où un développement de niches de clientèles et des différenciations de comportement marquées en fonction des générations

❹ Un contexte général et des évolutions de comportement de la clientèle qui renforcent l'importance de la communication

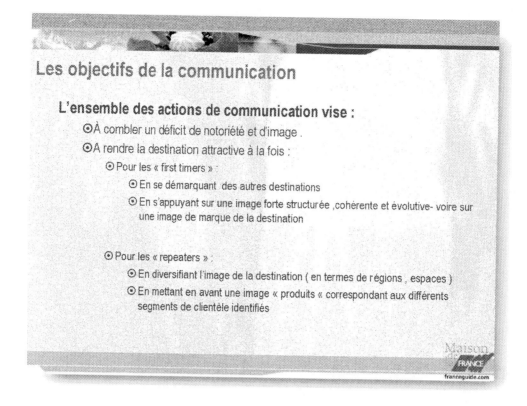

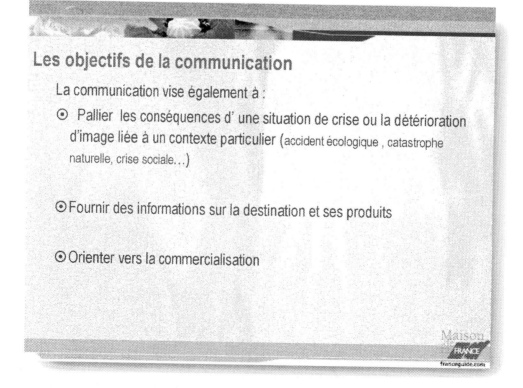

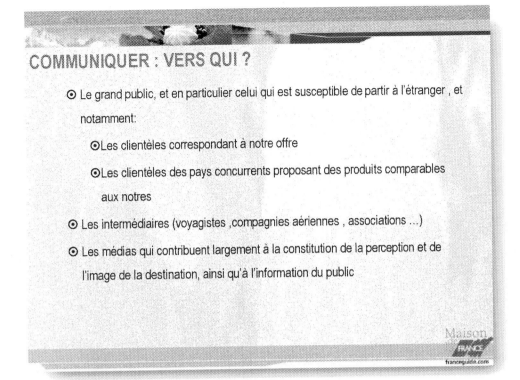

COMMUNIQUER : VERS QUI ?

⊙ Le grand public, et en particulier celui qui est susceptible de partir à l'étranger , et notamment:

⊙ Les clientèles correspondant à notre offre

⊙ Les clientèles des pays concurrents proposant des produits comparables aux notres

⊙ Les intermédiaires (voyagistes ,compagnies aériennes , associations ...)

⊙ Les médias qui contribuent largement à la constitution de la perception et de l'image de la destination, ainsi qu'à l'information du public

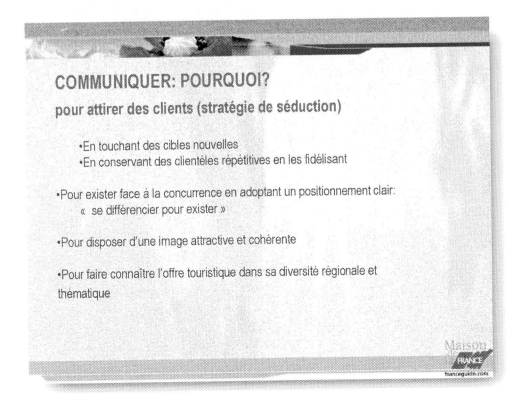

COMMUNIQUER: POURQUOI?

pour attirer des clients (stratégie de séduction)

•En touchant des cibles nouvelles
•En conservant des clientèles répétitives en les fidélisant

•Pour exister face à la concurrence en adoptant un positionnement clair:
« se différencier pour exister »

•Pour disposer d'une image attractive et cohérente

•Pour faire connaître l'offre touristique dans sa diversité régionale et thématique

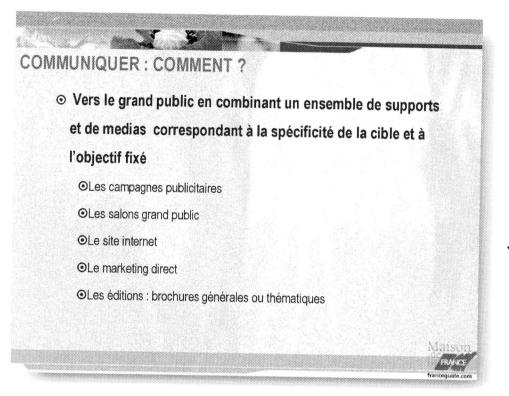

COMMUNIQUER : COMMENT ?

⊙ **Vers le grand public en combinant un ensemble de supports et de medias correspondant à la spécificité de la cible et à l'objectif fixé**

⊙ Les campagnes publicitaires

⊙ Les salons grand public

⊙ Le site internet

⊙ Le marketing direct

⊙ Les éditions : brochures générales ou thématiques

COMMUNIQUER : COMMENT ?

⊙ **Vers les intermédiaires qu'il convient d'informer de toute nouveauté dans l'offre de la destination :**

⊙ Par l'envoi de newsletters générales ou thématiques

⊙ Par la diffusion de manuels de ventes

⊙ Le site internet

⊙ Par l'organisation d'eductours

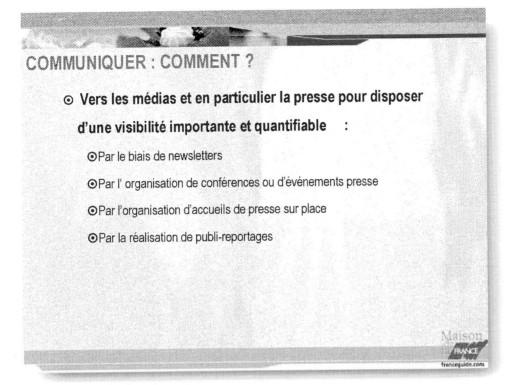

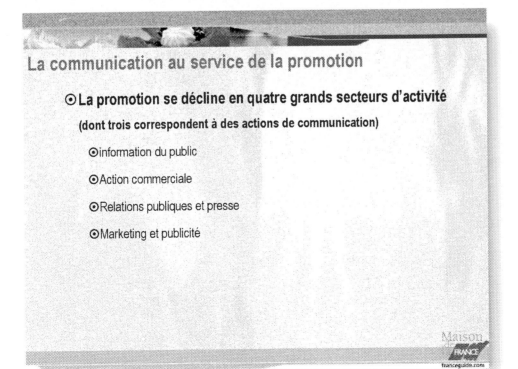

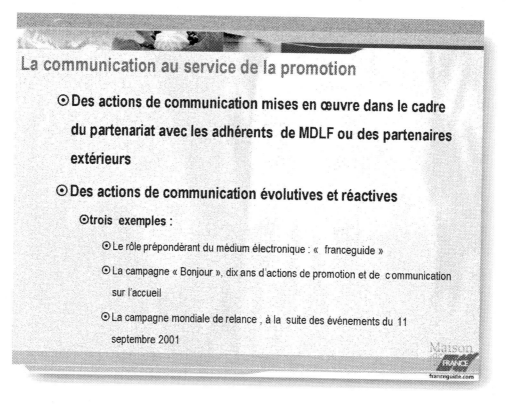

Internet , un outil d'information et de communication interactive

Internet , un outil d'information spécifique

Un site évolutif au service du grand public

⊙ Mise en place en juin 2002 de la nouvelle version de franceguide.com, portail officiel du tourisme français , en 9 langues et 4 langues asiatiques en sites allégés.

⊙ Des contenus enrichis et mis à jour régulièrement par le siège de MDLF et également par les bureaux à l'étranger qui mettent en ligne des articles adaptés à la demande de chaque marché

⊙ Un contenu orienté à la fois sur une offre thématique(16 thèmes développés en 2003) et des idées de séjour par région

⊙ Des liens avec l'ensemble des membres de MDLF

⊙ Des informations diversifiées et riches permettant à tout internaute de trouver l' Information recherchée

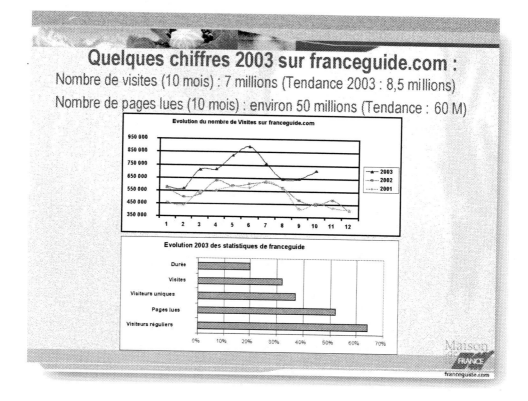

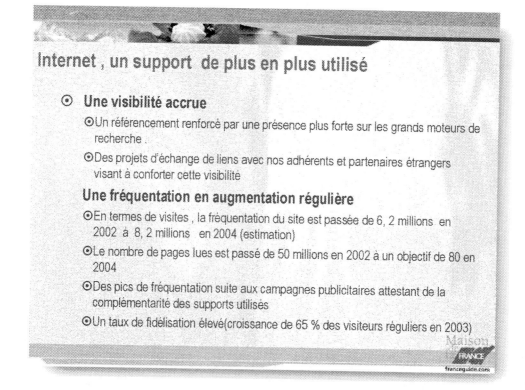

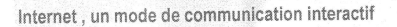

Internet , un mode de communication interactif

Le développement de l'e-marketing direct

⊙ Le consommateur devient le « **consommacteur** » d'une offre personnalisée

⊙ Constitue un outil de fidélisation des clients

⊙ Permet la mise en place d'informations personnalisées

⊙ Constitue un outil d'aide à la commercialisation pour les partenaires

⊙ Permet la mise en place d'une analyse du comportement des consommateurs

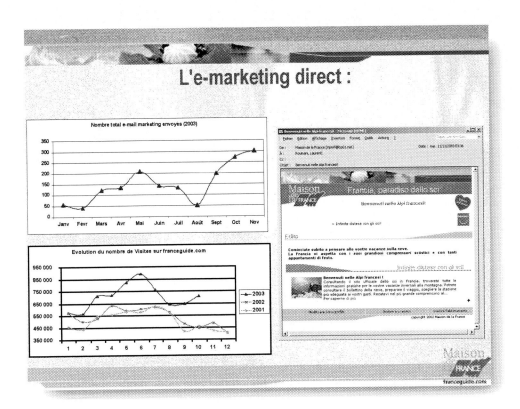

L'e-marketing direct :

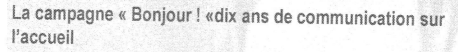

La campagne « Bonjour ! «dix ans de communication sur l'accueil

Un objectif initial: informer sur l'accueil

⊙Les premières étapes :

⊙Une démarche d'information institutionnelle intitulée « Bonjour-tout l'accueil en un seul mot »(1994)

⊙La campagne s'ouvre au secteur privé « l'accueil est le sourire de la France » (1994)

⊙La mise en place de contrats –accueil avec les grands réseaux de professionnels (1997)

⊙« La France accueille le monde »signature de l'ensemble de la communication autour de la Coupe du monde de football (1998)

⊙« La France invite tout le monde à la fête » :célébration des festivités de l'an 2000

⊙En 2001 la campagne est confiée à MDLF

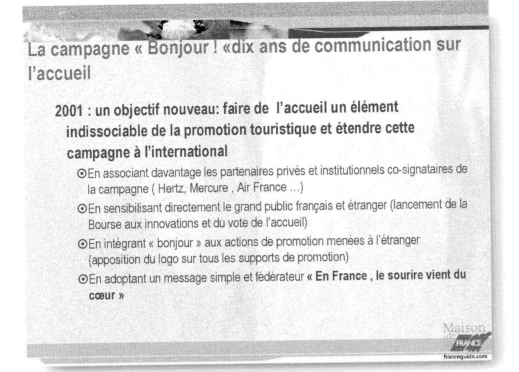

La campagne « Bonjour ! «dix ans de communication sur l'accueil

2001 : un objectif nouveau: faire de l'accueil un élément indissociable de la promotion touristique et étendre cette campagne à l'international

- En associant davantage les partenaires privés et institutionnels co-signataires de la campagne (Hertz, Mercure , Air France ...)
- En sensibilisant directement le grand public français et étranger (lancement de la Bourse aux innovations et du vote de l'accueil)
- En intégrant « bonjour » aux actions de promotion menées à l'étranger (apposition du logo sur tous les supports de promotion)
- En adoptant un message simple et fédérateur « **En France , le sourire vient du cœur** »

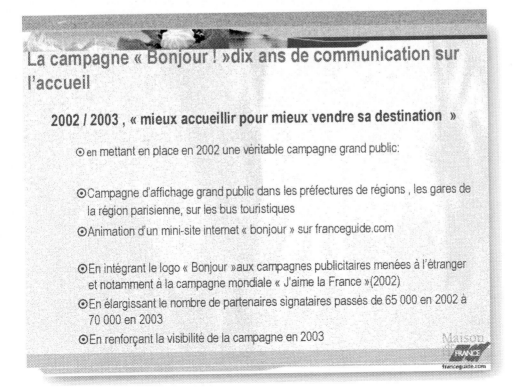

La campagne « Bonjour ! »dix ans de communication sur l'accueil

2002 / 2003 , « mieux accueillir pour mieux vendre sa destination »

- en mettant en place en 2002 une véritable campagne grand public:

- Campagne d'affichage grand public dans les préfectures de régions , les gares de la région parisienne, sur les bus touristiques
- Animation d'un mini-site internet « bonjour » sur franceguide.com

- En intégrant le logo « Bonjour »aux campagnes publicitaires menées à l'étranger et notamment à la campagne mondiale « J'aime la France »(2002)
- En élargissant le nombre de partenaires signataires passés de 65 000 en 2002 à 70 000 en 2003
- En renforçant la visibilité de la campagne en 2003

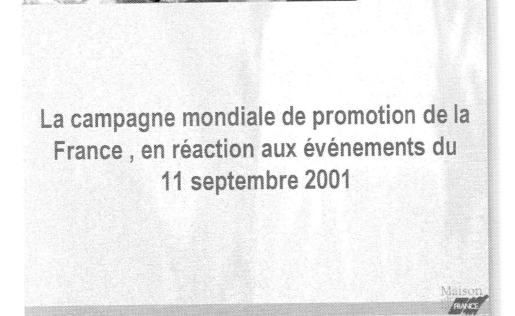

La campagne mondiale de promotion de la France , en réaction aux événements du 11 septembre 2001

Une campagne mondiale réactive

Le contexte :

⊙ Une chute de 30 % des voyageurs internationaux , touchant particulièrement les touristes longs courriers

⊙ Affectant particulièrement : le tourisme d'affaires , le tourisme des jeunes , l'hôtellerie haut de gamme , le tourisme organisé

⊙ Une tendance à privilégier les destinations de proximité

⊙ Une situation économique morose

La réaction

⊙ L'annonce par le Premier Ministre d'une « campagne mondiale de promotion de la destination France »

⊙ Le lancement dès février 2002 de la campagne visant à la relance de la demande sur les marchés concernés (principalement les marchés européens , mais aussi les Etats-Unis , le Canada , le Japon)

⊙ Un budget de 15 millions € a été consacré à cette campagne

Une campagne mondiale réactive

Les principes de la campagne :

- ⊙ La rapidité de réalisation et de lancement compte tenu du changement du contexte touristique mondial intervenu après le 11 septembre
- ⊙ Une campagne partenariale , avec des renvois sur les offres spécifiques de chaque partenaire
- ⊙ Une campagne déclinable par marché , et par produit
- ⊙ Un « fil rouge « décliné sur tous les supports de communication , fonctionnant comme un logo, applicable à tous les pays , tous les publics : le cœur rouge signé « j'aime la France « utilisé sur tous les marchés

Une campagne en deux temps :

- ⊙ Une campagne télévisée générique pour lancer l'opération (spots TV de 30 secondes sur plusieurs chaînes pan-européennes et la chaîne française LCI)
- ⊙ Une campagne déclinée par marché ,comportant des campagnes presse , des actions de marketing direct, du publi- rédactionnel , des campagnes radio, des brochures spécifiques

Maison de FRANCE
franceguide.com

ITALIE

• EXEMPLE

Corsica. La bio vacanza.

-Revue " Francia ", tirée à 80.000 ex. (principale édition en Italie)

- Campagnes de publicité en partenariat avec deux régions : Corse (dans la presse news magazine et le métro à Milan), et Bourgogne (dans la presse news magazine et tourisme mais aussi sous la forme d'un " folder " encarté dans un magazine touristique)

MONDIALE

Maison de FRANCE
franceguide.com

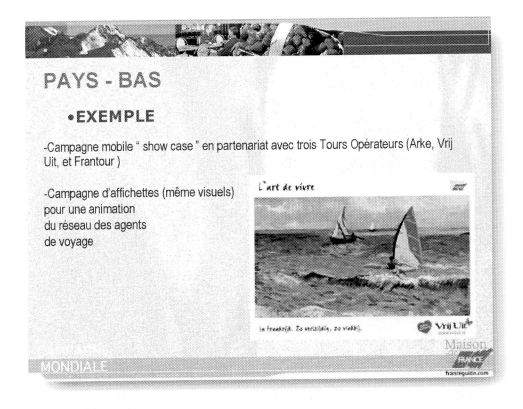

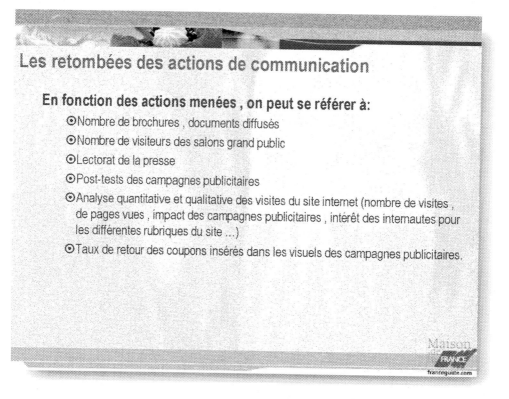

WHAT MATTERS NOW: TRENDS 2004, AFFLUENT TRAVEL IN AN UNCERTAIN WORLD

THOMAS WALLACE
Editor, Condé Nast Traveller

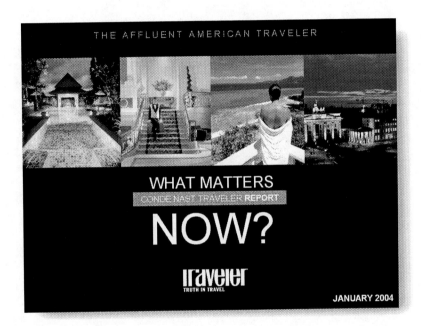

ACCLIMATING TO AN UNCERTAIN WORLD

DESTINATIONS WILLING TO TRAVEL TO:

	Mar '03	Jan '04
New York City	97%	97%
London	97%	97%
Rome	96%	96%
Berlin	90%	93%
Paris	86%	91%
Mexico City	90%	91%
Japan	81%	90%
Hong Kong	58%	86%
Brazil	91%	84%
Thailand	77%	81%
Bali	60%	74%
Vietnam	57%	73%
Turkey	48%	56%
Egypt	33%	46%
Jordan	30%	38%
Israel	27%	32%

Source: CNT email poll, March 2003 and January 2004

DETERMINED TO TRAVEL

- 90% have NOT changed travel plans due to recent events affecting airlines/airports

- 85% have NOT changed preference between American and International carriers

- 83% agree with armed 'sky marshals' aboard U.S.-bound flights

Source: CNT email poll, January 2004

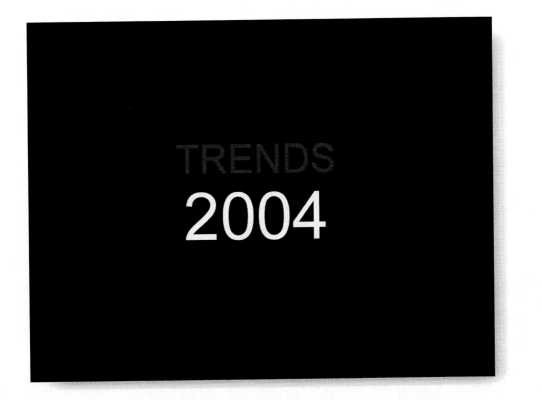

1 VALUE REMAINS PARAMOUNT

- Value ranks #1 when choosing a destination
- Cost (airfare and accommodations) has become less of a factor when choosing a destination (dropping in rank from #2 to #4)

- How is the VALUE of a destination defined?

	Oct '02	Apr '03	Oct '03
Friendly people	58%	74%	77%
Location of accommodations	74%	74%	76%
Good service	78%	80%	71%
Easy to get around	77%	66%	67%
Diversity of activities	77%	56%	66%
Low cost	3%	48%	41%

Source: CNT email poll, October 29, 2002, April 29 and October 29, 2003

2 FUNDAMENTAL MOTIVATION FOR TRAVEL REMAINS CONSTANT

- Culture continues as the #1 motivation for travel

Rankings	Oct '03
Culture	1
Stress Relief	2
Family Travel	3
Adventure	4

Source: CNT email poll, October 29, 2003

3 FULFILLING THE DREAM

- 75% agree: "Now is the time to take my dream vacation."

DREAM DESTINATIONS:

Rankings	Oct '03
Europe	1
Australia/New Zealand	2
South Africa	3
Far East	4
South America	5
USA	6
South Pacific	7
South Asia	8
Indochina	9
Southeast Asia	10
Caribbean	11
Arctic	12
Middle East	13
Central America	14
Mexico	15
Canada	16

Source: CNT email poll, October 29, 2003

TOURISM LIBERALIZATION WITH A HUMAN FACE - BREAKING DOWN THE BARRIERS TO FAIR TOURISM TRADE

GEOFFREY LIPMAN

Special Advisor on Tourism Trade and Services,
World Tourism Organization

Some years ago Alvin Toffler described "Future Shock" - the challenge for people and institutions to cope with the accelerating pace of change.

Even Mr. Toffler did not foresee the helter skelter geopolitical, social, economic and cross-cultural trauma of the new millennium - and its post 11-S intensification.

Nor could he fully anticipate the incredible magnification effect of 24 on 7 global multimedia. Reverberated every hour on the hour. Increasingly available in real time on personal wireless devices. And the 24hr News services with so much airtime to fill and so connected topically & commercially to our sector.

What he did predict however is that those who recognize and adapt to the phenomena will prosper. And those who ignore it will die.

To paraphrase Mark Twain, despite the fragility of Tourism to these mega trends, the rumor of our demise is rather premature.

Au contraire, the good news is that as a socio-economic phenomenon Tourism is adapting, surviving and over the long term growing dynamically. Simply because borders are opening, transport is becoming more available to more places and more people, have more disposable income and want to use it to travel.

I don't want to play down the seriousness of the short term slow downs in the figures of the past 3 years, the capital squeeze on the overextended airline sector, or the severe impact that security will have on costs and on congestion.

But the long term trends are incredibly positive, even with adjusted growth rates, this industry will double over the next two to three decades - in some regions much faster. It just won't be a smooth ride - because we are so connected to central politico-commercial activity. We have to adapt to the "Future Shock Syndrome".

This is not just important for those of us living in the *tourism goldfish bowl* but it is great news for the countries who understand that tourism is an industry that punches above its economic weight. That it stimulates other sectors of the economy (as we saw so graphically during the Mad Cow and SARS outbreaks). And that, properly managed - i.e. sustainably - it has all sorts of social benefits that other sectors can't deliver on.

The other piece of good news is that WTO itself is also adapting rapidly to provide the leadership that the sector needs in these trying times. And in doing so, is establishing a policy framework aligned to evolving global decision-making structures.

The Secretary-General has stressed the importance of our becoming the Untied Nations specialized agency - and it must be said that this is only a result of his vision and perseverance. Let me add one dimension - the UN itself is rapidly becoming the accepted focal point for good global governance and under the leadership of Kofi Annan is continuously adapting itself for that task - as for example with its new Panel on security and development.

No sector of the economy is better positioned to help build peace and development.

- Every peace agreement includes tourism exchange as one of its first components - take Iran's offer to help rebuild Iraq by sending tourists or India and Pakistan restarting relations through air service.

  As for security - writing in the World Economic Forum's Davos Agenda the Finance Minister of Afghanistan says " For Thailand it was really Tourism that provided a sustainable answer to drug cultivation. For us we must first look at security, but then in the medium term its ecotourism"

  Few people know that WTO has quietly been driving tourism activity to help build post conflict futures in East Timor, Sri Lanka, Rwanda and even DPR Korea.

- And when it comes to development, Tourism is the best option for the world's poorest countries. It's a universal export in the services sector, where the global economy is expanding and where they have so few alternatives. It's already the primary source of foreign exchange in most poor countries - particularly in Africa where the need is so great.

  It's an area where they have comparative opportunity in natural resources, culture, and tradition to tap the ecotourism boom. It breeds SME's and entrepreneurs, activates infrastructure and spreads jobs around the country, invigorating rural and depressed areas.

- And look at the prospects for the large developing countries such as China, India, South Africa and Brazil. Countries who will be massive two-way tourism traders over the next decade.

WTO is passionate about its commitment to poverty alleviation, embodied in our strategy of "Liberalization with a Human Face".

A strategy which responds to the new global Agenda manifest in the Millennium Development Goals which seek to halve poverty in the world's poorest countries by 2015. To the Summits of Doha on Trade, Monterrey on Debt Relief, and Johannesburg on sustainability. And also to the spirit of the Global fora of Davos on economics, Mumbai on social issues and Barcelona on culture.

Under this strategy, we are linking our Global Code of Ethics to the Millennium Development Goals. Integrating strategies on fair trade, poverty alleviation and sustainable development; prioritizing the interests of the world's poorest nations with Africa at the fore

In the past two years, WTO has diligently pursued this work. Supporting community initiatives, working with development agencies & banks, helping countries place tourism at the core of their Poverty Reduction Strategy Papers and putting in place a new mechanism called ST-EP (Sustainable Tourism - Eliminating Poverty) to bring new funds, research and projects into play.

Leading the WSSD Johannesburg implementation strategy for tourism to create a framework of indicators and best practice models.

Highlighting fair trade and development benefits in our work with the other WTO, and initiating export training programmes with the International Trade Centre & UNCTAD.

We have advanced a proposal for expanding air service to what we call Essential Tourism Development Routes, modelled on US and EU practices and now under joint study with ICAO. Because you must have adequate competitively priced air service to get tourism off the ground

And we have launched a dedicated Africa Programme, linked to NEPAD, to give new resources and increased investment in tourism development.

Our Assembly gave a ringing endorsement to the further intensification of these efforts within the UN family, convinced that tourism - which links people, builds livelihoods, supports communities and provides services exports for poor countries - is well placed to assist in meeting the major challenges facing the world today - peace, poverty, sustainability and fair trade.

We live in a world, where uncertainty is certain. Where complex issues are becoming more complicated. Where Summitry is providing a sea change in globalization. And where the spotlight of the media is strong and tough. As it should be.

During CNN's travel forum in London the question was raised as to whether the media was being objective in its coverage. I think it's the wrong question. The issue is are we being realistic in our understanding of what we can expect.

We can either bleat and frankly not change anything. Or we can get on with our job, diligently and openly in the belief that if your strategy is right you will ultimately shine in the media spotlight. In WTO we believe our "Liberalizing with a Human Face" strategy is right for our sector and right for our times.

GRUPO DE REFLEXIÓN II

El turismo como fuerza económica

PANEL II

Tourism as an economic force

TABLE RONDE II

Le tourisme comme force économique

- **INTRODUCCIÓN / INTRODUCTION / INTRODUCTION**
  Marc Meister,
  Managing Director, SERGAT Spain

- **"SPAIN MARKS" - PRESENTACIÓN DE LA CAMPAÑA PROMOCIONAL**
  Javier Piñanes Leal,
  Director General, TURESPAÑA

- **POLITICS OF TOURISM - BRIDGING THE PUBLIC/PRIVATE SECTOR COMMUNICATIONS GAP**
  Christopher Brown,
  CEO, Tourism Task Force

- **THE POWER OF TV IN TOURISM COMMUNICATIONS**
  Gary Wardrope,
  Commercial Director, Travel Channel

- **TRANSFERRING KNOWLEDGE IN TOURISM**
  Donald Hawkins,
  Eisenhower Professor of Tourism Policy, George Washington University

INTRODUCTION

MARC MEISTER
Managing Director, SERGAT Spain

Ladies and Gentlemen, it is a pleasure to welcome you to this morning's second panel discussion, on Tourism as an Economic Force.

My name is Marc Meister, Managing Director of Sergat España, Spains specialist agency in Tourism Marketing & Communications.

Before making some general remarks on our topic let me present to you our distinguished speakers.

To start off, Mr Javier Piñanes, Director of Turespaña, will speak on "Spain Marks" as an example of a national tourism promotion campaign.

Sr. Piñanes is very well qualified to speak on tourism promotion both in the field abroad and at head office in one's own country. He was deputy director of the Spanish tourism office in Frankfurt and then director of that group's office in Berlin. Anyone who has seen the deluge of German tourists all over Spain throughout the year will know how successful Sr Piñanes' work has been.

After Germany, Sr Piñanes became Deputy Director-General for promotion at Turespaña, the Spanish Institute of Tourism, here in Madrid, before being promoted to his current post as Director-General.

Our second speaker, Mr. Christopher Brown has since 1992 been managing director and Chief Executive Officer of the Tourism Task Force, Australia's national lobby group for travel and tourism. He will be speaking on "The Politics of Tourism — bridging the public and private sector communications gap."

The Tourism Task Force brings together the chief executives of Australia's 200 largest institutions in travel, tourism, leisure and infrastructure. Mr. Brown played a leading role in Sydney's successful Olympic bid. He is a vice president of the World Tourism Organisation's Business Council and the regional representative of the World Travel and Tourism Council.

Our third speaker will be Mr. Gary Wardrope, Commercial Director of Travel Channel television in London, who will speak about "The Power of TV in Tourism Communications". The strength of television as a communications medium is more than self-evident, but in the case of tourism it has a particular power in offering the mass market of viewers special access to countries and sights which they might never otherwise have considered as potential destinations

And last but not least, Professor Donald Hawkins will bring a keen academic eye to "Transferring Knowledge in Tourism."

He is the Eisenhower Professor of Tourism Policy at George Washington University in Washington, D.C., and has been active in tourism education since 1970. Professor Hawkins is active in UN-funded research on tourism development with biodiversity conservation and the sustainable use of water and energy resources.

Before handing over to our first speaker, let me make some brief remarks.

The importance of tourism as an economic force is broadly well known and I do not intend to bore you with pages of statistics to back up this point. However some figures are necessary to illustrate it quite impressively.

The WTTC forecasts a growth on a trend line of 4.6 per cent per year from 2004 through 2013. For the year 2003, the latest reference, it estimated the direct economic impact of travel and tourism at 3.7% of global GDP, or US$ 1.28 trillion, responsible for a total of over 67 Million jobs. Taking the broader impact of travel and tourism through secondary suppliers and other effects we come to 10.2% of the global GDP with the staggering figure of US$ 3.5 trillion and 194.6 million jobs. Within that latter total are US$ 1 trillion in exports, services and merchandise. Also included are US$ 686 billion in capital investment, or 9.6% of the global total and US$ 224 billion in government expenditures, some 3.9% of the worldwide figure.

Looking forward 10 years, the projections are for US$ 2.3 trillion of expenditure and 83.9 million jobs in the travel and tourism industry narrowly defined. For the broader overall economic impact of travel, the numbers are US& 8.9 trillion and 247.2 million jobs.

Sometimes mentioning all these very impressive figures which certainly underline the tremendous economic force which our industry is on a global scale, we tend to forget what tourism is all about: it's a people's business: by people - for people. We should not lose the perspective that tourism, in order to be viable in the long run, must serve not only consumers but suppliers, hosts and their communities, must help cross cultural exchange and fertilisation, must help to foster mutual respect and understanding, must help create enriching experiences on both ends, must help improving economical and social conditions of the suppliers at the same time as preserving their natural environment. Unless the children of this world, say in Tanzania, Bolivia, Laos, on the Marquise Islands or wherever, in the future understand and see by themselves that tourism enriches their lives, we will have failed. It's up to all of us to plan and ensure that the arithmetic juggling of figures translates into positive , peaceful experiences and prosperity for the present and future generations to come all around the globe.

With that as background, I now turn the dialogue over to our panel members. Following their presentations, we will have an opportunity for questions and answers.

"SPAIN MARKS" - PRESENTACIÓN DE LA CAMPAÑA PROMOCIONAL

JAVIER PIÑANES LEAL
Director General, TURESPAÑA

1. LA MARCA TURÍSTICA ESPAÑA: LA PROMOCIÓN TURÍSTICA

Es evidente que la promoción turística en los mercados exteriores es un instrumento importante de creación de imagen de país. En ocasiones, la primera, y a veces la única, que percibe el ciudadano extranjero al que se le quiere convencer de que visite ese país

La Administración Turística española viene realizando promoción turística y trabajando en la creación y consolidación de la marca España como destino turístico desde comienzos del siglo XX, cuando en 1928 se creó el Patronato Nacional de Turismo, dependiente del Ministerio de Instrucción Pública y de Bellas Artes. Puede parecer sorprendente la continuidad del enfoque en la creación de la marca turística España a lo largo de casi un siglo.

Muchas veces se ha reprochado al turismo español ofrecer una imagen de destino turístico masivo de sol y playa. Nada más lejos de la realidad. La corriente turística desde el centro y el norte de Europa hacia el Mediterráneo en busca de la luz, el sol, el clima y una determinada forma de vivir, obedece a impulsos profundos y tendencias sociales muy potentes. La promoción turística ha incidido en estas tendencias y ha sido especialmente activa cuando la coyuntura, las circunstancias económicas o conflictos internacionales han afectado al sector turístico, a su rentabilidad y a su estabilidad, poniendo en peligro una fuente fundamental de divisas.

Sin embargo, la imagen que siempre se ha transmitido de España ha sido la de un país con una rica herencia cultural, producto del encuentro de civilizaciones, que ha generado uno de los patrimonios artísticos más variados y originales y con unas manifestaciones no sólo del pasado, sino también vivas y actuales en las que se expresa la vitalidad del pueblo español del presente.

Este enfoque ha sido permanente en la creación de la marca turística. Los primeros años hasta finales de la década de los 60 la publicidad se dirigió hacía un turismo eminentemente cultural, de alto nivel social, y sin una estacionalidad o ubicación geográfica determinada. En estos años se encuentra el slogan más conocido de esta etapa del turismo de nuestro país: "España es diferente".

Posteriormente y hasta prácticamente finales de los 70, la publicidad fue centrándose sobre todo en el sol, las playas y las fiestas, buscando un turismo más lúdico y masivo.

Durante la década de los 80, la publicidad ha ido cambiando hacía un turismo más selectivo al que se ofrecen muchos más atractivos. En esta época se incorpora el slogan "Everything under the sun", que es posiblemente uno de los eslóganes más brillantes, duraderos y eficaces de la reciente publicidad española.

En 1991 el slogan "Todo Bajo el Sol" llevaba utilizándose nueve años y suponía un auténtico reto acometer su renovación. El nuevo slogan "Passion for life" remite a un turismo cada vez más activo y vivo, acorde con nuestro carácter y forma de entender la vida que mueve a quien nos visita a disfrutar de unas vacaciones que nunca la dejarán indiferente.

En 1997 y bajo el slogan "Bravo Spain", se crea una nueva línea de comunicación con el objetivo de:

- Transmitir la imagen de España hoy como país moderno, vivo, creativo, innovador y a la vanguardia de Europa.
- Demostrar la gran diversidad de la oferta turística de España.
- Potenciar el binomio calidad-diversidad.
- Fomentar una segunda visita al país fuera de la temporada de verano.
- Captar un turismo de mayor capacidad de gasto.

2. CÓMO NOS VEN: LOS ESTUDIOS SOBRE LA IMAGEN DE ESPAÑA

Transcurridos tres años desde el inicio de la creatividad "Bravo Spain", se planteó la necesidad de hacer una valoración de sus resultados y afrontar una nueva creatividad. Para realizar este análisis, se llevó a cabo un estudio a finales del año 2000 con el objeto de medir el grado de penetración de la Campaña de Publicidad de Turespaña en los mercados europeos elegidos de Alemania, Francia y Gran Bretaña, se puso de manifiesto, una vez más, que uno de los principales activos con que cuenta España como marca en el mercado turístico, es su logotipo. Éste es reconocido e identificado con España por un 75% de los europeos, un porcentaje que lo sitúa en los niveles de reconocimiento de las grandes marcas multinacionales. Además, el logotipo de Miró, de acuerdo con los resultados de este estudio, tiene un extraordinario poder para evocar los principales rasgos de la personalidad de España: carácter, sensibilidad creativa, vitalidad, innovación.

Los principales rasgos de la imagen de España como destino turístico, de acuerdo con el citado estudio ("Diagnóstico y Recomendaciones estratégicas para la comunicación de España"), se pueden resumir en los siguientes puntos:

- España es percibida como el destino que ofrece mejor relación calidad-precio.
- España es considerada el destino que ofrece las mejores playas.
- España también es valorada como el destino más hospitalario y con mejor trato humano.
- España es el destino donde los turistas perciben una mayor sensación de libertad y una elevada sensación de seguridad.
- España precisa una imagen más destacada como destino cultural.
- España precisa una imagen más destacada como destino gastronómico

Por otra parte, las conclusiones en lo referente a la imagen de España que se extraen tanto del estudio realizado para la Oficina española de turismo en Berlín por la empresa NIT, como del realizado para la Oficina Española de Turismo en Bélgica por la empresa WES, son bastante coincidentes, lo que lleva a pensar que en general los centroeuropeos tienen una imagen bastante parecida de nuestro país como destino de vacaciones.

Las principales características que hacen de nuestro país un buen destino de vacaciones son las ligadas a nuestro turismo de sol y playa: el clima, la calidad de las playas y su ubicación junto a la costa.

Además, destacan también la amplia variedad de actividades y su vida nocturna (oferta complementaria), además de su ser ideal para vacaciones familiares, y nuestra hospitalidad.

Los belgas destacan también España, frente a otros países mediterráneos, en lo que se refiere a calidad de nuestros hoteles y un nivel de precios razonable, mientras que para los alemanes estas características son aplicables a España en un nivel algo menor.

Sin embargo, todos los estudios coinciden también en que España adolece de falta de imagen como destino de turismo cultural. Según el Estudio de Turismo Cultural editado por Turespaña, en una encuesta a turistas culturales europeos sólo el 17 % mencionan que España tiene una oferta amplia y diversa de este producto, y su valoración general en este producto está muy por detrás de la otorgada a otros países como Grecia, Italia y Francia.

España registra, frente a su competencia, un posicionamiento plenamente competitivo en el territorio emocional, sin detrimento del componente funcional.

El mapa de posicionamiento es el del país que mejor compatibiliza los ejes de exotismo, proximidad y sensación de libertad alcanzando un buen equilibrio como destino turístico.

3. LA NUEVA CAMPAÑA COMO ELEMENTO DE RENOVACIÓN DE LA IMAGEN DE ESPAÑA: *SPAIN MARKS*

En base a este posicionamiento, los objetivos estratégicos que se definieron para la Campaña de Publicidad de Turespaña de 2002 y 2003 habían de contar con los siguientes elementos básicos:

- Consolidación del liderazgo a través de la calidad como elemento diferencial de la oferta turística española. No confundir con lujo: calidad=satisfacción de las expectativas del cliente. Sistema de Calidad Turística Española.
- Riqueza cultural: transmitir la idea de que España es un destino imprescindible para un turista interesado por la cultura. Cultura en sentido amplio.
- Reflejar el componente emocional que se ha destacado en el posicionamiento (hospitalidad, carácter español, calor humano, ritmo de vida, sensación de libertad, fiesta, alegría, relax, familia).
- Flexibilidad para adaptarla a las circunstancias cambiantes de la situación internacional y a las distintas tipologías del mercado.
- Capacidad para su utilización en campañas cooperativas con Comunidades Autónomas, marcas interregionales (España Verde, Pirineos, etc.), y empresas (Paradores, líneas aéreas, touroperadores).
- Diversificación
- Proyección exterior de España. Consolidar el liderazgo de España en su publicidad turística.
- Teniendo en cuenta las conclusiones del estudio de imagen, y de acuerdo con las especificaciones del concurso de creatividad, la selección recayó en la campaña Spain Marks previa comprobación de su acogida, en los principales mercados emisores de turismo hacia España

La campaña trabaja bien en muchos frentes, cubriendo los objetivos de la comunicación publicitaria de un destino turístico.

- Es una campaña novedosa que pronostica un alto nivel de notoriedad e impacto.
- Alta capacidad de motivar emocionalmente.
- Moderniza la imagen de España. Impulsa una imagen latente de país transformado y moderno de calidad.
- Innova y lidera en comunicación en el sector turístico, transformando los códigos comunicacionales vigentes.
- Despierta / Revitaliza el interés hacia España como destino.

Traduciendo estos planteamientos a cifras, en los últimos 6 años (1997 - 2002) la Administración Turística del Estado, a través de Turespaña, ha invertido 99, 3 millones de euros en la Campaña de Publicidad. En el año 2003, la inversión de Turespaña ha sido de 23 millones que, unidos a la aportación de las CC.AA. en las campañas conjuntas, ha alcanzado los 40 millones. Para el año 2004, el presupuesto es de 26,7 millones de euros, a los que se sumará la aportación aun no definida de las CC.AA.

3.1- Objetivos y realización de la campaña - Creatividad

El diseño de la línea de comunicación actual de la campaña huye de planteamientos convencionales en la publicidad turística y es innovadora e impactante en el estilo de los mensajes. Está basada en la variedad de la oferta turística nacional, fundamentalmente dirigida a un turismo cada vez más exigente y menos concentrado en épocas concretas del año, a través de un tono en la comunicación que transmite calidad, individualización, diversidad y modernidad.

Publicis ha sido la Agencia elegida para desarrollar la creatividad de la campaña de comunicación que Turespaña realiza desde 2002.

El objetivo que Turespaña estableció para esta campaña era presentar España como un destino turístico diferente, especialmente en comparación con el resto de los países de la cuenca mediterránea, y haciendo un especial hincapié en la calidad como elemento diferencial de la oferta española: calidad cultural, calidad gastronómica, calidad natural.

España no es sólo un lugar (playas, monumentos, gastronomía); es un viaje de los sentidos y del alma. Es una forma de entender la vida.

Sólo en España la vida se concibe de una forma mucho más rica, apasionada, más completa: se vive plenamente.

Por eso, todo aquel que haya pasado por España nunca volverá a ser el mismo. Llevará una señal, una marca: La huella de su paso por España.

El viajero y su marca: El principal protagonista de la campaña será el público al que va dirigida, el turista extranjero y se mostrará transformado por la huella que ha dejado en él su paso por España.

Cada original se centra en una temática turística concreta, relacionada directamente con la huella que ha producido.

Además, la campaña incorporará un lema, una firma, que simboliza la personalidad de España como destino turístico:

"SPAIN MARKS"
(España marca)

Este lema se traduce a cada una de las lenguas de los países en los que se realizará la campaña, así como el texto alusivo a la temática turística y la huella que ésta deja en el viajero.

La campaña se realiza en Francia, Alemania, Portugal, Italia, Holanda, Bélgica, Rusia, Polonia, Dinamarca, Noruega, Suecia, Estados Unidos, Canadá, Gran Bretaña, Finlandia, Japón, Brasil, México, Singapur y Japón y contará con más de 25 originales.

Más allá de un destino turístico

Al estar basada en nuestros valores sociales y culturales, la campaña contribuye a mejorar la percepción de España como país, y no sólo como destino turístico. Además, dada la gran trascendencia y el alcance de esta acción publicitaria, "SPAIN MARKS" se convertirá en un claro exponente de la construcción de la marca España en el mundo.

La agencia de publicidad

Publicis España es una de las agencias líderes en el sector publicitario español. Pertenece al Grupo Publicis, el primero de Europa y cuarto del mundo. Entre sus clientes se encuentran empresas como L'Oreal, Loterías y Apuestas del Estado, Coca Cola, Mahou, Hewlett Packard, y el Grupo Recoletos.

3.2- Ventajas de la campaña SPAIN MARKS (España marca)

De acuerdo con el informe del instituto de investigación Tourism & Leisure y Táctica, la campaña España marca, de Publicis España, *"se posiciona como la campaña más adecuada, porque sabe transmitir con mayor intensidad los valores y beneficios de España como destino turístico. La campaña presenta un proceso de comprensión del mensaje más ágil y directo, además de una mayor transversalidad y versatilidad en presentar valores, beneficios y generar interés. La campaña disfruta, además, de una gran notoriedad"*.

También de acuerdo con los resultados expuestos por dicho informe, *España marca es una campaña sugerente, que aporta innovación en comunicación en el sector turístico. Es apta para un líder. Se trata de una campaña con alta capacidad de movilizar emociones representadas en los rostros de los protagonistas. Se transmite con fuerza el hecho de que se ha vivido una experiencia y se ha sentido el país. La propuesta de emociones conecta con la imagen que se tiene de España, pero dándole un nuevo enfoque en la comunicación, que transmite la imagen de un país moderno. La idea que se interpreta del slogan de dejar huella expresa bien el resultante de la experiencia esperada de cualquier viaje: conocer y aprender sobre los países y sobre uno mismo. El viaje como posibilidad de crecimiento personal".*

The Politics of Tourism - Bridging the Public/Private Sector Communications Gap

CHRISTOPHER BROWN
CEO, Tourism Task Force Australia

There are three real issues that I think we need to talk about in communications. My background is more predominantly in that of the public affairs, public relations and, of late, crisis communications, rather than some of the experts in the marketing field and promotional field.

The headline issues that I've always approached and that I think we need to approach when it come to communications in our industry is honesty. You can try and "spin" it all you like, but eventually you'll get caught out. If you're promising something that does not exist, if you're spinning to the point of distraction, if you're not honest with your community - be it your customers, your internal staff, stakeholders, shareholders, or the media - you will get caught out, tragically and controversially, as in my part of the world endured the SARS crisis of last year. I think had some government and others been more honest at the beginning, some of the hysteria would not have flowed and I think everybody learnt a lesson about being honest and about your community particularly when it comes to crisis security and disease issues.

It's also about ingenuity. As honest and as credible as we have to be, it does not mean you cannot try and spin, it does not mean you cannot try and manipulate, it does not mean you cannot try and put the best possible focus on your product. I will use a positive example in recent times: New Zealand - Australia's "little brother", which has done so remarkably well off the back of the "Lord of the Rings" phenomena to convince the world that Middle Earth does exist. (Luckily you have to fly to Sydney to get there mostly, so it's about time we get to play off of their hip - they have done it off us for years.) They have been able to use, both in the marketing message and the public relations message to tell the world to come down and see "Middle Earth on Earth". It has been a very innovative and ingenious approach of their marketing.

You need to be pro-active. And I can come back to the African example. Some very ingenious comments made earlier by some of the colleagues, friends from Africa. And I suppose the best spin I can put on that is pro-activism. (It was great to see Becky Anderson here at the end taking a whole lot of cards, getting a whole lot of story ideas. I guarantee there will be some CNN focus on Africa in the next little while.) And that was pro-activism. People having the courage to stand up and say : "What's wrong, how do we fix it, what do we do about it?" And then to follow through and then develop the story ideas. One thing that I can guarantee in my experiences in communications: the media will not come looking for you unless there is a problem. So if you have a good story to tell, you have got to chase them. And if there is a problem, you'd better front up and be honest about it because it will overtake you.

Lastly it's about reality. Do not promise what does not exist because the thing I learnt in advertising from David Ogilvy as a trainee many years ago is: "Happiness occurs when reality is greater than expectation". For years, Australia kept selling Cairns as a tropical beach destination in North Queensland.

People would arrive and look at the mud flats and say: "The brochure said there's a beach. Where's the beach?" Well, the ultimate bit of spin is that the Queensland state government has now built a beach in Cairns so that the destination can actually live up to its promotion. And it's working very well.

In terms of media: be pro-active, always. But always also understand your media. There is nothing worse than finance journalists being pitched a story about rugby scores. You have to understand the media you deal with. We have to understand the timing pressures, the deadline pressures. They are not homogeneous. Some journalists want you to do all the work, and in reality you might get away with most of what you want because they are happy if you put it to them by deadline. Some are strong investigative journalists - they do not want to hear PR pap. They want to get involved in deep significant pieces. So it's very much always about understanding the media. There is no down side to understanding the media as much as possible.

Spend, spend, spend. It is going to get expensive, ladies and gentlemen. If you want to play the global media, it is going to cost you. It is going to cost you a lot. And that is spending on actual airtime, that is spending on professionals to help you do the job, that is spending on research and monitoring and following up and doing clippings because if a job is worth doing, it is worth doing it properly. I guarantee you in communications, it is worth doing it properly.

Use professionals, be professional. Go and hire the best PR people you can find and get them to do the job. Do not muck around. Do not get the person who was doing photocopying last week and make them the PR person this week. It is too important to be done in an amateur way. It is very important that you use the best in-house and external professionals to do that. It is also very important that you empower those professionals.

Do not have the PR boss reporting to the third-level marketing director. The PR manager reports to the CEO or Deputy CEO! It is a standard rule of communications because that boss is the one the media is going to come to quickly. They need to have access to their person, their advisor, their "spin doctor". So empower that person, invest in them, train them, resource them, support them in what they do because you might often think that the director of sales or the director of operations is the most important. Those two people probably will not make you lose your job but the director of public affairs can probably help save your job and help you get a better job and a better salary and a better return. So we have to stop relegating communications and PR to the bottom of the pile professionally and put it up where it deserves, much near at the top.

When it comes to communications in tourism, as we know, it is mostly about the message. Tourism is a fairly unique beast. Every single country on earth has a tourism product - some better than others, without a doubt. But pretty much everybody has a product to some degree of quality. Not everybody produces coal and wool, not everybody produces silicon chips or computer programming, not everybody produces *foie gras* and fine wine. **But everybody has a tourism product.** There are some different levels of access. There are different levels of ability to build infrastructure, of quality hotels and airport and others. But pretty much, the world is catching up, it's almost homogenous.

What the point of difference is, is the message, is the marketing, is the communications. That's where you can beat your neighbour. That is where New Zealand could get in front of Australia in the last few years because they invested and spent and were smart as we sat still and got fat and lazy and thought we had done the job. And now we are back to re-compete and get back out there into the world. But that is the point of difference. It's also a lot cheaper. It's an awful lot cheaper to run a PR campaign than to build new freeways, toll ways and airports around the nation. It's a lot easier and quicker to go after the world with a message about how magnificent your tourism product is than trying to attract billions of dollars to invest in new hotels and other infrastructure. Never underestimate the reinforcement of the message to all of those who give us the funds to go and invest in that message. **The message is what largely makes the difference in tourism because we are not selling a washing machine, we are selling a human experience.** We are saying to families: "Bring your children here and have a holiday. Trust us with your memories, with the magic."

And it is pretty hard to sell the magic without a good message. And whichever medium you choose - there will be a bunch of people who will tell you their medium is the best during the course of this Conference - use a medium. Essentially, it is important that we sell, we continue to sell, we never stop selling, and we get up and sell again tomorrow. Because the customers are being sold to by your neighbours if you are not selling yourself.

Look at Australia, here is a classic example. In the past twenty years we have gone from nothing and non-existent - nobody knew where we were, everybody thought we were Austria - into now being one of the global leaders in tourism. I am very proud that Australia will in the next few month rejoin the WTO and take its rightful position diplomatically in tourism. But I am prouder that over the past twenty years, with not a lot of money, with a smile and a shoeshine, we got out there and hit the road and 'sold' Australia to the world.

Now, we had some advantages along the way, like the Olympic Games, Gay Games, Rugby World Cup, we have had Expos and other major events and we have done them well. But we basically sold a message. And we have gradually improved our infrastructure. But still, when I leave here at 5 o'clock this afternoon, it will take me the best part of 26 hours to get home. And only way you overcome that problems is by selling the message to everybody: "It's worth it! It's worth travelling 26 hours to get to Australia from Spain because that is the price you pay for paradise." It is simply about a message, about selling. And Australia has done that after the last couple of years very well. We're about to do it again very well, when we re-emerge with a new global brand in the next few months.

Now turning attention to public-private partnerships. I have the pleasure of sitting on a domestic tourism public- private partnership arrangement in Australia - called See Australia. The federal government said to us, we will get into the business of promoting Australia to Australians, if you can bring industries and state governments to play. So they put up 8 million dollars, the state governments collectively put up 4 million dollars, the industry put up 8 million dollars.

See Australia had a very successful public-private partnership approach to domestic marketing. Similarly, as most NTO's do, in working with the private sector to get money. But it's important that that partnership works. In public-private partnership it requires different things of the different partners. But what is basically required is commitment. Commitment in dollars, political commitment, commitment to go the whole haul and not to give up half way. And there are too many examples of that. I know that in Spain, there are attempts now to build a greater public-private partnership in marketing and I applaud that because it must be public-private. Because with all due respect, public servants aren't the people to go to for ad campaigns, and private tourism operators aren't the best people to understand the politics of the industries, but together they are a hell of a partnership. **And we must always commit ourselves to that partnership. We need industry to sign on to "brand" and not just "product". We need government to sign on to retail not just generic promotion.** And together the two dynamics do work in bridging the marketing the public-private sector gap.

It is also important that you get your community to sign on to your message. Paul Hogan (Crocodile Dundee) launched Australia's ad campaign a few years ago. But the probably best ad campaigns he ever did were campaigns in Australia telling Australians what he had told the world, and challenging us to live up to the message he had sold the world. It was very important that in the new branding we are doing at the moment, that Australians feel and own the brand we are going to sell to the world.

Fosters, the Australian beer, discovered during the Olympic Games - as they were the sponsors for the Olympics - that the rest of the world would soon realise that Australians don't drink much Fosters. Imagine going to Ireland and finding that Guinness really is not the beer that is drunk, or going to Holland and finding out that Heineken is not that popular. Fosters is really not a beer drunk in Australia by many Australians, but we sell it to the world as "Australian for beer". The downside for the brewery was they had to flood every pub with free Fosters for the period of the Games so that it looked like we were drinking it when foreigners walked into the door. So there are some upsides to some of those problems. And I'll drink any beer if it's free.

The other side to what I was talking about was public affairs and policy and PR in a public-private dynamic. **It is interesting when you think about communications by governments and by industry, as to how much they differ.** Government always wants to talk to the public about their destination, industry always wants to talk about their product. And that's understandable. Each have a different imperative to their different stakeholders. The government always wants to tell industry that everything IS okay. Industry always want to bleat to the government that everything IS NOT okay. And there are understandable dynamics and we need forums like mine in my country and others in another countries to enable discussion. Simply sitting in the corner and sniping at each other gets you nowhere.

We have had a recent experience in Australia developing a White Paper. We were very lucky to get extra 235 million dollars out of the federal government. But we have had two years of bad news in the newspapers, almost talking tourism down because the opportunism is that governments only respond when there is a crisis, governments do not respond when things are good, because governments say to you: "It's your time, you pay the money". But fortunately we have been able to work through that and get the outcome needed.

So in conclusion, let me address another element of the public-private sector partnership. Some years ago, a crisis scenario in Australia was an oil slick on the Barrier Reef. Unfortunately, in the less secure world we now find ourselves in, the new crisis scenario plan in Australia is about the Opera House being blown up. We have to plan for awful things like that and have PR contingencies. The Federal Government sensibly put a media contingency plan together, but they did not intend to contact industry until Day 3 for a briefing. And I said, "you might wait until day three to talk to us, but CNN will call us two minutes after it has blown up".

So understand that in that partnership of communications both sides have a role to play, all sides need to commit in particularly to funding and everybody needs to commit to professionalism, honesty and integrity in all their communications in whatever industry we serve.

Thank you for listening to me.

THE POWER OF TV IN TOURISM COMMUNICATIONS

GARY WARDROPE

Commercial Director, Travel Channel

The Power of TV in Tourism Communications

- Television- From the comfort of your home
- Easy to use, simple to understand
- Sells the sizzle
- Provides great detail- from facilities, culture, hotel, room
- Trustworthy
- Everyone has a TV

travelchannel LANDMARK TRAVEL CHANNEL LIMITED travel deals direct

Why is TV perfect for the Travel Market

- Travel is time, place, price and its perishable
- Moving pictures are more powerful and emotive- TV inspires
- TV is dynamic- prices , products can be changed according to the market
- TV is tactical
- Can cut costs of distribution- paper, agent

travelchannel LANDMARK TRAVEL CHANNEL LIMITED travel deals direct

What are our products- Revenue Model

- Travel Channel
- 80 countries, 30 million homes across Europe, Africa and soon the Middle East
- Subscription and Airtime Model

- Travel Deals Direct
- Commission based selling packages in USA, cruise, ski, cities and rest of the world with all major operators

travelchannel   LANDMARK TRAVEL CHANNEL LIMITED   travel deals direct

Who are Landmark Travel Channel

- Multi Media company in Virginia and Atlanta
- Television, radio, internet, newspapers
- Weather Channel

travelchannel   LANDMARK TRAVEL CHANNEL LIMITED   travel deals direct

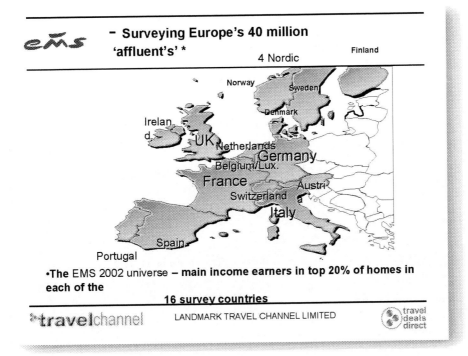

- Surveying Europe's 40 million 'affluent's' *

•The EMS 2002 universe – **main income earners in top 20% of homes in each of the**

16 survey countries

LANDMARK TRAVEL CHANNEL LIMITED

The ☆travelchannel **transmission 'footprint'**

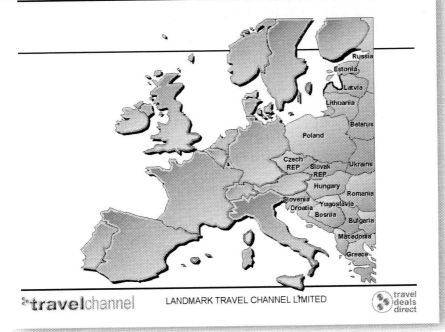

LANDMARK TRAVEL CHANNEL LIMITED

Growth of Digital TV UK

- Sky – 7 million homes
- Cable –NTL and Telewest 2 million
- Freeview- DTT-2 .5 million
- 45% of population in UK have digital- 11.5 million
- Analogue switch off 2010
- France- 4 million, Germany-2.5 million,Scandinavia 1 million, Portugal- 1 million
- Broadband-2.1 million cable to PC, 1.1 million ADSL, 1 million cable

travelchannel   LANDMARK TRAVEL CHANNEL LIMITED   travel deals direct

The Players-

- Editorial

- Travel Channel-UK and Europe, Middle East
- Sky- UK

- Transactional-UK Only

- Travel Deals Direct
- Thomas Cook
- TV Travel Shop
- Going Places
- Sky

travelchannel   LANDMARK TRAVEL CHANNEL LIMITED   travel deals direct

Benefits of Digital TV?

- Clearer picture- no hiss , no fuzz
- Can get more information down the pipe- therefore more channels possible, more cost effective for broadcaster, theme channels can run at fraction of the cost
- Interactivity-Convergence
- Customer is in control- get what they want, when they want

travelchannel   LANDMARK TRAVEL CHANNEL LIMITED   travel deals direct

Opportunities for Travel Supply Chain

- Airtime spot campaigns on targeted editorial channel in UK and across Europe
- Production of editorial shoots, adverts , videos, rights?
- Transactional commission based plays with operators and direct
- Sponsorships- Theme Months
- B Roll-own your own content for website, TV etc.
- Convergence- integrate website with TV
- Extensive database of properties/information

travelchannel   LANDMARK TRAVEL CHANNEL LIMITED   travel deals direct

TRANSFERRING KNOWLEDGE IN TOURISM

PROF. DONALD HAWKINS
Eisenhower Professor of Tourism Policy, George Washington University

By Dr. Donald E. Hawkins, Eisenhower Professor of Tourism Policy, School of Business and Public Management, George Washington University, Washington, DC, dhawk@gwu.edu

Transferring tourism knowledge is a very broad topic to cover in a brief paper so I want to focus mainly on higher education institutions role in transferring knowledge into practice. Let me begin by defining knowledge:

"An understanding of something and the ability to use that understanding through study and experience"[1]

KNOWLEDGE TRANSFER NETWORKING APPROACH

As the Chairman of the WTO Education Council, George Washington University intends to propose that that our members adopt a comprehensive networking approach emphasizing the responsibility of higher education institutions to transfer knowledge to the governmental, commercial and civil society components of the tourism sector.

According to the American Productivity and Quality Center (APQC), knowledge transfer is a cyclical process. The ultimate goal of knowledge transfer is knowledge use. As obvious as that may seem, many organizations have little idea if the knowledge they attempt to share is actually being used.

APQC recommends that networks be formed "to study how outstanding organizations design and deploy successful approaches to identify, capture, and share information and knowledge so that use and reuse are optimized. The ability to rapidly identify and transfer superior practices is an important source of competitive advantage. As the economy grows, transfer and reuse will be the fastest way to grow without adding undue costs. No matter the industry, reusing successfully demonstrated practices can lead to shorter cycle times, faster ramp-up, higher customer satisfaction, better decisions, and lower costs."[2]

---

[1] The Newbury House Dictionary of American English, Monroe Allen PUBLISHERS, 2000, P. 479

[2] APQC is a pioneer in knowledge management (KM). Based on the experiences of more than 350 organizations implementing KM, APQC has captured the best practices and created a proven methodology: APQC's Road Map to Knowledge Management Results: Stages of Implementation(tm). Since its 1995 knowledge management symposium, APQC has conducted 14 KM-specific consortium benchmarking studies. For details, go to: http://www.apqc.org.

The knowledge transfer process described in Figure 1 describes the creation of knowledge and its transfer though identification, collection, review, sharing, adaptation, adoption steps leading to its use.

Figure 1. Knowledge Transfer Process

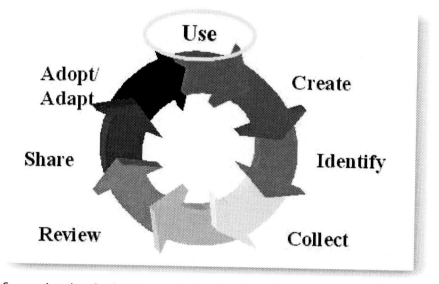

Source: American Productivity and Quality Center (APQC)

As stated earlier, using and reusing accepted practices can lead to the improvement of organizational effectiveness. Scientific, professional and trade networks in the tourism sector have given increasing importance to benchmarking to improve the performance of organizations, employing processes similar to the APQC approach described above. Wober[3] describes internal and external benchmarking approaches. Internal refers to the functions and activities of an organization at the same or different locations. External benchmarking involves the use of (a) best practices regardless of sector/industry or to improve performance and learn from others; (b) comparative analysis of performance objectives, strategies, and activities of competitors in a sector/industry to improve competitiveness; and (c) policies, strategies, information systems, training programs designed to improve a sector/industry. Wober classifies benchmarking in tourism to encompass profit-oriented firms, nonprofit organizations and destinations. Most of the benchmarking initiatives have been focused on profit-making firms, particularly in the hospitality industry. Fewer initiatives have been undertaken for non profit or destination organizations.

HIGHER EDUCATION'S ROLE IN KNOWLEDGE MANAGEMENT

Higher education institutions have begun to recognize that they play an increasingly important role to play in knowledge management (KM). As Hallal has stated: "In an age when knowledge has surpassed capital as the strategic factor driving the global economy, KM deserves some portion of the enormous effort now expended on accounting, financial analysis, capital investment and the vast infrastructure devoted to sheer money.[4]

---

[3] Wober, Karl W., Benchmarking in Tourism and Hospitality Industries, CABI, 2002, p. 3

[4] Halal, William E., The Logic of Knowledge: How a Knowledge Economy Differs from a Capital Economy, unpublished paper, George Washington University, Washington, DC, p.2.

Throughout history, higher education institutions have been challenged to both create and disseminate knowledge. Often, our efforts have been characterized as an "ivory tower" approach not related to practical realties. Today, higher education's role, in my judgment, should be to facilitate KM, which can be operationally defined as transferring knowledge into practice through research, teaching, and service, as described in the figure below:

Figure 2 Transferring Knowledge into Practice

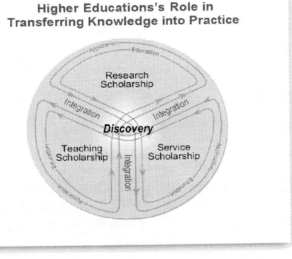

Teaching, research, and service scholarship can lead to the transfer of knowledge to practice through the functions of discovery, integration, application, and education, as described below:

Discovery of Knowledge. Discovery involves being the first to find out, to know, or to reveal original or revised theories, principles, knowledge, or creations. Academic discovery reflects "the commitment to knowledge for its own sake, to freedom of inquiry and to following, in a disciplined fashion, an investigation wherever it may lead."[5] Discovery includes identifying new or revised theoretical principles and models, insights about how empirical phenomena operate, and original creations in literature, performance, or production in the arts, architecture, design, video, and broadcast media.

Integration of Knowledge. Integration involves "making connections across the disciplines, placing the specialties in larger context, illuminating data in a revealing way, often educating non specialists, too". Integration creates new knowledge by bringing together otherwise isolated knowledge from two or more disciplines or fields thus creating new insights and understanding. It is "serious, disciplined work that seeks to interpret, draw together and bring new insight to bear on original research." It means "interpretation, fitting one's own research - or the research of others - into larger intellectual patterns."[6] Integration brings divergent knowledge, artistic creations, or original works together. Integration may occur within or between teaching, research, and service scholarship.

---

5 Boyer, Ernest L., Scholarship Reconsidered: Priorities of the Professorate, The Carnegie Foundation for the Advancement of Teaching, 1990, p17.
6 Boyer, op. cit. pp18-19.

Application of Knowledge. Application involves bringing knowledge to bear in addressing significant societal issues. It engages the scholar in asking, "How can knowledge be responsibly applied to consequential problems? How can it be helpful to individuals as well as institutions?"[7] Application involves the use of knowledge or reactive activities for development and change. With the first two functions, scholars define he topics for inquiry. With application, groups, organizations, community, government, or emergent societal issues define the agenda for scholarship.

Education. Education involves developing the knowledge, skill, mind, character, or ability f others. It "means not only transmitting knowledge, but transforming and extending it as well." Education stimulates "active, not passive, learning and encourages students to be critical, creative thinkers, with the capacity to go on learning…. It is a dynamic endeavor involving all the analogies, metaphors, and images that build bridges between the teacher's understanding and the student's learning. Pedagogical procedures must be carefully planned, continuously examined, and relate directly to the subject taught."[8]

NETWORKING THROUGH OUTREACH STRATEGIES

Outreach is a networking concept that describes a wide range of activities that involve universities can employ to create, identify, collect, review, share, and adopt/adapt knowledge leading to its use in practice. Outreach is not synonymous with "service" nor is it limited to cooperative extension and continuing education. Rather, outreach should be inherent in teaching, research, and service-i.e. :

Outreach research includes a wide spectrum of cooperative discovery, application, and creative problem-solving interactions between the university and external audiences. It includes policy and applied research, technology transfer partnerships, demonstration projects, creative works in the arts, and related interactions between university scholars and external audiences to discover, explore, and disseminate knowledge in practice.

Outreach teaching includes instruction and interpretation through cooperative extension and continuing education. Presentations to non-academic and professional audiences, the World Campus, and other extensions of instruction to benefit society are also outreach teaching.

Outreach service involves faculty sharing their expertise with a variety of audiences including service to the various professional and learned societies, participation in community affairs as a representative of the university, and service to communities, governments, and corporations. It includes clinical service delivery, participation in task forces, authorities, public hearings, professional performances, and other venues based on the expertise of faculty members."[9]

The examples which follow demonstrate outreaching networking approaches involving universities and the tourism sector:

---

[7] Ibid, p22.

[8] Ibid, pp23-24.

[9] Unified Knowledge System Concept for Overall Performance Evaluation, Pennsylvania State University, February 2001
http:/keystone21.cas.psu.edu/uniscope

OUTREACH RESEARCH EXAMPLE: SUSTAINABLE TOURISM CRC (STCRC)

The Sustainable Tourism CRC (STCRC) was established under the Australian Government's Cooperative Research Centers Program to underpin the development of a dynamic, internationally competitive, and sustainable tourism industry. The STCRC is a not-for-profit company owned by its industry, government and university partners.

STRC's vision is innovation driving a dynamic, internationally competitive and sustainable tourism industry. STRC's mission is the development and management of intellectual property (IP) to deliver innovation to business, community and government enhancing the environmental, economic and social sustainability of tourism - one of the world's largest, fastest growing industries.

DESTINATION AUSTRALIA is STCRC's integrated, multidisciplinary research program, focusing on three key areas:

- Sustainable Destinations
- Sustainable Enterprises
- Sustainable Resources

STCRC diffuses its research outputs to industry through:

- Collaboration with industry and government partners
- Spin-off enterprises
- Licensing its intellectual property
- Business tools, kits, manuals and expert systems
- Conferences, workshops, seminars
- Published reports, fact sheets and extension flyers
- Internet-based information services
- Training products, courses and programs
- International consulting services.

Recent accomplishments of the Sustainable Tourism CRC include the following:

1. Bringing tourism into the major Australia Government research and development initiative - the Cooperative Research Centers program
2. Strengthening collaborative links between industry, tourism research organizations, educational institutions and government agencies.
3. Funding post graduate sustainable tourism research issues
4. Focusing the collective export potential of Australia's leading tertiary level tourism, travel and hospitality providers.
5. Assisting the industry understand and value the benefit of a research based, strategic knowledge approach to addressing complex tourism issues
6. Assisting the Australian Government's decision to (a) re-join WTO (b) take an active role in the establishment and development of the APEC Tourism Working Group (c) establishing and hosting the APEC International Centre for Sustainable Tourism AICST.
7. Establishing or supporting spin-off companies to take the intellectual property generated from CRC research to the marketplace.

8. Leading the Australian/South Pacific research into WTO's ST - EP Program.
9. Providing Australian focus for the following tourism research agenda:
   - Tourism environmental management research (Wildlife Tourism, Mountain Tourism, Nature Tourism, Adventure Tourism)
   - Tourism engineering design & eco-technology research (Coastal and marine infrastructure and systems, coastal tourism ecology, Waste management, water supply and associated environmental impact studies, Physical infrastructure, design and construction)
   - Tourism policy, products and business research (Consumers and marketing, Events & sports tourism, Strategic management, business planning, and development, Destination management and regional tourism, Tourism economics and policy, Indigenous tourism)
   - E-travel and tourism research (Electronic product and destination marketing & selling, IT for travel and tourism online development, Rural & regional tourism online development, E-business innovation in sustainable travel and tourism)
   - Tourism education
10. The CRC has also established dedicated research centers at partner Universities:
    - Centre for Regional Tourism Research at Southern Cross University
    - Centre for Tourism Risk Management, University of Queensland
    - Qantas Chair in Tourism Economics, U. of New South Wales.
11. Publications: a large volume of high quality research generated by the CRC's projects can be viewed on the CRC website publications catalogue
12. Providing research and operational horse-power and support to Green Globe throughout the world.[10]

STCRC is developing Australia's long-term tourism research capacities through a vigorous postgraduate research education program, supported by scholarships for students in industry-designed projects, and by developing and distributing education and training products.

The Cooperative Research Centers Program is a major research and development initiative of the Australian Government. This program was established to boost the competitiveness of Australia by strengthening in collaborative links between industry, research organizations, educational institutions and relevant government agencies. It aims to bring the highest quality research providers and industry together to focus on outcomes for businesses and communities.[11]

OUTREACH TEACHING EXAMPLE: E-LEARNING COOPERATION MODEL

Distance learning, online education, e-learning and other terms have surfaced in the last decade to describe a variety of approaches to using the Internet and other information technologies to enable instructors in one place to deliver learning experiences to students located in other places, sometimes continents away.

The field has grown dramatically because e-learning offers a number of higher education advantages for certain student populations over the traditional single-site classroom approach, such as[12] :

---

[10] Correspondence from Steve Noakes, General Manager, STCRC, January 2004.

[11] Source and for further details, go to http://www.crctourism.com.au/

[12] Adapted from Mark Kassop "Ten Ways Online Education Matches, or Surpasses, Face-to-Face Learning." The Technology Source, May/June 2003. (Available online at http://ts.mivu.org/default.asp?show=article&id=1059).

1. Student-centered learning rather than faculty-centered instruction.
2. Writing intensity that improves written expression
3. Highly interactive discussions involving all students rather than just extraverts
4. More closely geared to interests of lifelong learners
5. Rapid feedback to questions and submitted assignments.
6. Learning flexibility in a time-deficient world
7. A more intimate community of learners
8. Expanded learning opportunities for those tied to their residences.

Two institutions of higher education with TedQual-certified programs - the Université du Québec à Montréal (UQAM) and The George Washington University (GWU) - have developed an E-learning Cooperation Model to enhance the delivery of tourism education in developing countries. This development was stimulated by the opportunities provided by the Memorandum of Understanding on Cooperation signed in 1999 between The World Tourism Organization (WTO) and The World Bank Group.

The Model is based on the project proposal entitled "Information Technology (IT) Strategy for Tourism Education in Africa - a Joint Initiative of the WTO and the World Bank Group" which received the support from the WTO Commission for Africa during its XXXVII Assembly, Seoul, Republic of Korea, 24 September 2001. While we focus on Africa in this elaboration of the Model here, it may be applied to any developing regions in the world.

Figure 1 summarizes the E-learning Cooperation Model, which begins with:

■ Digitalizing contents of all existing WTO GTAT courses for delivery online or on CD-ROM; and

■ Adapting digitalized program contents from participating TedQual-certified institutions, and developing new content where needed. For example, the GWU Accelerated Master of Tourism Administration (AMTA) graduate degree program, which meets TedQual standards, offers a bank of 15 courses now delivered online. Graduate courses from other TedQual certified institutions might be incorporated in the curriculum options, as well. UQAM can assist the translation of such courses into the French language and add content directly relevant to Francophone countries in Africa.

We anticipate that implementing this Model will produce the following constructive outcomes:

■ At least one group from the GTAT series of seminars and courses, which contents have been digitalized and offered to tourism managers in public and private sector workplaces, will be presented in each of the WTO member states in Africa;

■ At least one university from each of the WTO member states in Africa will present a high quality program in management of tourism, employing IT tools for tourism education;

■ At least one university from each of the WTO member states in Africa will apply for TedQual certification. GWU and UQAM, in collaboration with other interested TedQual-certified institutions, will offer capacity-building activities and direct mentoring to these TedQual candidates.

Figure 3. E-Leaning Cooperation Model

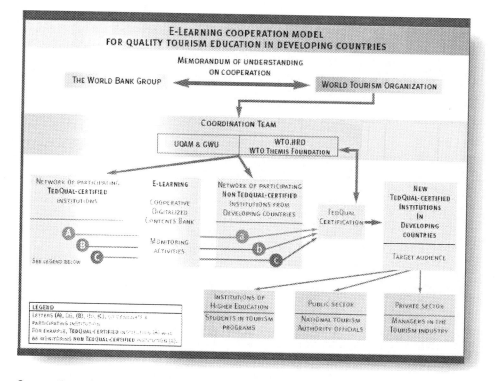

Source: *François Bédard, UQAM-CIFORT (2003)*

We are also exploring the ways and means by which this model might also be developed for the Indian Ocean and other regions of the World. The WTO Education Council is currently surveying its members to determine their distance learning capabilities and interest in joining this network. For example, George Washington University through its Blackboard E-Learning platform also an extensive series of continuing education unit (CEU) courses that lead to a Tourism Destination Management and Marketing Certificate and an Event Management Certificate. With development assistance funding, we are planning course series delivered through customized workshops enhanced by distance education learning for a tour operator certificate in Jordan, a rural tourism certificate in Morocco, an educational travel certificate in North America and a Sales Academy for the International Association of Visitor and Convention Bureaus.[13]

OUTREACH SERVICE EXAMPLE: DEVELOPMENT ASSISTANCE NETWORK FOR TOURISM ENHANCEMENT (DANTE)

As one of the largest global industries and employers, tourism has a significant role in the economies of both developed and developing countries. According to the World Bank's "World Development Indicators" 2002 report, more than 70% of the world's poorest countries are reliant on tourism as a key economic growth engine. Acknowledging this, development assistance projects are increasingly using tourism as a means of fostering sustainable development. However, there is a paucity of information

---

[13] For complete information on these programs, please go to http://www.gwutourism.org/

concerning appropriate engagement levels and policy guidance for development assistance in efforts to enhance tourism revenues for developing economies. There are difficulties in balancing the public sector role while maintaining a competitive private sector environment; also in balancing community needs and dealing with social issues Development assistance for tourism only really has a history of 20-30 years, and in most countries, sustainable tourism is an ongoing social, economic and environmental process of trail and error.

In 2001 George Washington University's International Institute of Tourism Studies (GWU/IITS) began a project to populate a database of world-wide donor funded tourism projects. The incentive for this initiative was the absence of consistent information about the sources or benefits of tourism projects in developing countries, and the missed opportunity to learn from experiences that would undoubtedly be of value to all stakeholders. During the past two years of research by GW's IITS, 363 ongoing projects, from over 20 different donors, with a total value of more than US$9.43 billion estimated for period 2001-10, have been identified; refer to Table 1 below for further details.

Table 1. Development Assistance Funding Estimates 2001 -2010

Region	Funding (US $ Billions)	Number of Projects
Asia and Near East	3.58	89
Latin America and Caribbean	1.58	138
Africa	.65	89
Europe and Eurasia	3.62	47
Total	9.43	363

Internet access to this database and the process of learning from it and utilizing it as a development tool, are the foundations of the DANTE initiative. The existence of DANTE as an interactive resource base would offer a range of benefits to tourism developers, stakeholders and donors as well as a credible platform for knowledge exchange and international co-operation. Donors are unified in support of the Millennium Development Goals (MDGs) and improved knowledge management and international cooperation are key elements in the strategy for achieving the MDGs. DANTE offers an opportunity, in a highly visible sector, to promote and deliver improved collaboration, knowledge management and the promotion of sustainable tourism practices.

DANTE aims to become a leading global partnership that promotes sustainable tourism initiatives with development assistance resources. It will achieve this by facilitating information exchange, knowledge applications (tools, practices, case studies, models and lessons learned), training programs and co-operation and understanding between the private sector, governments and civil society. DANTE will anchor this knowledge management system with core values of transparency, collaboration, accuracy, user-friendly accessibility and shared responsibility.

The development of sustainable tourism involves diverse stakeholders who all have significant roles and information requirements at different times. These stakeholders tend to have well-defined parameters within which they communicate and operate. In order to build partnerships and create genuine knowledge sharing between these stakeholders, the operational characteristics and information pathways of each stakeholder group need to be understood and facilitated to interface with DANTE and thereby each other.

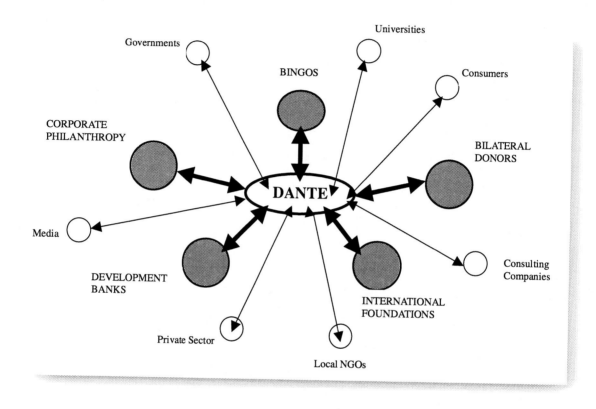

DANTE design activities will focus on the cluster groups represented in this schematic diagram. It is expected that primary relationships for DANTE will be established with the stakeholders represented by the darker circles, with particular emphasis on donor policies and practices. The outer ring of stakeholders represents the ultimate user beneficiaries of DANTE. DANTE seeks to establish an on-going dialogue between developing country needs and donor policies related tourism development. To assist with this formidable task, DANTE is in the process of creating regional centers in the Asia Pacific region in cooperation with the University of Hawaii's School of Travel Industry Management and in Europe with key collaborators.

GWU/IITS has spent the past two years gathering data and populating the database and a website is under construction. The architecture of this site is still in a formative stage, but it will aim to be user-driven with levels of entry tailored to user-profiles. Some of the key activities underway follow:

Community of Practice. GWU/IITS has also catalyzed the process of creating a "Community of Practice" network of professional staff with expertise in sustainable tourism from donor agencies in North America and is encouraging a similar development through networks in Europe and Asia. These virtual communities will help guide and promote awareness of DANTE in donor agencies in the coming months and contribute to the content of DANTE in the future. UNCTAD has agreed to facilitate information exchange under their Sustainable Tourism for Development collaborative initiative:

http://tourism.unctad.org/QuickPlace/sustainable-tourism-for development/Main.nsf/h_Toc/E972857E85B32490C1256D4B00299FA2/?OpenDocument

Internet platform - Activities are focused on creating a working platform for DANTE which will be enhanced and fine-tuned. The six months leading to the launch will be geared towards adding content to DANTE and improving and promoting the network. The months following the launch will be oriented towards follow-up of the Tourism Policy Forum disseminating outputs and recommendations. Post-forum work on DANTE will incorporate refinements and be focused on positioning DANTE as the leading sustainable tourism Internet portal. It is envisaged that DANTE will become a focal point for a best practices and development assistance guidelines.

WTO Education Council Knowledge Management Forum on Development Assistance - One of the key activities towards the development of DANTE is to focus the WTO Education Council Forum planned for June 2 and 3, 2004 in Madrid on development assistance polices and practices. In the lead-up to the Forum, a series of "Think Tanks" or "Roundtables" have, or will, will occur in European locations, Washington DC, and Bangkok. It is anticipated that follow up activities will continue through 2004 and 2005 culminating in a major report to WTO's General Assembly in 2005.

Delivering Training through DANTE - The DANTE network will provide an opportunity to deliver targeted and meaningful training to a range of potential user groups. During the market research period of development, training needs will be identified and courses formulated to meet these needs. Several universities, including GWU already deliver distance-learning programs via the Internet. DANTE will not compete with these courses, but will offer extensions and specifically tailored professional development. There is potential for DANTE to work with other partners at a local level to deliver training with a priority emphasis on identifying and accessing funding from foundations, corporate philanthropy, and multilateral/bi-lateral donors. This would be a cost effective way to reach grass roots tourism entrepreneurs (such as community based tourism businesses), destination management organizations, higher education institutions, NGOs and protected area managers in developing countries.

CONCLUSION

Higher education institutions have a critical role to play in transferring knowledge into practice. This paper provides a rationale for colleges, universities and other training institutions to facilitate knowledge though outreach activities involving research, teaching and service. Three practical examples are provided to illustrate an outreach approach. On going partnerships between higher education institutions and the tourism sector at all levels are needed to transfer knowledge into practical use.

REFERENCES

Boyer, Ernest L., *Scholarship Reconsidered: Priorities of the Professorate,* The Carnegie Foundation for the Advancement of Teaching, 1990.

Frechtling, D.C with contributions from Bedard, F and Hawkins, D. *E-Learning Cooperation Model for Tourism Education in Developing Countries,* TedQual, No. 6, 1/2003. WTO.Themis Publication.

Halal, William E., The Logic of Knowledge: How a Knowledge Economy Differs from a Capital Economy, unpublished paper, George Washington University, Washington, DC

Ruhanen, L and Cooper, C., *Developing a Knowledge Management Approach to Tourism Research,* TedQual, No. 6, 1/2003. WTO.Themis Publication.

Wober, Karl W., Benchmarking in Tourism and Hospitality Industries, CABI, 2002.

GRUPO DE REFLEXIÓN III

Cuando las culturas colisionan

PANEL III

When cultures collide

TABLE RONDE III

Le heurt des cultures

- **INTRODUCCIÓN / INTRODUCTION / INTRODUCTION**
  Mariano López,
  Decano, Cámara de Periodistas y Comunicadores de Turismo

- **COMMUNICATING CULTURAL DIVERSITY IN INTERNATIONAL TOURISM**
  Richard Lewis,
  CEO, Richard Lewis Communications

- **ON THE WAY TOWARDS THE DREAM SOCIETY?**
  Rolf Jensen,
  Chief Imagination Officer, Dream Company A.S.

- **COMMUNICATIONS: A STRATEGIC TOOL FOR TOURISM DEVELOPMENT**
  IN POST-CONFLICT COUNTRIES
  Scott Wayne,
  Principal, SW Associates

INTRODUCCIÓN

MARIANO LÓPEZ

Decano, Cámara de Periodistas y Comunicadores de Turismo

Gracias por su asistencia y bienvenidos a esta nueva sesión de TOURCOM. Si me lo permiten, antes de abordar el tema de esta mesa redonda, voy a presentarles durante unos minutos la Cámara de Periodistas y Comunicadores de Turismo de España.

La Cámara es -según creemos sus asociados- una respuesta práctica y solidaria a la necesidad de avanzar en la eficacia de la comunicación y en la calidad de la información turística.

En un país como España donde el sector turístico es sobresaliente, la comunicación y la información del sector no siempre alcanzan el nivel que los profesionales nos exigimos y que la sociedad demanda.

La Cámara intenta resolver al menos parte del problema trasladando el debate sobre comunicación e información al plano de las necesidades y objetivos de los comunicadores y los informadores.

La Cámara agrupa cerca de cien socios, todos profesionales en activo, que representan a los principales medios de comunicación vinculados al sector turístico español en la prensa escrita, la radio, Internet y la televisión, junto con los responsables de comunicación de las principales empresas privadas y organismos públicos de este sector y los responsables de los departamentos universitarios implicados en la investigación y docencia del turismo.

Al reunir, así, a los principales actores de la comunicación y la información turística, la Cámara actúa como lugar de encuentro que pretende contribuir al fortalecimiento de las relaciones entre comunicadores y periodistas, y que se orienta a la búsqueda de soluciones para obtener una mayor calidad en la comunicación y la información de la que se beneficie, finalmente, el lector, el oyente, el espectador o el internauta.

Pretende, también, la Cámara mejorar el conocimiento del sector turístico que tienen quienes poseen la responsabilidad de servir a su difusión. Y facilitar la relación de los profesionales de la información y la comunicación del sector turístico español con comunicaciones e informaciones, comunicadores e informadores, de cualquier punto del globo.

Y como ejemplo práctico, como resultado de este proyecto y de este esfuerzo, hoy tengo el placer de anunciarles el nacimiento de la página web de la cámara de periodistas y comunicadores de turismo. www.camaraturismo.org Les invito a que la descubran y participen en ella.

Ahí al lado tenemos FITUR. Por primera vez, y gracias a esta web que hoy presenta, podríamos decir, su esqueleto, con motivo de TOURCOM, todos y cada uno de los comunicadores de las diferentes ciudades, provincias, comunidades, países, empresas y organismos que participen en la FITUR 2005 podrían situar su comunicación en un mismo canal al que saben que van a acceder los precisos destinatarios de su mensaje.

Por primera vez, gracias a esta web, los profesionales de la comunicación y la información van a disponer de los informes, estudios, estadísticas y documentos emitidos por el sector, entre ellos, esperamos, los muy valiosos informes elaborados por la propia OMT.

Por primera vez, el periodista y el comunicador van a contar con un medio propio creado por ellos mismos para ayudarles a organizar, reunir y valorar noticias, enlaces, fuentes estadística, informes, papeles de trabajo y directorios de trabajo del sector.

Me tienen a mí y a los miembros de la Cámara a su disposición para ampliarles información sobre esta web y sobre la Cámara, cuyos socios les piden que se animen a entrar en la web, a participar con sus sugerencias, noticias o mensajes, y a formar parte por supuesto de la misma Cámara.

Gracias a los ponentes, a la OMT, y a ustedes por permitirme comunicarles esta noticia, que no estaba en el programa pero que creo, que creemos desde los socios actuales de la Cámara, que es una gran noticia para TOURCOM en la medida en que aporta una herramienta y quizás un modelo para mejorar, insisto, la calidad y las relaciones de la comunicación y la información turística.

Y volviendo al programa, tenemos el honor de contar con tres extraordinarios comunicadores para abordar, desde diferentes perspectivas, las exigencias de la comunicación y la información en el marco de lo que ha venido en llamarse la "colisión de las culturas".

Un problema -la colisión de culturas- del que sólo me van a permitir que les recuerde un dato: Europa Occidental, Japón y Estados Unidos representan las tres cuartas partes del total del turismo emisor del mundo. Tres de cada cuatro turistas proceden de estas áreas. ¿Podemos entonces hablar del turismo como un movimiento que facilita la "invasión cultural", la colisión permanente? ¿Es el turismo, por el contrario, un factor que reduce esa colisión en la medida que facilita el conocimiento mutuo? ¿O existen matices, muchos matices, infinitos matices? ¿Qué valores se ponen en juego, actúan, con este movimiento? ¿Cuáles emergen, cuáles chocan, cuáles se imponen en la aldea forzosamente global?

Para hablar y debatir sobre ello, contamos, primero con Richard D. Lewis -les animo a leer su currículo y el del resto de estos ponentes en la documentación facilitada-, CEO de Richard Lewis Communications, es autor de una obra clásica para el estudio de este fenómeno: "Cuando las culturas chocan". Habla doce idiomas, dos de ellos orientales, y ha vivido y trabajado en numerosos países europeos y asiáticos, donde ha sido reconocido por su mérito y su contribución al estudio de un fenómeno sobre el que cada vez, y gracias a personas como él, hay mayor sensibilidad, preocupación y necesidad de respuesta. Tiene la palabra Richard D. Lewis.

Rolf Jensen, es el Chief Imagination Officer, de una compañía, Dream Company, que trata de ayudar a la mayoría de las multinacionales líderes en su necesidad de anticipar, representarse, el futuro y solucionar los retos que supone el cambio, no siempre gradual y no siempre interpretable en clave de progreso. Mr. Jensen es autor del libro "The Dream Society. De la información a la imaginación. From information to imagination" y, además, un gran viajero, miembro de la Real Sociedad Geográfica de Londres.

Mr. Jensen nos va a hablar de una vieja preocupación kantiana, ahora que estamos en el centenario del filósofo: ¿caminamos hacia delante o hacia atrás? ¿Existe un camino? ¿Progresamos? ¿Avanzamos hacia la sociedad que deseamos, con la que soñamos?

Scott Wayne, principal de SW Associates, es un renombrado experto en programas de desarrollo turístico, programas que, como ustedes saben, abarcan multiplicidad de materias e involucran, necesariamente, a casi todos los estratos de una sociedad. Además es autor de varios libros de viajes lo que revela no sólo su pasión viajera y su conocimiento sino también, y para mí, más importante, su curiosidad.

Scott Wayne va a hablarnos de una herramienta estratégica para el desarrollo turístico -la comunicación- especialmente necesaria en aquellos países que han salido de un conflicto.

COMMUNICATING CULTURAL DIVERSITY IN INTERNATIONAL TOURISM

RICHARD D. LEWIS
CEO, Richard Lewis Communications

Tourism, professionals and cultural sensitivity

Tourism is undoubtedly the fastest-growing industry in the world, but it must be marketed in different ways around the globe. The tour operator must be aware of diverse speech styles, different listening habits and specific audience expectations. Presentations have to be quite different in countries such as the USA, Japan and Russia. In this article we give some examples of a variety of communication patterns in half a dozen countries. We also refer to differences in values, attitudes and the use of time.

SPEECH STYLES

The following diagrams illustrate communication patterns in Italy, Finland, Germany, Japan, the USA and the UK. It is important to note the importance of **coded speech** in the British speech style.

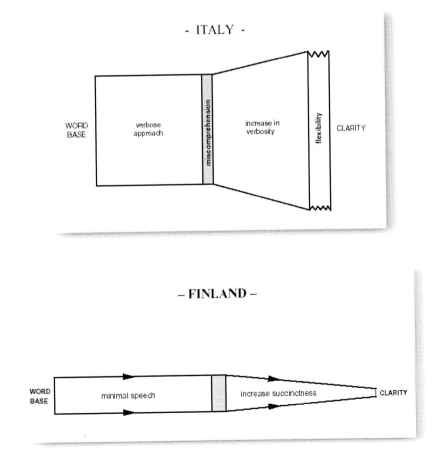

– GERMANY –

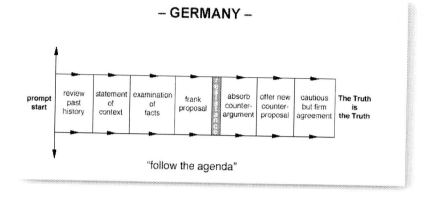

"follow the agenda"

– UK –

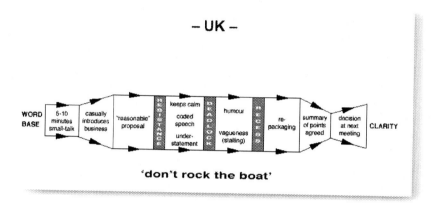

'don't rock the boat'

- USA -

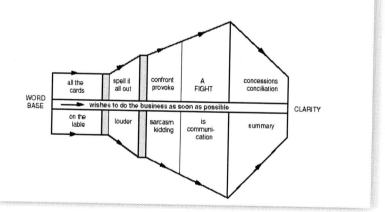

– JAPAN –

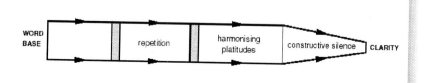

BRITISH UNDERSTATEMENT AND CODED SPEECH

Match up the expressions in the left hand column with suitable equivalents from the right hand column:

What we say	**What we really mean**
That's one way of putting it	What a stupid analysis
That's a good question	I don't know the answer
It's not bad	It's excellent
We'll certainly consider that	We won't do it
I'm not quite with you on that one	That is totally unacceptable
There is some merit in that	I can't reject it outright
Let me make a suggestion	This is what I've decided to do
That's very perceptive	That's just what I've bee saying for the last three years
I'll call you	I won't call you
We'll have to review your position	You're going to be fired
That might be just a bit tricky	It's impossible
Hm…that's an interesting idea	You can't really mean this
I've seen better	It was dreadful
You *could* be right	It's highly unlikely
I think I've got the message	You don't have to tell me ten times
You could say that	I wouldn't
I agree, up to a point	I disagree
It's not for me to influence you either way	This is what I strongly advise you to do
We must have a meeting about your idea	I don't want to discuss it now

The next two diagrams show audience expectations in 9 different countries and two basic presentation styles to sell to best effect.

AUDIENCE EXPECTATIONS DURING PRESENTATIONS

U.S.	U.K.	GERMANY
• humour • joking • modernity • gimmicks • slogans • catch phrases • hard sell	• humour • a story • "nice" product • reasonable price • quality • traditional rather than modern	• solidity of company • solidity of product • technical info • context • beginning - middle - ending • lots of print • no jokes • good price • quality • delivery date
attn span : half hour	attn span : 30-45 mins	attn span : 1 hour +
FRANCE	**JAPAN**	**SWEDEN**
• formality • innovative product • "sexy" appeal • imagination • logical presentation • reference to France • style, appearance • personal touch • may interrupt	• good price • USP • synergy with Co. image • harmony • politeness • respect for their Co. • good name of your Co. • quiet presentation • well-dressed presenter • formality • diagrams	• modernity • quality • design • technical info • delivery dates
attn span : half hour	attn span : 1 hour	attn span : 45 mins
MED/ARAB	**FINN**	**AUSTRALIA**
• personal touch • rhetoric • eloquence • liveliness • loudness • may interrupt • want "extra" talk afterwards	• modernity • quality • technical info • modest presentation • design	• matey opening • informality throughout • humour • persuasive style • no padding • little contexting • innovative product • essential technical info • personal touch • may interrupt • imaginative conclusion
attn span : short	attn span : 45 mins	attn span: 30 mins

PRESENTATION STYLES

RESERVED	EXTROVERTED
for: **UK** **Germany** **Finland** **Japan**	for: **USA** **France** **Latin America** Australia
quiet unhurried polite factual understated impersonal restricted body language reserved recommending laid back medium eye contact efficient convincing humorous	loud and clear brisk direct imaginative overstated personal overt body language theatrical persuasive intense strong eye contact dynamic charismatic witty

Cultural diversity is evident in different styles of communication, as is shown in the following examples:

A German marketing executive, well known for making convincing presentations of his company's product on his own territory, was told by his British colleagues that his style was too intense. The Americans on the other hand told him he lacked "punch". In Tokyo a polite audience of twenty buyers gave him no feedback and did not pursue the product.

In Stuttgart the secretary of a company president, fluent in English, was almost fired when she said "Who are you?" to a powerful American CEO who phoned and asked to speak to her boss.

An Indian engineer, on his way to Sweden for a 6-month assignment to Volvo, was badly delayed by late aircraft departures and he phoned the company to say he would arrive well after midnight. The company informed his landlady, Mrs Svensson, to wait up for him and have a hot meal ready. This she did and when he eventually arrived she said: "I suppose you would like a hot meal?" The Indian, who was very hungry, replied in the polite Asian manner "Oh no, I couldn't possibly put you to the trouble at this hour." Mrs Svensson, somewhat surprised, then said "Oh well, good night then" and went to bed.

Pierre, a French advertising manager went to England to propose a new strategy to the Chairman of their British subsidiary, who replied: "Hm, interesting idea - we must have a meeting about that." When Pierre asked if the proposal was accepted the Englishman replied "We shall certainly consider it". Pierre reported back to his French colleagues that the proposal was going ahead, though it never did.

What these examples show is that a good command of the customer's language (in these instances, English) can prove completely inadequate if it is not accompanied by knowledge of the cultural habits of the people. Effective presentations in Britain are low key; Americans want and need the hard sell; in Japan what one says has no importance - only humility and harmony-creation will get the business. "Who are you?" to the Anglo-Saxon ear sounds hostile. Mrs Svensson was unaware that in most of Asia one accepts an offer or a gift only after first declining it twice. Pierre did not realise that his English colleague was using coded speech to reject his idea in an indirect, courteous manner. (Hm, interesting idea = Forget it. We must have a meeting about that = I don't want to discuss it. We'll certainly consider it = We won't do it).

Cultural diversity is not something that is going to go away tomorrow, enabling us to plan our strategies on the assumption of mutual understanding. It is, in itself, a phenomenon with its own riches, the exploration of which could yield incalculable benefits for us both in terms of wider vision and more profitable policies and activity. People of different cultures share basic concepts but view them from different angles and perspectives, leading them to behave in a manner which we may consider irrational. We should, nevertheless, be optimistic about cultural diversity. A nation's culture is its blueprint for survival and, hopefully, success. It is an all-embracing blueprint plotting a group's entire way of life, including a shared system of values, social meanings and agendas, passed on from generation to generation. Bold is the child that challenges the assumptions of parents, teachers and peers! Cultures are especially resilient at national level. Governments have a vested interest in their citizens' sharing cultural values in order to reduce the potential for future cultural conflicts. Schools, therefore, transmit culture to large numbers of young receptive students who are given the same information, values and concepts and in the same language.

History is taught thoughtfully, often being "remodelled" to consolidate shared values and myths. Such interpretations are all part of the ongoing process of defining a national identity.

With globalisation, the need for standardisation of systems, procedures and goals becomes greater. But managers will also be under pressure to understand how to organise and lead multinational teams, whose values, traditions and communication patterns spring from cultures widely different from their own.

The use of time:

WHERE TIME MOVES IN A MYSTERIOUS WAY

Westerners race against time, but business decisions in Asia are arrived at in a variety of ways.

In the travel business, time, time-tabling and schedules are important. In many countries trains, buses, aeroplanes and even boats are expected to leave and arrive more or less on time. In Switzerland and Germany this means on the dot. In other lands - Italy, Brazil etc - "on time" might mean half an hour (or half a day) later!

In the world of tourism, travel agents and tour operators have to organise their clients' programmes on the basis of dates, days, sometimes hours or minutes. Just how long should one devote to a particular sight or attraction? Will different nationalities want to see different things, or allocate different periods of time to this and that? How much free time or freedom of movement should one include in a busy programme? Is it true that Americans say things like :"I'm in Romania, so it must be Tuesday?" Do diverse cultures look at time in different ways?

How do people manage their time? Northern Europeans, Americans and Latins all share the belief that they can manage their time in the best possible way. In some Eastern cultures, however, the adaptation of man to time is seen as a viable alternative. Time is viewed neither as linear nor subjective, but as cyclic. The evidence, they reason, is everywhere; each day the sun rises and sets, people grow old, die and are succeeded by their children. It has been this way for 100,000 years. Cyclical time is not a scarce commodity. As they say in the East, when God made time, he made plenty of it.

Accordingly, business decisions in Asia are arrived at in a different way from the West. Westerners typically expect decisions to be made quickly and current deals to be treated on present merit, irrespective of the past. An Asian cannot do this. The past formulates the contextual background of the present decision, about which in any case, as an Asian, he must think long term - his hands are tied in several ways, An American sees time that has passed without decision or action as "wasted" time. The Asian, in contrast, does not see time racing away unused but as coming round again in a circle where the same opportunities will re-present themselves and when he is so many days, weeks or months wiser.

Hence, in business, the Western chain of action is matched by Asian reflection. The American goes home at the end of the day with all tasks completed. The Germans and Swiss probably do the same. The Frenchman or Italian might leave some "mopping up" for the following day. The Thai attitude to time, by contrast, has been described as a pool that you gradually walk around. It is a metaphor that applies to most Asians, who, instead of tackling problems immediately in sequential fashion, circle round them for a few days - weeks even - before committing themselves. Hence, after a period of reflection, certain options may seem worthy of pursuing and others quietly dropped.

The Chinese similarly "walk round the pool", but they also have a keen sense of the value of time. This is most visible in their attitude towards taking up other people's time, for which they apologise. Punctuality is also considered important, more so than in many Asian countries. Indeed, when meetings are scheduled between two people, it is not unusual for a Chinese person to arrive up to half an hour early "in order to finish the business before the time appointed for its discussing". It is also considered polite to announce shortly after the start of a meeting that one will soon have to leave - the aim, again, is to economise on their use of your time. The Chinese will not go, of course, until the transaction has been completed, but the point has been made.

There is clearly a double standard at work here. The Chinese penchant for humility demands that the interlocutor's time be seen as precious; on the other hand, they expect time to be liberally allocated to the consideration of the details of a deal and the nurturing of the relationships surrounding it. They frequently complain that Americans on business in China always want to hurry. The American sees the facts as having been adequately discussed; the Chinese feels that he's not yet attained that degree of closeness - the sense of common trust and intent - that is for him the bedrock of this deal and future transactions.

The Japanese are distinguished by the meticulous manner in which they segment time. This does not follow the American or German pattern, however, where tasks are assigned in a logical sequence aimed at maximising efficiency. The Japanese are not so much concerned with how long something takes but how time is divided up in the interests of propriety, courtesy and tradition. In a conformist and regulated society, the Japanese like to know at all times what point they are at and where they stand. The mandatory two-minute exchange of business cards between executives meeting for the first time is one of the clearest examples.

Indeed, the Japanese does not enter into any activity with the casual, direct manner typical of the Westerner. The American or northern European has a natural tendency to make a quick approach to the heart of the thing. The Japanese, on the contrary, must experience the 'unfolding' of the significant phases of an event. This is partly Asian indirectness, but also the Japanese love of tradition, the beauty of ritual and the compartmentalism of procedure. Above all, when dealing with the Japanese one can assume that they will be generous in their allocation of time. In return you should try to do 'the right thing at the right time'. In Japan, form and symbols are more important than content.

It is not easy for a person of one nationality to appreciate how much or how little importance those of another culture attach to time. My friend travelled recently from Bombay to London with a 75-year- old Indian lady who was going abroad for the first time to meet her son and newly-born grandson in England. The plane was 3 hours late and the British airline representative came repeatedly to the good lady to offer his apologies for the delay. He was more than kind in his attentions. My friend understood however that the obvious nervousness of the Indian lady was due to a combination of factors. Firstly she was about to leave her homeland for the first time. She had never flown before and was very worried how her fragile health might be affected by hurtling along at 35,000 feet. She would arrive in a land whose officials might be unfriendly, whose language she could hardly speak. The climate was reputedly cold and damp, the food perhaps strange and unpalatable. The grandson had been ill and her son was understandably uneasy. With all this on her mind the old lady could not have cared less whether the plane left on time or not.

ON THE WAY TOWARDS THE DREAM SOCIETY?

ROLF JENSEN

Chief Imagination Officer, Dream Company, A.S.

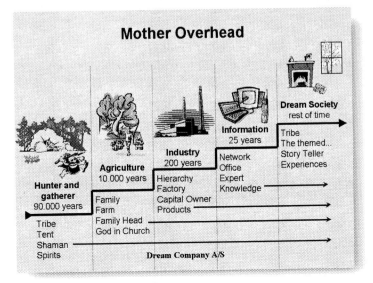

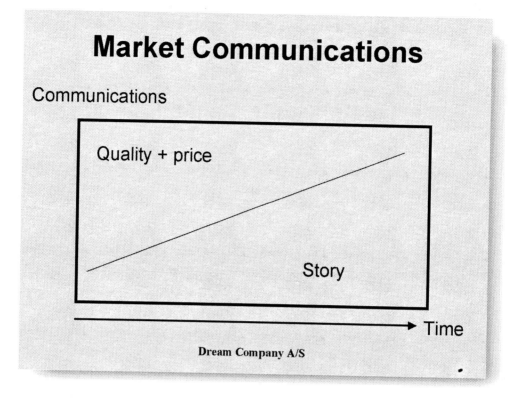

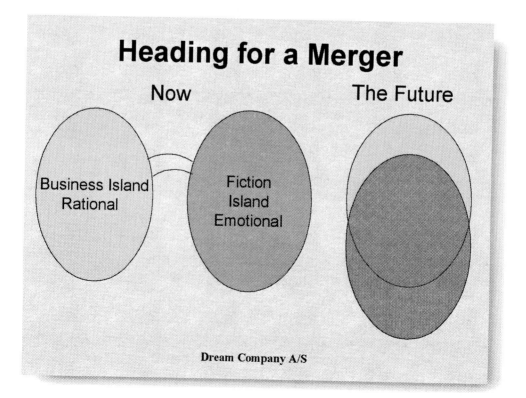

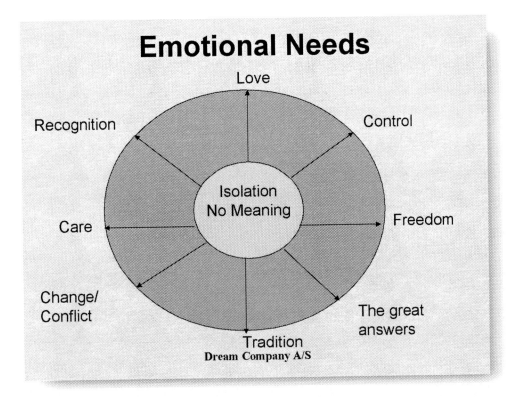

One Illustrative Example

- Detergents are traditionally about control (cleanliness)

- Unilever moves into love and tradition (www.rituals.com)

Now: cleanliness+love+tradition

Dream Company A/S

Now Comes the Storytelling Part

- Rules are made to be broken?......

- No, obeyed!

- Using the rules of fiction in advertising and branding, in communications

Dream Company A/S

Principle # 1:Feel it

- What is strongly believed in, will be believed

Dream Company A/S

Principle # 2:Make it Personal

- From the general to the personal and specific

- It works even with mice!

Dream Company A/S

Principle # 3: The Law of Conflict

- Only Conflict fascinates

Dream Company A/S

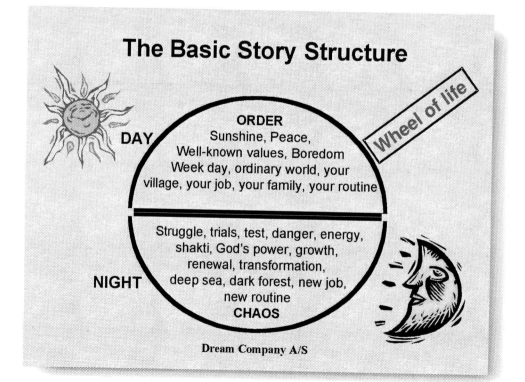

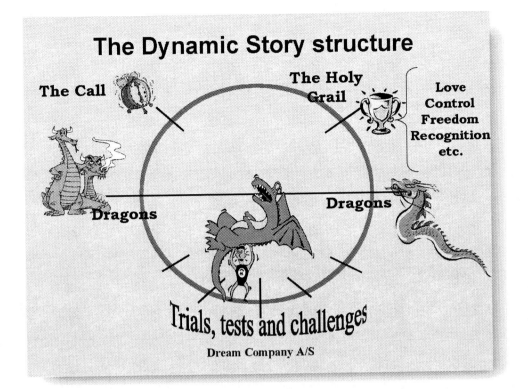

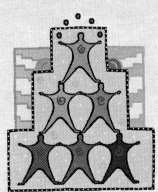

A Travel Communication Story

- Protagonist: Tourist
- Helper: Airline
- Antagonist: Money, time
- Fairy mother: The communication
- Audience: Family and friends
- The goal: New experiences

Dream Company A/S

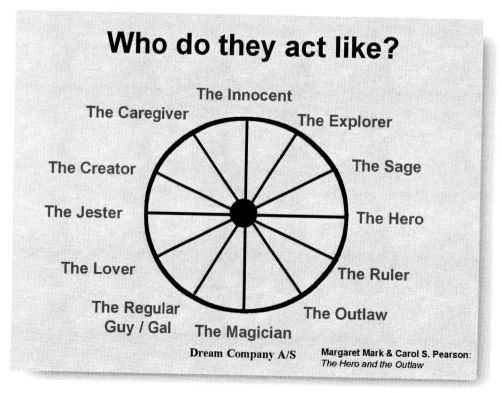

Who do they act like?

The Innocent

The Caregiver

The Explorer

The Creator

The Sage

The Jester

The Hero

The Lover

The Ruler

The Regular Guy / Gal

The Outlaw

The Magician

Dream Company A/S

Margaret Mark & Carol S. Pearson:
The Hero and the Outlaw

Thank You!

- "Create the Future – or the Future will create you!

- "If you feel the future as headwind, you are walking in the wrong direction"

- WWW.DREAMCOMPANY.DK

Dream Company A/S

COMMUNICATIONS: A STRATEGIC TOOL FOR TOURISM DEVELOPMENT IN POST-CONFLICT COUNTRIES

SCOTT WAYNE
Principal, SW Associates

Developing tourism in countries that are virtually unknown as tourist destinations is a challenge. Add to this challenge a recent history of war and ethnic conflict in some countries and the obstacles seem practically insurmountable. The obstacles are not insurmountable, especially if a communications-driven approach is one of the "tools" in the country's development "toolkit".

At the core of the challenges often in post-conflict countries are, not surprisingly, issues related to infrastructure - either it is in need of either being rebuilt or constructed from scratch. The infrastructure is a key to unlocking access to existing tourism products in the country or helping to spawn the creation of new products. In fact, as demand for existing and potential products increases, this demand can be a catalyst for improved infrastructure. In other words, increased demand for tourism can generate demand and revenue for financing infrastructure.

How is this demand created? By communicating to existing and potential markets what the destination has to offer. In a perfect world of no competition, this is easy, but competition means a continual, non-stop targeted messaging. In post-conflict countries, this communications is even more essential because often the country's tourism offer is overshadowed by its recent past of war and conflict.

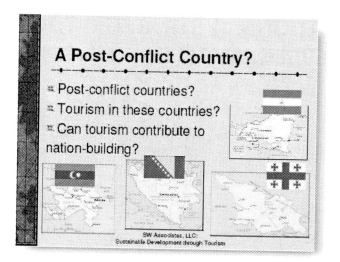

There is no official definition of a post-conflict country, except perhaps one that has been ripped apart by war and conflict and is supposedly well enough past the fighting and people killing each other to begin putting itself back together again. It can be considered a very positive signal when a variety of groups in civil society, government and business begin getting more and more interested in tourism.

Is tourism a realistic development option for countries that have been known recently more as war zones than as peaceful places to visit? Can tourism contribute to nation-building?

Well, call me an optimist, but I believe that it can and, in fact, in some post-conflict countries such as Bosnia-Herzegovina, Croatia, Azerbaijan, Georgia and Nicaragua to name a few... it can and in some respects is doing just that.

I'm going to turn to a couple of specific examples in Bosnia-Herzegovina where, at the time of TOURCOM, I was working on a USAID tourism competitiveness initiative. First, however, it's worth having a look at some of the common challenges these countries and many others that have been in similar situations have faced and continue to face.

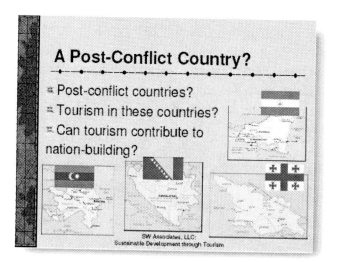

At the top of the list of challenges is one that is directly related to communications ‡ the image of the country or even specific destinations within the country.

Even worse, though, is probably no image, a lack of information, a blank slate. For a very small minority of travellers, this is appealing, but they don't add up to much of an economic impact for a country.

This is entirely dependent on the information - both in terms of imagery and words - that people receive about the place. For the vast majority of travellers, the negatives easily outweigh the positives, the potential threats and risks over actual situations. Destinations and, in fact, entire countries that do succeed in this information game become brands that attract buyers and inspire sellers.

A second key challenge is also communications-related - a poorly developed, presented and marketed product. Tourism is great because it is one of the most malleable industries; you can practically make a tourism "product" out of anything - a field (where a battle was once fought), a small building, a desert plain (Las Vegas), a swamp (Disney World)... the list goes on and on.

A place can be set up to receive visitors, but if there is no information distributed and packaged about the place, it remains like a never-opened book gathering dust on a shelf. If you can't inform the market, the market moves like a divining rod to those places that do inform and persuade the investor, tour operator and ultimately traveller to invest or visit.

The third key challenge is really the result of the other two - poor image or no image, no brand, a lack of information and awareness in the market - add up to a country or destination that just is not competitive with its neighbours and competitors farther a-field. And if the country is not competitive regionally or internationally, it is not going to attract much investment either domestic or foreign direct investment.

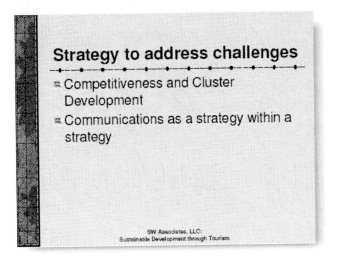

At the heart of this theory is that industries tend to cluster geographically to increase their competitiveness. Basically, it is just commonsense - if a major car manufacturer establishes itself in Flint, Michigan, then the companies that supply the manufacturer with tires, windshields and the multitude of other parts that go into manufacturing a car will find it cheaper and more cost-effective to "cluster" near the manufacturer.

Tourism is a logical industry for clustering because it is intrinsically geographic. Visitors go to a destination. Services are created or repositioned at that destination to serve the visitors. A variety or cluster of services is realized according to the products that are offered. And the offer depends on what is communicated to potential investors, service providers, local residents and visitors - thus getting back to the importance of information. In this sense, tourism is a major stepping stone towards the development of the destination and country.

With all of this mind, let's return to the example briefly mentioned before - Bosnia-Herzegovina - where the approach has emphasised communications - communications with the public to raise awareness about tourism as an economic option, with the industry to better realize their potential, and with other stakeholders particularly among the multitude of governmental authorities in the country.

As part of the former Yugoslavia, Bosnia-Herzegovina was a popular tourism destination, which is not surprising. The landscape is some of the most beautiful in the region. And despite a number of years of inhospitable conditions, people throughout the country can be overwhelmingly hospitable and welcoming to visitors.

In addition, the country's spas, while not luxurious or competitive with spa resorts in more developed destinations, attracted many Yugoslavs and other visitors throughout the region and are again beginning to attract visitors.

The same with the ski slopes around Sarajevo, which hosted the 1984 Olympics, and are now again crowded in the wintertime. Rafting and kayaking have been catching on in the north.

The list of existing and potential tourism activities in Bosnia-Herzegovina goes on and on. The country's destinations and activities are gradually being rediscovered, but, not surprisingly, there are still many challenges to unravel.

Following one of the most horrific conflicts of the 20th century, Bosnia-Herzegovina has no shortage of challenges. Nation-building is at the top of the list. In 1995, to get the adversaries of the war to lay down their arms and make peace, the Dayton Accords created a less than ideal political structure, but one that all of the parties could more or less agree on and use to begin the putting the pieces of their country back together again.

Lord Paddy Ashdown, who was appointed High Representative for Bosnia by the nations that hammered out the peace accords, says that "The next big issue for Bosnia is the ludicrously tangled and complex system of government in this country. We have 13 prime ministers, 13 ministers of education, 13 ministers of the interior for 3.7 million people."

How is this "tangled and complex system" an issue for tourism development? Well, unfortunately, a similarly tangled web of governmental authorities currently exists for tourism. Not surprisingly, the industry is confused about how and with whom to work with in government on communicating and advancing their interests.

These political realities have no doubt impacted infrastructure development in the country, especially in relation to potential tourism growth. It is simply a huge challenge to obtain a consensus from multiple political authorities. Air access is limited both in terms of the airport and air connections. Air Bosna, the only locally-based carrier went bankrupt. Rail access is also limited but slated for improvement. Roads are also slated for improvement as part of the European Union's major highway development initiatives. There are also no truly international standard accommodations in the country. Marketing efforts by both the public and private sectors are limited mainly to a few brochures and inadequate web-based information. Over a million landmines are still buried throughout the countryside. You get the picture.

Given these challenges, it is also a challenge to attract tourism investment. Very few international investors have ventured into the market. The risks are still perceived as too high. The recent acquisition of the Sarajevo Holiday Inn by an Austrian company, however, will probably communicate a more positive, confidence-building message to potential investors though.

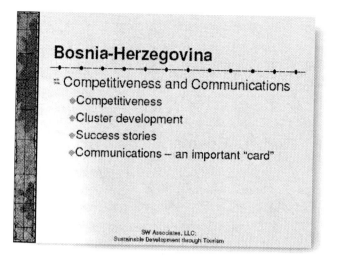

Faced with these challenges, the key question for us on the USAID Tourism Competitiveness Initiative was what could be accomplished in only a year to help put Bosnia-Herzegovina on the international tourism map. In other words, what could be done to help the country compete internationally and especially regionally?

One of the main purposes of the Initiative was the creation of a tourism cluster, which was described earlier. And then the cluster, with the assistance of the Initiative, could pursue joint activities. Rather than try to create new activities, though, the Initiative sought ways to combine existing ones into new products or itineraries and then work with the cluster members in communicating these "success stories" to key constituencies. These "constituencies" included:

*Government - The Initiative Team believed that it was important for Government officials throughout the various authorities mentioned previously to be made aware that tourism was dynamic and growing, rather than languishing and fragmented. Otherwise, it would be difficult to address issues that slowed or stymied potential growth.

*Media - Communicating with and through the media was also very important because it was a key channel for advocacy with the Government, a means of creating stronger cohesion within the industry itself, and of course a means of communicating with travellers, both domestically and internationally. Success breeds success, but not if the successes remain unknown.

*Public - Creating a more positive image of a destination begins within the country among the citizens of that country. Fortunately, Bosnia-Herzegovina is far ahead in this respect. Ask any Bosnian to describe a beautiful place in the country and he or she will not hesitate to whet your appetite to explore. The public outside the country, though, still has not heard these messages. This is an opportunity for the tourism industry of Bosnia-Herzegovina.

The communications challenges were addressed by creating a "Communications Toolkit" for the Cluster Members and getting them involved with World Tourism Day on September 27th. The toolkit was a straightforward set of materials that could be used by a company or organization to help them communicate success stories to the constituencies mentioned above. In addition, the cluster members were encouraged to recognize World Tourism Day as a "lightening rod" for attracting attention about the importance of tourism for the country. And then related to that day, the Initiative launched a Tourism Poster Competition with arts schools around the country.

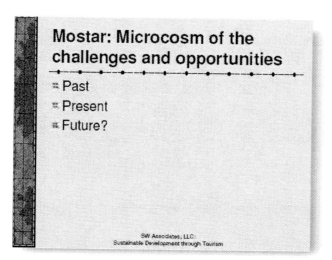

The city of Mostar in the Herzegovina region was a microcosm of the challenges and opportunities for tourism development throughout the country.

The war sliced the city down the middle between a Muslim east and a Catholic west. In the process, over a thousand buildings were destroyed or damaged, many of which were historic monuments, some dating to the city's founding in the 16th century. The old town, which was and still is predominantly Muslim, was almost completely destroyed, although there was equally substantial damage in the Catholic half of the city.

The destruction of the Bridge truly encapsulated the severing of the city. Before the war, the Bridge was a symbol of ethnic unity - linking the east and west banks of the river Neretva. Built almost five centuries ago, it was a tourist attraction. Visitors flocked to Mostar to visit the Bridge. The bridge was the heart of the city, a symbol of integration.

When the Bridge was destroyed, it was as if the spirit of Mostar was forcibly extracted from the city. Today, many people in the city, in both halves of the city, are working to recapture that spirit.

Until early 2004, Mostar was, in effect, two cities. There were two of everything or more. Before the war, there was one city administration. After the war, there were seven. There were two soccer clubs in Mostar - one Catholic; one Muslim. There were even two sets of telephone directories. And then Paddy Ashdown declared that there would be a single city administration and, in effect, forced the consolidation of administrations.

In Mostar, however, tourism involving both sides of the city does not have to be forced. Tourism is, in a sense, a common language, something that the different ethnic groups can agree on. This requires communications at its most basic level - getting one group to sit down with another and agreeing on how tourism should be organized. It's happening in Mostar. Tourism is thus serving as a crucial bridge and bridge-builder.

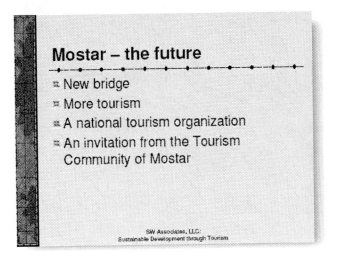

Despite the political divisions of Mostar, many of the people I spoken with who are working in or interested in tourism seemed quite intent on positioning Mostar, the region of Herzegovina and the country as a whole for that matter as a single tourist destination. Not as a Catholic or Muslim or Serbian Orthodox destination.

For TOURCOM, the Tourism Community of Mostar gave me a letter of invitation to give to journalists. They would like to invite journalists to the reopening of the Bridge and to share their rich history and heritage, the wine country of Herzegovina, the religious tourism of Medjugorje and the adventure travel opportunities in the mountains and rivers around the country.

A national level tourism organization is evolving, in part, through the World Bank-inspired poverty reduction strategy. And this will help magnify the bridging effect of tourism and, in fact, communicate or rather send a message that the country as a whole is a tourist destination.

As the Mostar Bridge reopens, it is a very positive symbol for the tourism industry of Bosnia-Herzegovina, as well as the country as a whole. In a sense, since the Bridge is a tourist attraction, it marks a turning point for tourism in the country. Visitors will flock to the Bridge because it represents the new Bosnia-Herzegovina, a country reunited and peaceful that wants to share the best of its past and present with visitors. A country that is back on the international tourism map.

GRUPO DE REFLEXIÓN IV

Responsabilidad del turismo - Comunicaciones del turismo
sostenible y Código Ético Mundial para el Turismo

PANEL IV

Tourism concern - Sustainable tourism communications
and the Global Code of Ethics for Tourism

TABLE RONDE IV

Responsabilité du tourisme - Communications du tourisme
durable et Code mondial d'éthique du tourisme

- **EL CÓDIGO ÉTICO DE LA OMT Y LAS COMUNICACIONES EN EL TURISMO**
  Diego Cordovez,
  Presidente del Comité Mundial de Ética del Turismo

- **COMMUNICATING TOURISM AS AN INSTRUMENT OF DEVELOPMENT**
  Anil Kumarsingh Gayan,
  Minister of Tourism and Leisure of Mauritius

- **COMMUNICATING SUSTAINABLE TOURISM: REACHING THE GEOTOURIST**
  Jonathan Tourtellot,
  Director of Sustainable Tourism, National Geographic Society

EL CÓDIGO ÉTICO DE LA OMT
Y LAS COMUNICACIONES EN EL TURISMO

DIEGO CORDOVEZ

Presidente, Comité Mundial de Ética para el Turismo

Se dice mucho que vivimos en globalización pero yo no voy a entrar en el tema si la globalización es buena o mala, y porque es buena o porque es mala. Pero si voy a establecer un hecho que es absolutamente claro, es una realidad, y es que el mundo actual es interdependiente y es cada vez más interdependiente, cada día es más interdependiente. Y por eso es que a partir de el final de la segunda guerra mundial una serie de organismos internacionales sobre todo presididos por las Naciones Unidas, han tomado una serie de iniciativas para ir en el fondo estableciendo un cierto orden en esa interdependencia.

La comunidad internacional reconoció desde el principio que era necesario que hubieran ciertos marcos de referencia dentro de los cuales se llevaran acabo actividades políticas, económicas financieras y en otros sectores de interés internacional. Así se estableció un sistema de seguridad colectiva que ha sufrido algunos tropiezos, particularmente en los últimos años, especialmente el año pasado y que por eso está siendo ahora objeto de un examen de las Naciones Unidas, por iniciativa del Secretario General a fin de establecer las rectificaciones que sean indispensables. Se estableció un sistema financiero internacional que también ha sido objeto de observaciones de varios sectores y que también ha sido objeto de ciertas rectificaciones a lo largo de los años, y hay todo un sistema de cooperación para el desarrollo. Un sistema que ha establecido a si mismo ciertos entendimientos, normas, compromisos, metas con respecto al desarrollo, con respecto a la reducción y eliminación de la pobreza y que también tiene todavía una serie de vacíos y una serie de defectos pero que creo tiene una característica muy interesante y muy importante y es que ha creado el hábito de cooperar. Y si hace unas pocas semanas hubo un grave desencuentro en la ciudad de Cancún sobre problemas de comercio, inmediatamente la comunidad internacional ha tratado de buscar alguna manera, algún camino de cooperación para enmendar el problema y para avanzar hasta ciertos objetivos que ya se habían definido.

La interdependencia ó la globalización es en el fondo un gran mosaico de acuerdos internacionales que han sido normalmente el fruto de iniciativas de un organismo internacional, a veces de un gobierno y a veces incluso de una persona. Pero que se han ido componiendo libremente, que los gobiernos los han negociado libremente, y que contiene fundamentalmente normas y metas también libre y mutuamente aceptadas.

En este mismo momento se han establecido ciertas metas, por ejemplo con respecto a la eliminación de la pobreza durante este milenio, se han establecido metas para la reducción del SIDA, se han establecido como esas otras metas y otros objetivos.

La Organización Mundial del Turismo que ha estado asociada con el sistema de desarrollo de las Naciones Unidas desde hace muchos años, y que ahora tiene ya el carácter de organismo internacional especializado del sistema de las Naciones Unidas, ha contribuido también desde hace mucho tiempo a la elaboración de normas en el sector del turismo porque, como decía, nuestro presidente, es una actividad, una industria fundamentalmente humana que en la misma forma que tiene una serie de beneficios puede también tener ciertos aspectos que requieren de un grado de normativa que es absolutamente indispensable.

Muy brevemente, les voy a explicar en que consiste el Código que ha aprobado la Organización Mundial en el año 1999, en una Asamblea celebrada en Santiago de Chile y también les voy a explicar brevemente cual es el objetivo del Comité que se estableció justamente para darle sentido práctico a este Código.

El Código es un código voluntario, ha sido, y por eso es que yo insistía antes en la palabra libremente, porque un poco como proponía el presidente Wilson, estos son acuerdos a los cuales los gobiernos han llegado por su propia voluntad, que han sido negociados entre ellos y en consecuencia, el código fundamentalmente constituye un compromiso adquirido por los miembros de la Organización y es el resultado de un esfuerzo común entre entidades del sector público, los gobiernos y entidades del sector privado.

El propósito del Código es el de servir de un marco de referencia para que quienes participan en el turismo en su sentido amplio, los turistas, los que reciben a los turistas, la gente que está conectada con el turismo para que todos ellos puedan juntos promover un crecimiento y un ordenamiento justo, responsable y sostenible del turismo mundial y cuyos beneficios sean para todos los sectores de la sociedad. El Código, como lo decía nuestro presidente, incluye una serie de principios y en general las buenas normas, lo digo yo como abogado, las buenas normas legales, son aquellas que se apoyan en un acuerdo fundamental sobre los principios que se persiguen mediante esas normas. Estos principios fundamentalmente tienen por objeto optimizar los beneficios del turismo en la economía, en el comercio, y al mismo tiempo, como decía nuestro presidente, eliminar aquellos efectos o consecuencias negativas que puede tener el turismo sea en el medio ambiente, en aspectos sociales etc.

Los nueve principios fundamentales que contiene el código publicado por la OMT son:

1. El turismo contribuye al entendimiento y al respeto mutuo entre hombres y sociedades. La idea es de que las sociedades comparten ciertos principios éticos y que pueden vivir en una diversidad de creencias religiosas, filosóficas etc. En consecuencia el turismo tiene que respetar esa realidad
2. El turismo es un instrumento de desarrollo personal y colectivo
3. El turismo es un factor de desarrollo sostenible
4. El turismo es un factor de aprovechamiento y enriquecimiento del Patrimonio Cultural de la Humanidad
5. El turismo es una actividad beneficiosa para los países y las comunidades de destino.
6. Establece algunas obligaciones con respecto a los agentes del desarrollo turístico
7. Establece el derecho al turismo
8. Establece el principio de la libertad de desplazamiento turístico
9. Establece el derecho de los trabajadores y de los empresarios del sector turístico.

Algunos de estos principios, en su detalle, establecen por primera vez como parte de una norma internacional ciertas responsabilidades para la prensa, por eso estamos aquí en esta conferencia. Establece ciertos principios sobre una total prohibición de la explotación de niños en la industria turística y establece una serie de otras normas que son fundamentalmente el resultado de la experiencia de muchos años de la Organización en la promoción del turismo mundial.

Entrando en el detalle sobre las disposiciones del Código, que tienen que ver con el tema de esta conferencia, el artículo sexto del Código, establece el derecho que tienen los gobiernos y las obligaciones que tienen también al mismo tiempo los gobiernos de informar a sus nacionales y a los nacionales de otros países sobre los riesgos de una actividad turística en un sitio determinado, en una época determinada. Y establece que esa información tiene que ser clara y justificada. En la mayoría de los casos esa información también tiene que ser consultada con el país del que se trata y que por cierto, tiene que ser proporcionada a la gravedad de las situaciones que existen en una situación ó en una circunstancia especial.

El artículo sexto también habla de las obligaciones y la contribución que también puede hacer la prensa en lo que se refiere a la promoción del turismo, y en ese sentido por cierto, habla de la importancia que tiene que la información que se provea se ajuste a la realidad, que sea correcta y que se desarrollen ciertos medios de comunicación como es evidentemente Internet para facilitar el turismo. Al mismo tiempo que se eviten situaciones en las que el turismo se promociona fundamentalmente con propósitos de explotación sexual. En este sentido, el Código es un primer esfuerzo a nivel internacional para establecer ciertas reglas.

La Organización ha querido que el Código sea un instrumento dinámico, viviente, y que sirva para los propósitos para los cuales fue redactado. Y por eso estableció para que se vaya promoviendo el conocimiento del Código, para que se vayan conociendo sus disposiciones y para que los países cada vez ajusten más tanto sus legislaciones y posibles, como ya hay varios casos, así como en todo caso, su conducta internacional en este sentido, ha establecido un comité que se va justamente a reunir en el mes de febrero por primera vez en Roma y cuya obligación fundamental es la de promover el conocimiento, la aplicación y la interpretación, todos aquellos aspectos que se refieren a la utilización, a la puesta en vigencia, a la puesta en vigor del Código en el futuro.

Hay algunos gobiernos que ya han hecho que el Código forme parte de su legislación interna. Hay otros que se han comprometido a ajustar su conducta internacional, a ajustar sus disposiciones internas, a los principios y disposiciones del Código. Hay otros países que han dispuesto que sea traducido a los idiomas de sus propios países e incluso de ciertas regiones específicas de sus países. Es decir, el Código empieza a irse incorporando al que hacer y al trabajo, y a la relación internacional de los países miembros, y lo que tenemos que hacer en el comité que se ha establecido justamente es apoyar esos esfuerzos, colaborar con los gobiernos para que el código sea más y más aceptado con las razones obvias para lo que fue redactado.

Tengo la convicción de que lo que se necesita es darle una posibilidad a ese comité, que los gobiernos lo apoyen en el sentido de que vayan estableciendo ciertas pautas, ciertas formas de actuar, un hábito de cooperar con el comité para que el Código cada día sea, deje de ser un instrumento legal y se vaya convirtiendo en un instrumento práctico en el accionar de los gobiernos.

Gracias.

COMMUNICATING TOURISM AS AN INSTRUMENT OF DEVELOPMENT

ANIL KUMARSINGH GAYAN

Minister of Tourism and Leisure of Mauritius

Dr. Dawid de Villiers, WTO Deputy Secretary-General,
Señor Cordovez, Proposed Chairman of the World Committee on Tourism Ethics,
Mr. J. Tourtellot, Director of Sustainable Tourism, National Geographic Society,

Excelencias,
Señoras y señores,

"Communicating tourism as an instrument of development" is the subject which I have been assigned. I must confess my difficulty in really grasping what is expected of me. I pray for your understanding if I do not live up to your expectations.

I am most grateful to the WTO for having invited me to participate in TOURCOM - First World Conference on Tourism Communications and I am particularly grateful for the suggestion made in the invitation letter to the sharing of ideas on how tourism can make this world a better place.

WTO AND MDGS

Now that the United Nations has qualitatively enhanced the status of the World Tourism Organisation into a specialized agency of the UN family, it becomes imperative for it to reassess its role in the light of the many programmes of the United Nations to promote a better life for the millions and millions of women and men worldwide who are surviving with less than US$ 1 a day.

Señoras, señores

You will recall that the UN General Assembly in the year 2000 adopted the Millennium Declaration. That was a political commitment at the highest level to undo the injustices of the past and to assist in the achievement of the Millennium Declaration Goals (the MDGs). The MDGs covered many sectors but the essential elements remained and continue to remain the reduction by half by the year 2015 of the number of people living in poverty, improving access to health, education and potable water.

Before concrete measures could be taken to further the aims of the MDGs, Sep. 11 happened and the focus of attention from poverty alleviation shifted to the global war against terrorism. The world changed dramatically after the terrorists' attacks and we are still adjusting to the new security environment. Terrorism and tourism are linked in a variety of ways. The impact which terrorism can have on tourism can only be imagined from what happened in Bali, Morocco, Tunisia and Mombassa. Tourists are sensitive creatures and no one can blame them if they shun dangerous places. The terrorists know that only too well and they have perfected the art of hitting where it hurts most.

Ladies and Gentlemen,

LEGACY OF COLONIALISM

History teaches us that the countries that attract the largest number of international tourists are in the rich West. They have assets and experience in the trade which newcomers find most difficult to emulate. These countries were also among the colonial powers. The development of tourism facilities was not a priority of the colonial powers. There can be no doubt that the legacy of colonialism together with the tensions and conflicts generated by the Cold War further hampered the development of tourism in newly independent countries, primarily in Africa. In any event the scarce resources of these countries had to go to health, education, and infrastructure but also sadly towards the purchases of "unnecessary" weapons.

AFRICA AND NEPAD

This was the case in Africa which is at present the most disadvantaged and impoverished region of the world. But things are changing for the better. The new leadership in Africa and the New Partnership for Africa's Development (NEPAD) have contributed largely towards the resolution of conflicts and the enhancement of awareness that there will be no development without peace and stability. From Liberia, Sierra Leone to Sudan there are windows of hope that are opening. Democracy and good governance are making significant progress. Diseases like HIV/AIDS and malaria are being tackled and kept in check. Any good news from Africa is most welcome. It is our hope that the return of peace will be conducive for tourism development in Sub-Saharan Africa. The potential for tourism is enormous and investment will be there when there is good governance and stability. You know as well as anyone that communicating tourism in the absence of stability, security and a predictable legal system is an exercise in futility.

COMMUNITY BENEFITS

Tourism does not mean simply putting up 5-star hotels with first-class services. Tourism can only succeed in developing countries if there is an obligation on sharing of benefits with the community. The benefits must trickle down to the ordinary people not only in terms of jobs and supply of services but what is even more important is to ensure that the people are also stakeholders in the continued viability of the tourist enterprise.

MUTUAL COOPERATION

The people who are affluent and who can afford relatively expensive holidays are mostly living in the rich countries. The development of a tourism industry in a developing country will inevitably rely upon the reservoir of tourists found in the rich countries. What some people may construe as dependence is in fact a sound platform for cooperation.

TRAVEL ADVISORIES

Let me say something about the power of the media and the impact of adverse reporting in respect of emerging tourist destinations. What large cities and big countries can absorb in terms of negative "news" or publicity becomes catastrophic for these tourist destinations. I wish to make reference here to what has caused tremendous alarm in many tourism-dependent countries. I am referring to the travel advisory which countries issue unilaterally. This has become more common with real or perceived terrorist threats. We are not in any case suggesting that countries that have credible intelligence should be prohibited from warning their nationals who happen to be holidaying in another country about the risks of terrorist activity. What we take strong exception to is the unilateral character of the travel advisory and also to the fact that the same objective i.e. of taking protective measures can be achieved through an exchange of information at bilateral level. Should there be no measures taken as a result of the imparting of the intelligence then we could understand the unilateral issuing of a travel advisory.

In any other circumstances, we consider such unilateral action to be counterproductive and detrimental to developing countries.

I welcome the initiative of the WTO Secretary-General to convene a meeting to address this sensitive issue. My country would be prepared to participate in that meeting. The WTO's intention to address this problem and to devise new standards is long overdue. There remains the danger that the unilateral issue of travel advisories could be treated as disguised barriers to trade in services.

In the field of communications, it is far better to have no publicity at all than to have negative publicity. It is urgent that the international media get sensitized about the havoc that any kind of adverse reporting can have on a tourist destination. The market reacts immediately to such unwise reporting and, as we move in a direction of designing a partnership with the media, we hope that they would be more in step with our concerns.

As an employment generator in deprived areas, tourism plays a major role in poverty alleviation. This dimension, this human dimension, is simply overlooked when the media get to report without due regard to the consequences of their reporting.

COMPETITION AND COMMUNICATION

Tourism is an activity which thrives on competition. There is no room for complacency for anyone engaged in tourism. This is why we consider that competition is healthy and promotes creativity and innovation. The constant improvement of the tourism product in order to meet the demands of an increasingly sophisticated market is essential for the industry.

For the sustainable growth of the industry, communication in all directions at all levels and with all stakeholders becomes the key instrument. Every country must develop its own strategies for communication. These strategies are not static. They need to be closely monitored to ensure that there is value for money spent on communications.

We in Mauritius have found that close cooperation between hotels, airlines, tour operators and other services in the industry helps in maintaining and enhancing networks of communication.

Tracking trends and tastes are critical for the sustainable development of tourism. What makes this task extremely taxing is that trends and tastes evolve much faster than it is possible for the industry to adjust and take corrective measures. But we must learn to play according to the rules of the trade. Additionally, we should be on the lookout for new opportunities in order to be able to respond rapidly to them.

IMPORTANCE OF NATIONAL CARRIER

For tourism development in Mauritius we have through the Mauritius Tourism Promotion Authority over the years promoted the destination as safe, secure, modem with convenient air access. I spoke about dependency earlier on. There is one area where countries imperatively have to be present and that is in air services. Depending on other airlines to service the tourist industry is fraught with grave dangers and uncertainties. A national carrier will be committed to the destination and it has been our experience that our national airline has been always available to accompany the development of our tourism industry. We are convinced that at the present time the tourism industry in developing countries cannot succeed without the active participation of a national carrier.

WAY FORWARD

Tourism which contributes approximately 4.2% to the GDP of the global economy and employs about 8.2% of the world's economically active population is an activity that is of immense significance to developing countries. We cannot afford to lose any time in tourism development.

We believe that the end of conflicts, improvement of the global economy, receding fears about air travel and a general mood of optimism and confidence in the future will provide a welcome impetus to the tourism industry worldwide. The WTO must be commended for the role it has played in creating awareness about the importance of tourism for developing countries. The uncertainties associated with the trade talks and the likelihood of reaching agreement on trade distorting agricultural subsidies being remote, many countries, particularly the small ones, would be well advised in diversifying their economies and targeting tourism as a priority area for development.

The prospects are bright for this but, at the same time, the WTO must make its voice heard loud and clear on the necessity of working towards a level playing field between the rich and the poor as far as tourism is concerned. There must be a determined effort by the rich to encourage the development of tourism in developing countries.

One harmful consequence of globalisation and the weight of the major trading blocs in the other WTO (World Trade Organisation) is that small countries, especially the small island developing states (SIDS) are being crowded out of the global trading system. Trade liberalisation for many of them means the end of preferential trading regimes which enabled them to survive. They have inherent vulnerabilities for which the global trading system has no remedy. They are in a catch-22 situation.

One way to escape this trap is to embark on a programme of tourism development. These SIDS need special treatment and we urge the WTO to study their situation and to come up with solutions which must be long-lasting and sustainable. Most island developing states rely heavily on tourism receipts for their foreign exchange. These countries have no other alternative than to choose the path of tourism development. We hope that the media will help us in publicising the special plight of these countries.

We also urge the WTO to participate actively in the UN high-level meeting on Small Island Developing States which Mauritius is privileged to host at the end of August this year.

CONCLUSION

The unseen benefit of tourism is its contribution to understanding among peoples of different cultures. Tourism is really an instrument of peace and for peace. Through people-to-people communication tourism pushes the likelihood of a clash of civilization and cultures to the frontiers of impossibility.

As a force for good and understanding, tourism is unmatched. But as an instrument of development and holding out the realistic prospect of development and the achievement of the MDGs, tourism is unparalleled by the sheer spin-off effects for employment and wealth creation.

A better world is possible as long as the benefits of tourism are equitably shared. We are confident that the WTO will promote the partnership that alone will yield fairness and equity.

I wish to thank you all for your attention.

Muchas gracias.

COMMUNICATING SUSTAINABLE TOURISM: REACHING THE GEOTOURIST

JONATHAN TOURTELLOT

Director of Sustainable Tourism, National Geographic Society

A word about the National Geographic: We are a non-profit organization. You can think of us as an educational NGO. Our mission is the increase and dissemination of geographical knowledge, and we do this mainly through our media. We reach 70 million readers through our various magazines. One of them is National Geographic Traveler, which is, according to industry data, the world's most widely read travel magazine, at 5.7 million. We reach 200 million people through our cable television channels in 25 different languages and hundreds of millions more through other television programs, through maps, through books, through our website, home videos and so on.

Geography is, of course, about place. And tourism is also about place, but not necessarily all tourism, as we will see. In order to highlight this basic relationship between tourism and 'sense of place' we've introduced a new term, geotourism, which derives from "geographical character." Here's the definition of geotourism: *tourism that sustains or enhances the geographical character of the place being visited. By that we mean its environment, its heritage, its aesthetics, its culture and the well-being of its citizens.*

People often ask, "What is the difference between geotourism and ecotourism?" That's easy: *ecotourism* focuses only on nature; it's a niche. *Geotourism* talks about everything that goes into making a place - a place. Without question, it is sustainable tourism, but it focuses on the importance of place. It focuses on recognizing that there are opportunities to build on character of place, and so enrich both the travel experience and the quality of the locale.

Let's look at three overlapping types of tourism and how they each relate differently to character of place.

First, TOURING. This is the origin of the word "tourism." This style of travel depends totally on both the human and physical character of place, whether you're looking at a human-heritage site, like Machu Picchu, or a natural locale as with this hike in the mountains of Maui. Tourism of this type tends to have fewer impacts on the locale, while providing maximum benefit for local businesses and local people. The touring style requires preserving all the different elements that add up to character of place.

The next type, which we can call 'R and R' tourism - for Rest and Recreation - depends only on the *physical* nature of the place. You have to have beaches, you have to have a ski slope, you have to have lakes and rivers; but you do not generally depend very much on the human character of place-on local culture or heritage. This particular type of tourism encourages 'resort sprawl.' It can literally change the face of the earth, as resorts and vacation home subdivisions spread along seacoasts and into scenic mountain areas. You can see it on satellite pictures. It is a major development issue.

The third type of tourism we can call ENTERTAINMENT style. Here we have theme parks, convention centers, sports arenas, casinos, and outlet shopping malls that stock national and international brands. This type of tourism doesn't depend on character of place at all. You can do it anywhere. You can do it in the middle of a desert. And in fact one of the best known examples of it does rise from the middle of a desert - it's called Las Vegas. This type of tourism is industrial strength: high volume, high impact. If it is not sited and designed properly, it is the type most likely to have high negative environmental and aesthetic impacts. (For that reason, Las Vegas is actually in a comparatively good place for what it is.) Entertainment Style tourism does provide a lot of jobs. Because it tends to involve large companies, it has a lot of policy clout at high government levels. Governments make decisions based on this type of tourism.

Let me show you the next thing that tends to happen. When there is no policy about how tourism is handled, the destination-except for major cities-often sees a natural drift from the first style toward the third, driven by unguided market forces.

Here's how it works. Touring Style tourists are the first to discover a place. Then, as the destination increases in popularity, more hotels and resorts transform it into R and R Style, from which it's easy with yet more development to end up with Entertainment Style. By this time, the place no longer has the quality that first attracted Touring Style visitors, and they abandon it. Seacoast destinations are particularly vulnerable to this sort of thing. They can basically lose the original character of the destination through too much traffic and crowding. This happens so often that, in fact, academics have a term for it: The Butler resort life cycle.

When governments, as they often do, measure success in tourism in terms of quantity and not quality ("We counted ten thousand more tourists this year!"), they accelerate the trend toward overwhelming their destinations. It is very important that tourism success be measured, not by counting heads, but counting up the economic and social benefit to the location. Without policies to conserve what tourists are coming to see, the place may eventually find that it has no attractions at all.

Attracting the geotourist means focusing attention on a holistic way on all of the natural and human attributes that make a place worth visiting. That, of course, includes flora and fauna, historic structures and archaeological sites, scenic landscapes, traditional architecture, and all of the things that contribute to culture, like local music, cuisine as well as the agriculture traditions that support the cuisine, local crafts, dances, arts, and so forth.

It's additionally important that it benefit local people. The reason for this is to build that virtuous cycle wherein local people are benefiting from tourism, and that benefit in turn provides them with an incentive to protect what tourists are coming to see. It also provides local pride. Whether it involves the environment, as in Samoa, or local crafting traditions, as in North Carolina. An important part of this, that I have come to recognize more and more as I have worked in this field, is the importance of interpretive information-not only for tourists, but also for residents. The best interaction is for local people to help visitors to learn what the place is all about. And when you understand a place and appreciate a place, you become more interested in protecting that place.

That word 'enhances' is another important distinction in geotourism. Geotourism recognizes that you can improve things a bit. It can be done in two different ways. One is constructive tourism, by creating something suitable to the place that makes it better than it was before. Reykjavík, Iceland, for instance, put an elegant rotating restaurant on top of an ugly, conspicuous water tank. You get a magnificent view of the city from there. That's constructive tourism. The second way is restorative tourism, which helps to save something that might otherwise disappear, as with the old wooden ship that sailed the coast of the State of Maine in the United States. The last handful were saved when someone realized tourists would pay to sail on them. The Maine schooner fleet is in every way a success - an environmentally light footprint, beautiful to look at, and a fine heritage experience.

What, then is the geotourism market? How much do consumers really care about sustainability? In the United States, National *Geographic Traveler* sponsored a study by the Travel Industry Association of America to find out. The *Geotourism Study* is the first one we know of in the States that asked people extended questions about what they did when they traveled and correlated that with their attitudes are about sustainability. And, by "sustainability," we didn't just ask about the environment, but also about historic preservation, aesthetics, culture clash, and so on...

We found that over half of the American traveling public thinks that it's harder to find unspoiled places than it used to be. Almost three-quarters say they don't want their visits to harm the environment of their destinations. Eighty percent want outstanding scenery.

A cluster analysis on the data revealed that the top four of eight segments did most of the travel and spent most of the money. From the destination's point of view these are the four most important segments. We found that three of those four were very interested in sustainability, plus one of the bottom segments. These are the geotourists. They enjoy character of place, and they are predisposed toward doing what they can to protect their destinations. When we asked whether you would support travel companies that protect the character of a place, the four geotourist segments came out highest. What's more, these are the tourists most likely to read magazines, guidebooks, and newspaper articles about travel.

Unfortunately, there's not a lot in these media about sustainability or about how well a destination is managing itself.

Here's some of what we are doing about that at National Geographic. Well, we are trying to tell people about it. We have an online Sustainable Tourism Research Center. In Traveler we cover these topics in my "TravelWatch" column, and we give recognition to companies and tourism projects in a "Best Practices" sidebar.

In Traveler Magazine here, in addition to a column that I write, we also report in every issue on 'best practices' and give a particular example, such as the ECEAT environmental agro-tourism program in Poland.

In cooperation with Conservation International, we presented the first World Legacy Awards last year, announced in Washington by Queen Noor of Jordan. These are last year's winners. At the top is Ko Yao Noh, an island in Thailand, which won for destination stewardship; in the middle ATG Oxford, which won for its Heritage-Tourism work in Tuscany; and at the bottom is Wilderness Safaris of southern Africa, which won for Nature Travel. This year we have added a fourth category, General-Purpose Resorts and Hotels. The next awards are to be presented in early June. In our March issue, we'll be publishing the results of what we believe to be the world's first Index of Destination Stewardship, based on the informed judgments of over 200 experts from various fields and countries around the world. Some are probably in this room right now. The Index rates 115 well known destinations around the world on the basis of sustainability, tourism management, and success in retaining the assets that attract visitors. It should be interesting to say the least.

Lastly, we believe that many travel writers are also concerned about the decline in unspoiled destinations. We have chosen Tourcom, then, to announce release of the first version of this *Travel Writer's Guide to Sustainable Tourism and Destination Stewardship*. We invite all interested travel journalists to help create ever-improved versions of this manual over months and years to come. Tourism has become far too important a force in the world for us not to weave these important matters into our reporting. If WTO's figures are right, millions of jobs depend on it, including our own.

DEBATE - COMUNICACIONES DE CRISIS

DEBATE - CRISIS COMMUNICATIONS

DÉBAT - LA COMMUNICATION EN TEMPS DE CRISE

■ **INTRODUCCIÓN / INTRODUCTION / INTRODUCTION**
Deborah Luhrman,
Consultant and former Chief of Communication of the World Tourism Organization

■ **PARTICIPANTS:**
- **Dexter Koehl,**
  Vice-President, Public Relations & Communications, TIA
- **Sandra Lee,**
  Permanent Secretary for Economic Development and Labour of Hong Kong, China
- **Osmane Aïdi,**
  Président honoraire de l'Association internationale de l'hôtellerie et de la restauration (IH&RA) et Président de l'Union inter-arabe de l'hôtellerie et du tourisme

■ **CRISIS MANAGEMENT COMMUNICATIONS - WHO SHOULD I REALLY BE TALKING TO?**
Steve Dunne,
Managing Director, Brighter Management Group

■ **TRAVEL ADVISORIES AND NEGATIVE NEWS: A LOOK AT THE MAIN ACTORS AND THE RELATIONSHIP IN THEORY AND IN PRACTICE**
Christian Nielsen,
European Services Network

■ **CRISIS COMMUNICATIONS AND THE FUTURE OF THE AIRLINE INDUSTRY**
William Gaillard,
Director of Communications, IATA

INTRODUCTION

DEBORAH LUHRMAN
Consultant and Former Chief of Communications, World Tourism Organization

Good Morning Ladies and Gentlemen,

Welcome to Day Two of TOURCOM and to our debate on the timely topic of Crisis Communications in the tourism industry.

Before we start I would like to let you in on a little secret... **there is no such thing as a special crisis communications techniques.**

That's right. Crisis communications is simply good communications practices carried out quickly and efficiently during and after a crisis situation.

WTO defines a crisis as any unexpected event that affects traveller confidence in a destination and interferes with its ability to continue operating normally.

As the Secretary-General said yesterday in the inauguration-a crisis can be anything from a natural disaster like a hurricane, for example, to a deliberate terrorist attack on tourists themselves. In between, there are accidents, wars, or diseases-such as the bird flu currently affecting Southeast Asia. Crises can also be economic-like the Asia financial crisis or even big fluctuations in exchange rates.

The tourism industry has been battered by just about all of these crises over the past three years...and they've been coming at us one right after another. So our excellent panel of speakers this morning will take a look at some of the communications lessons that can be drawn from this recent series of crises.

I'd like to introduce them to you now:

Dexter Koehl is the Vice-President of Public Relations and Communications for the Travel Industry Association of the United States-which is the only organization that is involved in international tourism promotion on the national level. He'll be speaking about the response of the US travel industry to the tragic events of September 11th.

Then we'll hear from Sandra Lee, the Permanent Secretary for Economic Development and Labour of the Hong Kong Special Administrative Region, about the impact of the SARS crisis last spring and the actions taken by the government of Hong Kong to relaunch its important tourism industry.

We'll also hear from Dr. Osmane Aïdi, the Honorary President of the International Hotel and Restaurant Association...specifically about the communications response of the Arab world to the recent spate of crises.

Following these very pertinent case studies we're going to take a look at the bigger picture of crisis communications. Steve Dunne, General Manager of the UK travel public relations company Brighter PR will speak about how to focus your crisis communications and who to communicate with.

Christian Nielsen...who has published a very useful book called "Tourism and the Media" will look at ways of counteracting negative news and especially the impact of travel advisories.

And finally, our friend William Gaillard, Communications Director of IATA-the International Air Transport Association-will speak about crisis communications in the airline industry. In addition to dealing with lots of negative airline news himself over the past few years, Willy has developed a crisis training course for airline executives. So I know he has plenty of interesting information to share with us.

I don't want to rob too much time from this great panel, but I want to briefly explain what WTO has been doing in the area of crisis management. Just weeks after the September 11th tragedy, WTO set up what we call the Tourism Recovery Committee... made up of Tourism Ministers and private sector leaders from the most affected parts of the world.

This Committee has met several times to share information on consumer response and effective recovery measures... and in this way it has been instrumental in helping the governments involved make good policy decisions during this difficult period.

About this time last year I was asked to gather together the expertise from this committee into a booklet which is called "Crisis Guidelines for the Tourism Sector" . The guidelines are a series of measures designed to protect, maintain and enhance the reputation of a destination in times of crisis... a process which these days is being called reputation management.

Last year the crisis guidelines were made available free-of-charge on the WTO website and we also presented them in a series of regional workshops on Crisis Management in South Asia, East Asia-Pacific and the Middle East-so we had a chance to add quite a bit of experience to this body of knowledge on crisis management.

WTO's crisis guidelines advocate a proactive approach... just like the CNN presenter Becky Anderson recommended yesterday. If I had to boil down all the information into a few key messages, I would have to say that the secret to being prepared to successfully manage a crisis is to communicate more... in good times as well as bad.

During a crisis, communication needs to take place quickly, frequently and simultaneously on several different levels... with the travel trade, the media and directly with the consumer...all of which is much cheaper and easier nowadays thanks to internet.

WTO advocates an honest and transparent approach to communication in order to maintain credibility, because credibility is your most important asset in minimizing damage during a crisis and in rebuilding traveller confidence during the recovery period.

Following a crisis, WTO recommends that communication and promotion efforts be redoubled, through all the normal activities such as press conferences, news releases and electronic email bulletins... and then through the organization of special fam trips so the media, tour operators and travel agents can see for themselves the true extent of the damage.

There are many other tools to rebuild image that are talked about in the crisis guidelines... such as organization of special events, fiscal measures to keep tourism businesses from going bankrupt and the development of new industry partnerships... because sometimes it seems that it's only during bad times that the tourism industry can really band together.

I am sure our panelists can all offer good examples of some of these measures, so let's begin now with Mr. Dexter Koehl of TIA.

DEBATE - CRISIS COMMUNICATIONS

DEXTER KOEHL

Vice-President of Communications & Public Relations,
Travel Industry Association of America

Every one of us in the U.S. travel industry remembers where we were on September 11th, what it felt like to see the terrible attacks, and what it was like to manage a travel organization in the immediate aftermath.

While much of the nation could wait for the shock to subside, we had to move immediately into crisis management mode. I am going to share with you how Travel Industry Association of America staff assembled the travel industry's troops and launched a *ten-week counter offensive* literally before the smoke had cleared.

Almost immediately after the news had set in on September 11th TIA President and CEO Bill Norman began to consult with members of TIA's 15-person executive committee and a Travel Industry Recovery Coalition was formed representing 26 sectors of the U.S. travel and tourism industry. A message and battle plan quickly followed. We knew where we had to go and we had a plan to get there.

WEEK ONE: By September 17th the TIA senior staff team had created and begun to execute a recovery plan with two major goals: *Ensure safe, secure travel* and *restore travellers' confidence.* We needed to be unified as an industry. And we needed to bring as many other industry groups and the federal government on board with us.

Our first target was the news media. We had to seize the moment in the media and we did. As you would expect, the media were hungry for statistics, forecasts, literally anything they could get their hands on with regard to our industry. We recognized an opportunity to provide the industry with *one voice, one message* and *the tools to deliver that message.*

We gathered more than 50 of the top public relations and communications professionals in the travel industry via conference call and presented a *common message and strategy,* with all the tools to implement a unified industry PR campaign.

Our message platform was clear and simple: *"Travel is a fundamental American freedom.* We as an industry have a duty and responsibility to preserve and protect that freedom. We support the government's efforts to enhance safety and we as an industry must work together to restore consumer confidence in the safety of the U.S. travel product."

We provided talking points, facts and figures, sample letters to the editor, and other materials in a *special micro-site* on the TIA web site, www.tia.org. It became an easily accessible source for response for the industry.

The micro-site was an industry media clearinghouse that communicated to the U.S. and international media our availability as a source for timely information about the industry.

Over and over the public heard our message: Travel is a fundamental American freedom. A return to travel is a return to normalcy.

WEEK TWO: While our public relations campaign was underway, we were setting up our next phase-a national newspaper advertising campaign.

Our ad agency held two focus groups, one in New York City and one in the state of Ohio, and created several ads within ten days of the incident. What we learned was that consumers wanted to know what the industry was doing about safety and security. Consumers wanted an industry message to reassure them that things were being done to make it safe to travel.

In addition, they made it clear that they expected a "deal" or an offer to get them back.

WEEK THREE: TIA went ahead with its previously scheduled annual Marketing Outlook Forum in Atlanta with a revised agenda and communications tools for TIA members. This was an ideal setting to meet with almost 500 senior marketing executives and communicate our crisis strategy and message face to face. The timing could not be better - proving that sometimes luck is on your side.

We also launched the first round of national advertising October 2nd in eight newspaper markets across the country.

The ad was clean, simple and had a strong impact. Let me read it to you:

■ We see America as a land where the freedom to come and go as we please is a cherished right.

■ That's why America's travel industry has pledged its full support to the U.S. Congress and other federal agencies to ensure that travel is safe and secure.

■ After all, America was founded, expanded and made great by travellers.

■ And nobody can take that away from us. Not now. Not ever.

■ At the very bottom of the ad it said: SeeAmerica.org is a web portal to all U.S. travel industry sites supported by the Travel Industry Association of America, a non-profit organization representing all segments of the U.S. travel industry.

In addition to the paid advertising, the ad ran as editorial in newspapers around the country. The ad launched a comprehensive advertising and public service announcement or PSA campaign using *SeeAmerica* as a unifying brand.

SeeAmerica.org is a non-profit, non-commercial consumer web site that links to every travel industry organization in the US. It is a one-stop Internet location designed to get travellers to every travel site in America: cities, states, and companies.

This SeeAmerica.org web site and the SeeAmerica brand name had been promoted the previous year in the UK, Japan and Brazil. It now played an important role in linking the industry together domestically.

WEEK FOUR: The next advertising component was an advertising template with the message, "It's your country. See it. SeeAmerica." Our members downloaded this art from TIA's business-to-business web site, tia.org, and wrapped it around their own advertising messages.

We created a print public service announcement campaign for newspapers and magazines and for members to use in their own publications. It simply stated, "It's your Country, See it. SeeAmerica.org".

TIA member USA Today donated $1 million in media value to promote recovery through SeeAmerica advertising. Full page ads appeared in USA Today and banner ads ran on usatoday.com, their online web edition.

The template campaign then transitioned to a second phase as the Christmas holiday season approached. It centred on the theme of "give the gift of travel this holiday season".

WEEK FIVE: We remained focused on using the national brand, SeeAmerica, to leverage limited resources. Whether it was simply using the SeeAmerica logo in their ads or adopting the whole campaign, the industry benefited by leveraging our resources.

WEEK SIX: The U.S. National Parks and Forests announced that they would not charge entrance fees on Veterans' Day, the November 11 national holiday, to honor the sacrifices veterans had made.

We built on their idea and created SeeAmerica Day, as a Veterans' Day holiday promotion to encourage Americans to see their country, visit their monuments, visit friends-in short, we wanted to get people moving. We solicited offers throughout the industry to post on the SeeAmerica web site and then we announced it through a pictorial e-mail. This allowed us to make a national announcement quickly and at no cost. The e-mail was sent to all of TIA's 2,000 member organizations who, in turn, sent it to their customers, vendors and employees announcing their special offers.

Many cities in America offered free transportation, free entrance to museums and monuments or highly discounted rates for SeeAmerica Day. Hotel companies offered special SeeAmerica rates and some airlines did the same. And all of the offers were listed on the SeeAmerica web site with direct links to the site where the offer could be purchased.

WEEK NINE: Our most visible crisis communications effort came in week nine with a television ad campaign featuring President Bush and *real travel industry workers*.

Our industry owes an enormous debt of gratitude to Bill Marriott, Chairman of Marriott International, for personally calling his peers in the industry and soliciting dollars to fund this travel industry recovery television ad *which had no government funding*.

In addition to the paid advertising, we organized a news media blitz that was incredibly successful. We put the ad onto a world-wide satellite feed and methodically pitched the story to the media, city by city, country by country. In each case we localized the Bush ad story by offering top travel industry executives for media interviews.

The goal of the news media campaign was two-fold: First, to get the ad to run for free as often as possible; and second, to call attention to the ad so that when it ran, viewers would notice and remember the message.

And notice and remember they did. A national survey showed than an incredible 70 per cent of American consumers said they saw the Bush ad. And 55 per cent of the adult population of the U.S. accurately described the message. That was an astounding success.

In addition to the ad campaign, we took the SeeAmerica message to three of the biggest international trade shows of the year: World Travel Market in the UK, JATA in Japan, and Braztoa in Brazil. And at each event, TIA hosted traditional U.S. "Thanksgiving" holiday events with the local media, tour operators and other key U.S. travel partners, thanking them for supporting travel to the U.S. during this time of crisis.

WEEK TEN: In week ten we announced a partnership (Slide#21) between the industry and the U.S. Postal Service that leveraged the resources of both organizations to promote travel both within and to the United States.

The U.S. Postal Service agreed to print and release a set of stamps called Greetings from America featuring one stamp per each state for 50 unique stamps. TIA created a SeeAmerica Sweepstakes on the SeeAmerica.org web site. The Sweepstakes had 50 prizes of a one-week dream vacation for each of the 50 states, designed by each state tourism director. Each prize included a special dream itinerary with six nights hotel, a car rental and air transportation.

Posters showing the stamps and promoting the Sweepstakes were placed in state tourism information centers and in post offices around the country, guaranteeing exposure to more than 15 million people a day.

A PR campaign announcing the Greetings from America program generated more than 800 news stories with 70 million impressions. It ran in 209 U.S. television markets throughout the nation, including the top 25 markets.

In conclusion, what were the lessons we learned from this ten-week crisis communications campaign? They can be reduced to just four short points.

1. Develop a strategy and message and stay with it.

2. Engage the entire industry - and government too.

3. Leverage your resources so everyone can participate - in other words partner.

4. And finally, move quickly and take control of the situation - you can't afford to wait and let it control you.

Thank you.

DEBATE - CRISIS COMMUNICATIONS

SANDRA LEE

*Permanent Secretary for Economic Development and
Labour of Hong Kong, China*

Risk and crisis management is now very much an issue for all of us in the tourism industry. We face new challenges every day: from accidents such as the recent aircraft tragedy, to acts of terrorism such as the hotel bombings last year; war in the Middle East to economic turmoil in Asia; natural disasters in South America to new diseases on a global scale. From Iran to the USA, China to the UK, all of us have to deal with events outside of our control.

My remarks today will focus on the Severe Acute Respiratory Syndrome or SARS and how Hong Kong responded to the crisis. I will briefly cover the key stages of our response with particular reference to the travel and tourism sectors. I will also describe the recovery plan and how this has been implemented.

TOURISM RISK MANAGEMENT FOR THE ASIA PACIFIC REGION

In the recently completed report on Tourism Risk Management for the Asia Pacific Region prepared by the APEC International Centre for Sustainable Tourism, Sir Frank Moore wrote in the introduction:

"In times of crisis, for any tourist destination the first concern must be for visitors. Away from home, in unfamiliar surroundings, they are quickly disorientated and very reliant on their hosts and the host communities in general. Adequate planning for what has been seen as the 'unexpected' can be the difference between a well-managed problem and a human and economic disaster."

Mr. Francesco Frangialli said in his remarks that:

"... the strategies for reacting in a crisis and for recovering from it are remarkably similar from one tourism destination to another and from one crisis to the next".

I might add that this is true for all crises and at all levels from the smallest company dealing with the loss of a key employee to governments responding to natural (or unnatural) disasters.

THE STAGES OF REACTION

In my view, there are basically three stages in every crisis - the initial reaction when the crisis emerges and the facts are unclear; the consolidation stage as the nature and extent of the crisis becomes clear and the relief work becomes more organized; and the recovery stage when the emphasis turns to helping those who survive the crisis and the focus is on the future.

THE SARS CRISIS

In the same document, Peter De JONG the President and CEO of the Pacific Asia Travel Association (PATA) pointed out that:

"It took SARS to drive home just how economically dependant the countries of Asia-Pacific were on travel for their wellbeing."

I can easily illustrate this point by reference to Hong Kong.

For the first quarter of 2003, GDP growth in Hong Kong stood at 4.5% in real terms over a year earlier. However, the spread of SARS caused GDP in the second quarter of 2003 to fall to a 0.5% decline in real terms over a year earlier. The seasonally adjusted unemployment rate rose markedly, from 7.5% in the first quarter of 2003 to 8.6% in the second quarter.

The blow to inbound tourism and the travel-related sectors was most severe, particularly in April and May. From a positive 29% growth in visitor arrivals in the first two months of 2003, the number of visitor arrivals dropped substantially by 65% year-on-year (from 1.4 million in April 2002 to 490,000 in April 2003); and fell a further 68% (from 1.3 million in May 2002 to 430,000 in May 2003). Hotel occupancy rates in April and May plunged to 22% and 18% respectively, from a level of over 85% in the corresponding months of 2002.

What this meant in real terms is quite simple: from a vibrant and expanding sector prior to SARS the tourism industries were devastated. Hotels that had only recently had 'full' signs up now had no guests. Their F&B outlets were empty. Their shopping arcades deserted. Our Airlines cut flights and routes. Load factors fell as low as 20% from their previous high levels. Travel agents, shops, restaurants, bars and many other businesses in the sector were closing down. Staff were put on no paid leave or worse as businesses downsized. In short the tourism sector faced ruin.

In response, the government quickly put in place a low interest loan guarantee scheme targeted at the tourism sector to help employers pay salaries and cover other operating expenses. We waived licence fees and reduced certain rates and charges. All designed to help cushion the effects of the crisis.

FEAR OF THE UNKNOWN

SARS emerged as an unknown disease from an unknown source, with unknown methods of transmission and no known treatment. From a single index patient staying in a hotel in Hong Kong, the disease was spread to Canada, Vietnam, Singapore and eventually Europe and the USA. Hong Kong was faced with a nightmare situation: a disease that seemed to be very easily spread in a city with one of the highest population densities in the world. To compound the situation, Hong Kong is also one of the major gateways to China, in particular Guangdong where the SARS virus first emerged and is a major transportation hub in Asia with links to all corners of the Globe.

I do not want to describe in detail the medical response to SARS. There have been a number of detailed studies of this and anyone interested can access them on the Hong Kong Government's Department of Health website. Suffice to say that it took the concerted efforts of the World Health Organisation, the Hong Kong Government Department of Health, the Hospital Authority, and academics working together with overseas agencies such as the Centre for Disease Control to identify the virus and develop a treatment regime. The dedication, professionalism and care of our health workers was truly one of the best thing to come out of this situation. Unfortunately, even with all these efforts, eight medical staff were among the 300 people who died as a result of SARS in Hong Kong alone.

KEY LESSONS

SARS, as many of you will be aware, emerged initially in Southern China at the end of 2002 with cases growing in number through to February 2003. Unfortunately, information on this new disease was not released in good time despite the fact that there had been rumors and indications of something unusual in Guangdong Province but no official confirmation that there was a major problem. Once the SARS was brought into Hong Kong at the end of February 2003, it was too late to take steps to prepare and with the consequences that the disease was to have a far-reaching effect in Hong Kong and around the world.

This was the first real lesson: by not having access to accurate information we were not as prepared as we should have been and the situation quickly deteriorated.

Because the extent of the problem was not initially evident, the Government and the travel sector's initial reaction was to give reassurance to visitors and residents alike that there was little to worry about.

A classic example of this first stage was the handling of the Credit Suisse/First Boston Hong Kong Rugby Sevens. This is a major international sporting event, with 24 teams from all over the world. It has established itself as one of the pre-eminent events in the local calendar, attracting over 10,000 overseas visitors to Hong Kong in addition to the 25,000 local spectators. Scheduled to take place at the end of March 2003, just as the SARS situation started to deteriorate, the Hong Kong Rugby Union sought assistance from the Government to help them decide whether or not to cancel or in some way change the event. The Tourism Commission worked closely with the Department of Health and the Rugby Union to provide accurate information on what was known at that time about SARS. Detailed medical information was sent to all the participating teams to explain the situation before they arrived in Hong Kong for the tournament. At the start of the tournament the teams' management were briefed on the latest developments and steps were taken to protect the players from any risk of infection. Thanks to this direct and open approach, and even though three teams did pull out, these were replaced and the event went ahead successfully.

Through this experience, it became clear that there was a need to provide accurate information to our overseas contacts and, in particular, to the travel trade. A meeting was set up in early April at which travel trade representatives were briefed on SARS. This was followed by specific briefings for the hotel operators given their particularly important role in providing the most direct contact with visitors to Hong Kong.

At the same time, the Department of Health, in conjunction with the Tourism Commission and trade representatives, immediately started work on sector-specific health guidelines for hotels, the travel trade, airlines and transport companies. These guidelines covered relevant information as diverse as how to handle suspected cases for tour guides to hygiene for kitchen staff. A checklist of actions to be taken in each sector supplemented the guidelines.

Beyond the sector-specific action, Government quickly put in place comprehensive screening procedures at all ports and entry points to Hong Kong. The objective was to try to ensure that travellers on arrival were basically healthy, give each one information on what they should do if they experienced symptoms of respiratory tract infection and to facilitate tracing should cases subsequently emerge.

In view of the uncertainty over how SARS was spread, Government also took action to suspend all schools and to conduct home confinement for all those who had been in close contact with SARS patients: not just medical staff but also family members and casual contacts.

It is true to say that Hong Kong went from a vibrant, energetic city to a city in fear in the space of a few days.

COMMUNICATION, COMMUNICATION, COMMUNICATION

It was clearly evident that the only way to deal with the panic that was starting to get a grip was to use every possible means to communicate to the public the situation, accurately. Not only were traditional means such as daily press conferences and media briefings used but also emerging technologies were brought into play. At one stage, when rumours spread that there was an impending food shortage and the start of panic buying, SMS messages were sent out to all mobile phone users to assure them that there was no shortage of food and that there were adequate supplies to last months.

The importance of communicating the situation accurately to our overseas contacts was also recognised at an early stage. The Tourism Commission contacted the WTO to seek their assistance to disseminate relevant information to all member countries. The Hong Kong Tourism Board (HKTB) did the same with their contacts through PATA and also used their overseas offices to issue regular bulletins drawn up on the basis of information provided by the Department of Health. Even though the number of arrivals fell dramatically, it was important for the eventual recovery that our trade partners were informed of developments to establish the credibility of our messages.

DÉBAT - LA COMMUNICATION EN TEMPS DE CRISE

DR. OSMANE AÏDI

*Président honoraire de l'Association internationale de l'hôtellerie et de la
restauration (IH&RA) et Président de l'Union inter-arabe
de l'hôtellerie et du tourisme*

Mesdames, Messieurs,

Je remercie l'OMT pour l'organisation de cette rencontre.

Je souhaite vous transmettre une expérience que nous avons reçue dans le monde, qui est très large, très grande depuis le Koweït jusqu'au Maroc. Nous avons eu à faire face, pendant les dix dernières années, à plusieurs crises différentes par pays et dans toute la région.

Une des premières crises que nous avons souffert il y a une dizaine d'années est survenue lors de l'invasion du Koweït par l'Iraq et la première guerre du Golfe. Cette première guerre du Golfe a eu une conséquence très désagréable et catastrophique pour le tourisme même dans les pays qui étaient loin de la guerre : en Syrie, en Égypte, au Liban, des pays qui sont situés à plusieurs milliers de kilomètres de cette guerre, et, malgré cela, les Européens et les Américains ont eu l'impression que, si les événements avaient lieu dans un pays arabe déterminé, c'était la même chose dans tous les pays arabes.

En Syrie et au Liban nous avons fait un effort très particulier en 92-93. Nous avons organisé des expositions culturelles en Europe pour favoriser le tourisme culturel et nous avons eu recours aux médias. Nous avons invité des médias de plusieurs pays, sans exception (de la France, de l'Allemagne, de l'Angleterre...), des journalistes, des reporters de télévision. Un effort particulier a été fait dans la presse journalière, hebdomadaire, mensuelle, des programmes de télévision, afin d'offrir une image réelle de la vie dans cette région, une image qui n'a pas été altérée par cette guerre qui était lointaine.

Avant la guerre, nous avions des taux d'occupation, dans les grandes saisons, jusqu'à 90 pour cent. Après la guerre, ces taux sont tombés presque jusqu'à 2 ou 3 pour cent. Au bout de quelques mois, nous avons repris cet effort et la situation est devenue normale. Et ceci tant pour ce qui a trait à la guerre du Golfe qu'aux événements de Louxor. À Louxor, en Égypte, la situation a été traitée différemment. Un partenariat public-privé a été organisé pour des équipes complètes, guidées et dirigées par le ministre avec les administrations, l'Organisation mondiale du tourisme, les privés. Des tour-opérateurs ont visité plusieurs pays pour expliquer, donner toute assurance et garantir la sécurité dans ce pays.

Nous avons eu les mêmes problèmes après l'Intifada qui a eu lieu et les troubles qui se sont suivis au centre de la région entre Palestiniens et Israéliens, ainsi que les répercussions qui se sont fait sentir donnant lieu à ce que les touristes hésitent à visiter cette région.

Á l'Union inter-arabe pour l'hôtellerie et le tourisme, nous avons alors organisé un congrès au Caire et, en association avec l'Union arabe de l'aviation et des chemins de fer, nous avons réfléchi au problème. Vu que ces crises se succédaient et qu'elles étaient dévastatrices pour l'industrie du tourisme et de l'hôtellerie, nous avons essayé, avec l'Union arabe des médias et de la télévision, de faire un effort très particulier et de favoriser le tourisme régional, le tourisme de proximité, qui, surtout après le 11 septembre, avait diminué à cause de ces événements qui faisaient hésiter les voyageurs d'Amérique, du Japon, etc. de prendre des avions pour venir dans une région lointaine.

L'Union inter-arabe de l'hôtellerie et du tourisme, en association avec le l'Union arabe de télévision et de radiodiffusion, nous avons mis au point un programme hebdomadaire dans toutes les télévisions de 22 pays. Toutes les semaines, un pays était présenté à la radio et à la télévision, d'une part, pour projeter des reportages sur la réalité de la situation et, d'autre part, pour encourager les ressortissants limitrophes à se déplacer et faire du tourisme dans un pays proche. Ceci résulterait, d'un côté, plus économique, et, de l'autre, permettrait aux voyageurs d'effectuer des séjours plus longs. Et ceci d'autant plus qu'ils ne connaissaient pas les pays limitrophes, où ils pouvaient trouver ce qu'ils cherchaient dans les pays lointains.

En outre, ce partenariat public-privé a été matérialisé il y a deux ans à Tunis, lors de la réunion du Comité de crise de l'OMT à l'issue duquel des recommandations ont été faites aux organismes gouvernementaux afin de diminuer les taxes, la TVA, de reporter le paiement des créances ; parce qu'il ne faut pas oublier que les établissements touristiques et hôteliers ont souffert beaucoup de cette diminution du taux d'occupation. Il existait des créances auprès des établissements de crédits qui menaçaient la vie de ces établissements. Il y a eu donc une demande auprès des gouvernements pour essayer de donner des directives aux autorités compétentes, tant bancaires que financières, afin que soit reporté le paiement des impôts, de la sécurité sociale, etc. Il ne s'agissait pas de demander des exonérations, mais des reports des créances.

Il a été également recommandé de faciliter l'émission des visas d'entrée aux frontières, pour encourager les flux touristiques dans les pays et diminuer les formalités.

Avec ce programme de partenariat entre les établissements touristiques et hôteliers du secteur privé, et les télévisions, les médias, les radios, nous avons pu augmenter d'une manière considérable le tourisme interrégional, qui a pu ainsi diminuer l'influence très désagréable et très pénalisante qui a résulté des événements de septembre ou bien de la guerre d'Iraq.

Actuellement, après cette dernière guerre d'Iraq, de nouveaux programmes de promotion entre les secteurs public et privé sont mis en place pour, d'une part, augmenter le tourisme régional qui pouvait être un facteur déterminant pour la survie des établissements et, d'autre part, offrir des programmes internationaux afin de montrer la réalité des faits dans ces pays et ne pas laisser des doutes sur la situation qui y existait.

Merci beaucoup, mesdames et messieurs.

CRISIS MANAGEMENT COMMUNICATIONS - WHO SHOULD I REALLY BE TALKING TO?

STEVE DUNNE

Managing Director, Brighter Management Group

Good morning ladies and gentleman. My name is Steve Dunne, I'm Managing Director of the Brighter Management Group. It's a pleasure to be with you here this morning.

For those that may not know, Brighter Group specialise in advising and helping travel and tourism clients communicate with the marketplace both in the good times and, in keeping with this morning's theme of crisis management, the not so good times.

This morning, I've been asked to talk on Crisis Communications and specifically to answer the question "who should I be talking to?"

So, who should I be talking to in a crisis?

At first sight that may seem like a simple question with a very straightforward answer. Surely, in a crisis we talk to the media don't we? We also talk to the general public, or at least those impacted by our crisis - whatever that crisis may be. And, more often than not, don't we use the media to help us communicate with our customers - the public?

Now let me state right here and now that there is absolutely nothing wrong with that answer. Certainly, the media will beat a path to your door in the result of a crisis - of that you can be sure. It is also a safe bet that the public impacted by your incident will demand to know what is going on and will be hungry for your news.

However what I am here to suggest today, and these comments are based on the learning from the many crises that I, and my colleagues at Brighter Group, have been involved with in the travel and tourism industry these past few years, is that actually there is a series of communications channels that, at first sight may not seem so obvious as a communications channel at all.

I am here to suggest that, based on our experiences, if you can utilise these hidden channels of communication you can release their huge potential to aid your communications with the marketplace during the three classic stages of a crisis.

If you can utilise these channels, not only will you receive empathy and sympathy, but you will also be equipped with a communications tool that will educate, inform and reassure your target markets at a very critical time for your organisation - but they will do this from that most precious of all angles - qualified, independent, third party endorsement. To put it another way, we need to utilise the powerful leverage of the opinion formers and opinion leaders to whom the media and the public will flock during your crisis.

Now, I mentioned a moment ago the three classic stages of a crisis. What did I mean?

Crises, regardless of their nature or magnitude, go through three distinct stages. Those stages vary in length of time according to the nature of the crisis. Your organisation could go through all three stages in a couple of hours or maybe days or it could take months or even years to experience each stage - but each stage, I promise you, you will go through.

The first stage is what is known in the industry as the vacuum. This is where your crisis has just happened or is perhaps fermenting and about to burst onto the scene. During this stage there is little or no knowledge of the cause of the incident. Only that it has happened or is about to happen.

Details are vague but rumour will very quickly be rife. The marketplace and the media will be hungry for news but will be unable to find satisfactory answers - after all you may be busy finding the facts out for yourself. The media and the public will therefore seek the opinion of anyone they feel has the slightest knowledge, no matter how scant, of your country, service or product.

Inevitably, this will lead to speculation, often based on inaccurate knowledge of your organisation or country. The seeds of trouble for your recovery are already being sowed at this stage.

Stage two, sometimes known as the action stage, is where, for all concerned, the mists begin to clear. The details of your crisis are now largely known. The media are commenting on your approach and the travelling public, impacted by your incident, are making their decisions regarding their existing or future travel plans. At this stage the media is, and quite rightly should be, the principle form of communication to the market place. They are only interested in commentating on the crisis and how it is being managed.

Stage three is perhaps, in terms of crisis management, the most challenging stage for communications professionals. It's called the recovery period and as destinations such as Hong Kong after SARS, Egypt after Luxor and Bali after the terrorist strikes will vouch, it can take an organisation or destination many months or even years to pass through.

In stage three the media have lost interest in you and your crisis - at least the news desks have. They have moved on to other things. So now you may be getting little or no editorial coverage at all; the traveller has a mind set about your destination or product based on the speculation of stage one and your performance in stage two.

As your getting little or no editorial coverage the travellers perceptions are not being addressed. The traditional channels of communicating with your customer are closed to you. Your image has been seriously hurt and it's a long way back to recover your old positive reputation.

So, now that we know the stages we will go through if we are unfortunate to experience a crisis, what communications channels can we harness to help us manage the perceptions of our product in the eyes of the media and the travelling public both during the vacuum stage and the recovery stage?

What I would urge you all to do, when you go back to your offices and companies, is to seriously look at who your ultimate target market refers to for information, advice, knowledge or endorsement of your product and to then make a decision to harness them in your crisis communications process.

So, for example, if you are a destination or a resort, which tour operators and travel agents supply the largest number of visitors to your country? Where are they based? Who are the key contacts and what do they know of your contingency plans and capabilities for dealing with a crisis? Do they know who to contact within your organisation for accurate up-to-the minute information? Are you accessible to them?

Those same questions can be applied to airlines, hotel groups, and car rental and cruise lines. The list will be large and probably unique to you but the common component will be that they will be influential in talking to your ultimate target market and helping get you back on the agenda positively.

Once you have identified these influencers and opinion leaders make it part of your crisis-management planning to establish a network of communications channels with them and instigate a programme of education about your product but from a crisis management viewpoint. Let them know why you are doing this and what their role will be. After all, the chances are that any crisis for you will adversely affect their business - so it is in their interests to be in partnership with you.

And here is an important point. Do it now. You won't have time to establish the network and to educate it when your crisis breaks. But when it does break, the media and the travelling public will ask these organisations for their views on what is going on with your crisis and their speculation will be fuelled by the opinions of these organisations. What they know or don't know about your contingency plans or the extent of your problem and what you are doing to manage it will very quickly become the hard facts of the situation in the eyes of the media and the public.

And furthermore, if these organisations have anything less than a positive view of you they will not sell you, feature you in their brochures or include you in their itineraries. Any other marketing activity you undertake will become fruitless.

So let these organisations know what your contingency plans are; how you would cope with the range of crises you could possibly face and who, in the result of such a situation they can have access to for up to the minute information - a dedicated line only for the use of these organisations or a dark site on your web site which they can access for up to the minute qualified information.

Then, during the recovery stage of your crisis, your communications plan needs to focus very seriously on educating, reassuring and informing these groups as they will lead the way in passing your message through to the traveller, a message they will pass with the perception of neutrality and expertise about your destination or product.

So, think in your crisis management plan about taking trips of travel agents, tour operators, trade bodies or any other group to visit your resort, hotel or city immediately after your crisis has been resolved. Work with them to produce joint promotional material.

Hold special briefing sessions in their offices for their senior management and staff. Create interactive web programmes and information databanks.

Leave no stone unturned in your efforts to win their confidence and increase their knowledge of your product post crisis. And, unpopular though it may be, invest whatever it requires in terms of funds and resource to implement this programme. This is one thing you cannot do half-heartedly - after all it's your reputation at stake and the competition is tough. Someone else will be quick to take your place on the traveller's agenda.

I simply cannot emphasize enough how important it is to utilize these channels with crisis management in mind. Many make the mistake, after a crisis; of implementing a consumer advertising campaign coupled with media trips for influential journalists. That is a vital part of the campaign - yes but as many have found to their cost, if they do not embrace the influencers in the trade they will find that when the consumer arrives at the door of the travel agent the agent will not endorse his choice and may not even have the product available to sell because tour operators are simply not convinced about the destination. Given this situation one finds the ad campaign has given little return on investment.

An excellent example of how this approach has worked well is Egypt. Luxor had been a huge blow and then a couple of years later came 9/11. What the Egyptian Tourist Board did that impressed me was to work with the UK travel industry and harness the trade as influencers and opinion formers. They worked with the trade before the advertising broke to the consumer, ensuring that the agents were informed and knowledgeable and that tour operators were confidant enough in the product to provide itineraries. They kept the trade informed at every stage of the crisis.

The tour operator Kuoni who had withdrawn Egypt from their programme were so impressed with the communications programme that Egypt put in place that they produced a dedicated Egypt brochure within six weeks of the communications programme running. In short the combination of having the trade confidant and knowledgeable about Egypt in advance of the advertising campaign to the consumer and the general media campaign running alongside increased significantly the sales of UK visitors to Egypt in 2002/3.

So in closing ladies and gentleman let me reiterate my theme. The media has a vital role to play in communicating our message during a crisis. They can be a great friend in times of trouble. The news desks will cover our efforts to deal with the crisis and the dedicated travel writers will write with empathy and knowledge and be a positive aid in the recovery period.

But do remember that there are less obvious channels of communications that we should harness, just who they are may be unique to you, but have them you will.

So, ladies and gentleman here on this slide is some thoughts that I would like you to take away with you today :

- firstly, ensure that you have a positive attitude to crisis communications - learn to identify crises early and act quickly;

- secondly, be aware of the three stages of a crisis and what to do for each stage;

- have yourself a crisis management plan ready to go with every eventuality your destination or product may face;

- identify who your target audience will seek opinions from about you and your crisis.

Instigate a pre-crisis contact and awareness programme - it will be too late when the crisis starts. Thank you for your time this morning.

TRAVEL ADVISORIES AND NEGATIVE NEWS: A LOOK AT THE MAIN ACTORS AND THE RELATIONSHIP IN THEORY AND IN PRACTICE

CHRISTIAN NIELSEN
European Services Network

This is a typical image we have of tourism under normal circumstances.

Typical image of
tourism

This is tourism under duress. What happens to tourism when it's struck with a disaster; man-made or natural?

Negative (tourism) image

Structure of presentation

Travel advisories and negative news: a look at the main actors and the relationships in theory and practice

- Introduction & definitions
- Relationships between tourism, the media & travel advisories
- Bad news and tourism

| Introduction & definitions |

Basic tourism model

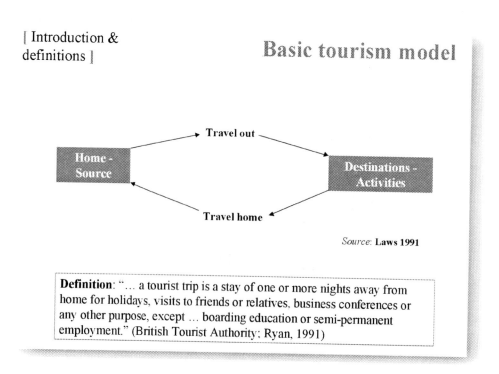

Source: **Laws 1991**

Definition: "... a tourist trip is a stay of one or more nights away from home for holidays, visits to friends or relatives, business conferences or any other purpose, except ... boarding education or semi-permanent employment." (British Tourist Authority: Ryan, 1991)

| Introduction &
definitions |

Basic media model

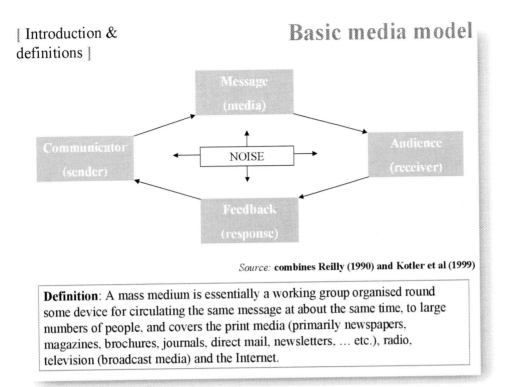

Source: **combines Reilly (1990) and Kotler et al (1999)**

Definition: A mass medium is essentially a working group organised round some device for circulating the same message at about the same time, to large numbers of people, and covers the print media (primarily newspapers, magazines, brochures, journals, direct mail, newsletters, ... etc.), radio, television (broadcast media) and the Internet.

| Introduction &
definitions |

Basic travel advisory model

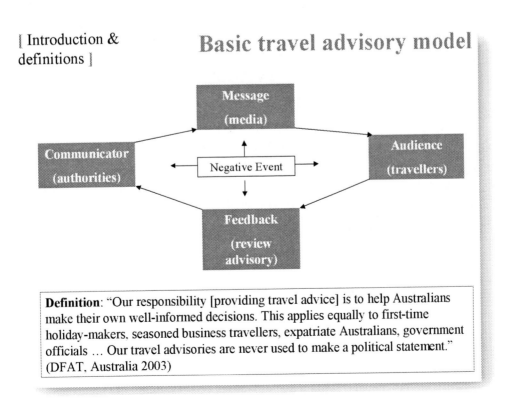

Definition: "Our responsibility [providing travel advice] is to help Australians make their own well-informed decisions. This applies equally to first-time holiday-makers, seasoned business travellers, expatriate Australians, government officials ... Our travel advisories are never used to make a political statement." (DFAT, Australia 2003)

[Relationships]

What's the connection?

"Promoting a destination in normal circumstances is a difficult task, but promoting a destination that faces tourism challenges – whether from negative press, or from infrastructure damage caused by natural disasters or man-made disasters – is an altogether more arduous task." (Nielsen 2001)

[Relationships]

When are advisories issued?

✳Travel advisories are issued traditionally by national authorities to ensure their citizens are well informed and prepared for travel abroad, helping them avoid danger and difficulty while away.

✳Different codes and standard phrases are used by governments, but several share raw information: notably Australia, NZ, USA, Canada and the UK.

✳Advisories are regularly updated, informed statements on the current risk of a destination based on multiple sources.

✳In Australia's case, the sources include assessments from embassies, high commissions and consulates about security in their locations; reports from Australians on the ground about difficulties faced; intelligence gathered (esp. threat assessments from the Australian Security Intelligence Org.)

[Relationships]

Tourist information search

✳But the big question is, who do people rely on for information about potentially risky travel?

✳And do people seek information from different sources along the path to making a decision to travel?

✳Adapting Baskin and Aranoff's (1998) figure 'Critical paths of influence in the adoption and changing of tourism ideas', a **disaster critical path** can be traced.

"**Three elements** are identified as leading to the creation of destination image: returning tourists through word-of-mouth reporting their experiences, the media, and the government of the tourist-generating region." (Hall & O'Sullivan 1996)

[Relationships]

Travel decisions and unbiased 3rd parties

Adoption stages Channel of influence →	Awareness	Interest	Evaluation	Trial	Adoption
Mass Media	♠♠♠♠♠	♠♠♠♠♠	♠♠	♠♠	♠♠
Biased Intermediaries	♠♠	♠♠	♠♠♠	♠♠♠	♠
Unbiased 3rd Parties	♠♠♠	♠♠♠	♠♠♠♠	♠♠♠♠	♠♠♠♠
Significant Others	♠♠♠♠	♠♠♠♠	♠♠♠♠♠	♠♠♠♠♠	
Personal Experience					♠♠♠♠♠

Scale of importance

♠ = very little...[to]

♠♠♠♠♠ = extremely

Paths

Critical path = _____

Disaster critical path = _____

Source: **Nielsen 2001, adapted from Baskin & Aranoff**

[Bad news tourism]

Tourism's Lazarus factor

"The only stories that get substantially reported by the Western media are natural disasters and the sporadic and sometimes violent attacks on visitors with immediate consequences for tourism-dependent local economies." (Lilley, 1999 – reporting on the aftermath of Hurricane Mitch in Central America)

BUT

"While travel confidence was gradually restored after the war, it was further dented by terrorist attacks in Riyadh, Casablanca, Jakarta and Mumbai. However these had far less impact than expected as the public seems to have grown accustomed to living in an unsafe world." (World Tourism Organisation statement, 29/10/2003)

[Bad news tourism]

Terror-tourism-media model

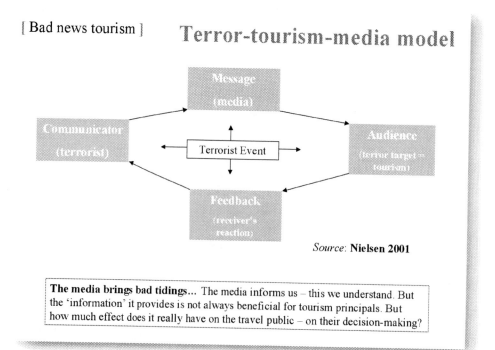

Source: **Nielsen 2001**

The media brings bad tidings... The media informs us – this we understand. But the 'information' it provides is not always beneficial for tourism principals. But how much effect does it really have on the travel public – on their decision-making?

[Bad news tourism]   # Media effects argument

Micro vs. Macro
✳although the media may succeed in conveying specific (micro) information to a population, it may do so in differing degrees to various status (macro) groups*

Alteration vs. Stabilisation
✳discusses the predominance of change as a media effects criteria in research because its easier to observe

Cumulative vs. Non-cumulative
✳differences in media effects research between influences that accumulate over time compared with single message changes

Long-term vs. Short-term*
✳experiments show reasonable, though relatively short-term effects, following exposure to a message, but dissipate with time unless additional exposure takes place

Attitudinal vs. Cognitive vs. Behavioural
✳early effects research centred on attitude change, moving on to 'learning' effects of the media

Media Content and Use*
✳content and form of media messages is analysed for its often subtle psychological effects (i.e. sex sells)

Source: **Nielsen 2001, from McLeod et al. 1991**

[Bad news tourism]   # Effective tourism communication

Draft press/news releases keeping in mind the following:
✳Develop a sense of newsworthiness

✳Professional approach to relations between tourist entities and the media*

✳Assess the probable impact of statements on different audiences

✳Dramatic stories sell themselves (which is the problem with negative news stories too!!)

✳Research results from the WTO or WTTC are newsworthy

✳Timing is very important*

✳Communicating with the media requires an adherence to accepted standards

✳Be sure all facts and figures are correct (and indicate source)*

✳Watch deadlines delivering info to the press/media

✳Give release instructions, e.g. 'for immediate release' or 'embargo until xx'

✳Write simply and objectively in 3rd person

✳Apply the Hey-You-See-So approval system; 'Hey' (gain attention), 'You' (identify audience), 'See' (subject), 'So' (plan of action or next move), to writing press material

| Bad news tourism |

Image reversal campaign

To get 'selective images' in the press, on the news, ... on TV ask these questions:

❋What image does the destination presently have in key markets?*

❋What are the cultural and social values of the source market – how do I target them?

❋How is info diffused in these markets? (mass media, grapevine, formal channels, etc.)*

❋What image do I want my destination to have? (sporting, 4 Ss, luxury, adventure, ...)

❋How can I influence these target markets? (advertise, wait, educate, ...)

❋When should I begin my image reversal campaign? (during negative event, after, ...)*

❋How much do I spend on the campaign? (bear in mind marginal utility)

❋Should I educate the host nation on how to handle tourists in the new situation?*

❋Once campaign is underway, how do I monitor its success?

Importance of image... "Place promotion is the conscious use of publicity and marketing to communicate selective images of specific geographical localities or areas to a target audience." (Ward & Gold, 1994)

CRISIS COMMUNICATIONS AND THE FUTURE OF THE AIRLINE INDUSTRY

WILLIAM GAILLARD

Director of Communications, IATA

Air transport is the backbone of the travel and tourism sector. If people have any doubts about the safety and security of air transport, it would have definitely a disastrous impact on travel tourism worldwide. At the same time, our industry sector is under constant watch by the media in terms of safety and security and there is a good reason for that: Air accidents provide spectacular images for television. They've got all the ingredients that bring audiences to television. The human tragedy, the grief the sorrow, the drama. It is anything that TV coverage needs and therefore, any kind of accident involving an aircraft will receive a completely undue share of coverage.

If one thinks of the tragedy which appeared in Sham El Sheik in Egypt just at the beginning of the year in which thirty-five tourists were killed in an air crash, in Europe, this matter has been at the forefront of news for the past month. I personally have been on television somewhere in Europe everyday since the 4th of January to deal with this particular incident. Imagine if we had an earthquake in the meantime, killing 50.000 people in Iran - how much coverage do you get, how much coverage do floods in parts of Africa get, killing hundreds of thousands of people. But, this particular issue, the fact that suddenly middle-class people, middle-class young people, middle-class young and healthy people die within seconds on their vacations has a tremendous impact on Western public opinion. And therefore, the amount of coverage that it gets is completely out of proportion with the sheer dimension of the tragedy. As I said, earthquakes, famines and disastrous floods don't get a tenth of the coverage that an air disaster gets because they involve people who are obviously far less influential in their society than the people who die in an aircraft.

Still, in spite of that coverage air transport is still by far the safest way to move. Just to give you one piece of statistics, which I think is also an interesting anecdote: in 1949, five hundred people died in a commercial aviation crash - in scheduled traffic at that time - but only nine million flew in 1949. Whereas last year, also about five hundred people died in scheduled commercial flights, but 1.6 billion people travelled last year. That shows you how safe air transport has become and actually how quick and safe it was in the 40's and 50's.

Airlines have always been quite good at handling their business continuity part of crisis. If an airline would have a crash, within hours, its full schedule would be served. The aircraft would still be landing and taking off and everyone getting on this aircraft and the whole process in the company going back to normal minutes after the tragedy. What airlines really have never focused on was the issue of crisis communications. Until the 1990's they did not understand that efficient management of crisis implied three pillars. One of which was crisis communications. It ought to deal with the public in terms of information and second, family assistance. The airlines very often did this very well before the 1990's, but they usually didn't talk about it. Or they didn't talk about it in an efficient way. And third, something

197

that the airlines have always done well - cooperation with the investigation authorities, with the idea not to punish anyone, but to make sure the same causes don't lead to the same consequences that we don't have a remake of such an accident in the future.

Everything changed in July 1996, with the TWA crash, the New York/Paris flight 747. Why did it suddenly come to that in 1996? Well I think there are many reasons.

First of all it occurred in New York which is the number one media center in the world with a certain brand of politicians who immediately got involved thinking that they probably could get some political capital out of being involved in a human tragedy.

Secondly, it was just before the Olympics, so all the attention was focused on the U.S. in terms of this big event. There had been a number of security threats and people were quite nervous about the Atlanta Olympics from that point of view.

The other factor is that twenty-four hour satellite television coverage had then reached its maturity. In the 1970's just to give you an example, there was the first crash of a jumbo jet. It was a Lufthansa flight in Nairobi, it was 1973. It took four days for images of the wreckage to reach Germany. German television had to assign a crew, they had to film, they had to come back, they had to process the film and they had to show it. These days we get images of planes burning on the runway within five minutes. There is a large number of airports around the world that have permanently fixed-cameras on their runways continuously filming. Remember the crash in Taipei in the late 1990s? When watching it on television in Japan, we could see the fire engines rushing towards the burning aircraft on television. So the television was there before the fire department got there. And it was at the airport. So, the immediacy of coverage is something that is completely new and the airlines in 1996 were not really ready for that.

And then there was the Internet. Most of the theories about what happened to TWA flight 800 came through the Internet, including all the hoax about missiles and things like that. And people in 1996, culturally, did not yet understand all the implications of the Internet.

So, faced with the situation and analyzing what had happened to TWA, we decided at IATA to create a service that the airlines could use. Not only to plan their crisis communications response, but also to train spokespeople who are extremely scarce in times of crisis and to prepare themselves to handle any eventuality. This service has, since developed, gone beyond the air transport industry or beyond the airlines at least. We have gone to advise oil companies, banks, aircraft manufacturers, engine manufacturers, and so on and so forth. It has matured so much that in two days it would become completely independent from IATA as a company with its own rights just because the scope of its activities has become so large. I don't' want to go on and describe what the service does, apart from the fact that it trains executives and airline spokespeople. It writes communications manuals, it sets up basically everything, including doc sites on the web to make sure that the moment the crisis hits - and speed is definitely the essence - the company is ready to react within minutes, with very, very strict targets about what has to be done within forty minutes, an hour, two hours, three hours and so on.

One thing which I think was quite innovative in what we did is that we decided that in the case of TWA, the airline was unfairly accused by New York politicians of not caring about family members and survivors. It had actually been doing an excellent job in dealing with family members and survivors, but in the end never talked about it. And perception is everything, perception is the truth. So if politicians perceive your company as not doing anything to help the families of those who perished in the catastrophes, then you did nothing. And therefore, one of the top priorities we've put always to airlines these days is a press conference right at the beginning. We have there a family assistance team, the top executives, the minister, the nurse, the psychologists that are going to be aiding the family assistance team that describes in details what is going to happen in the next few days, in the next few months and in some cases in the next few years to assist those who have lost their loved ones in the catastrophe. And I must say that the response by the public and the response by the media has been outstanding.

There are people who are finally recognizing the fact that the airlines are doing their job, because the airlines are telling them that they are doing their job. It is as simple as that.

I think I'll leave the rest for the debate. Thank you very much.

GRUPO DE REFLEXIÓN V

Una plataforma de las comunicaciones en el turismo para el futuro

PANEL V

Tourism communication platform for the future

TABLE RONDE V

L'avenir de la communication dans le domaine du tourisme

- INTRODUCCIÓN / INTRODUCTION / INTRODUCTION
  Mustapha Elalaoui,
  President & CEO, Strategic Communications Group

- INFORMATION, COMMUNICATION AND TOURISM IN THE EUROPEAN UNION
  Mathieu Hoebrigs,
  Principal Administrator - Tourism, European Commission

- TOURISM BRANDING - CONTEMPORARY CHALLENGES FOR NATIONS, REGIONS AND CITIES
  Richard Tibbott,
  Chairman, Locum Destinations

- FROM "HIGH-TECH" TO "HIGH-TOUCH" - IMPORTANCE OF DIRECT COMMUNICATIONS,
  MEETING AND EXHIBITIONS INDUSTRY
  Stanislava Blagoeva,
  President of ETTFA

- E-COMMUNICATION IN TOURISM - THE ROLE OF THE INTERNET,
  CHALLENGES AND OPPORTUNITIES FOR TOURISM
  Thomas Steinmetz,
  Publisher, e-Turbo News

INTRODUCTION

MUSTAPHA ELALAOUI

President & CEO, Strategic Communications Group

(summary)

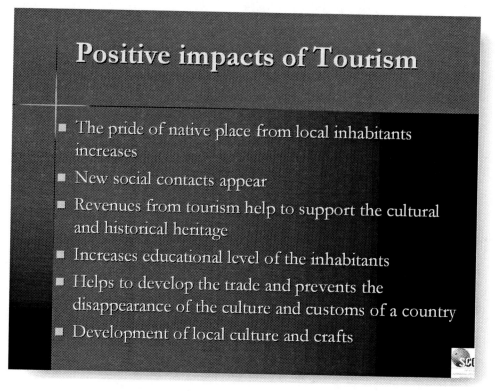

Positive impacts of Tourism

- The pride of native place from local inhabitants increases
- New social contacts appear
- Revenues from tourism help to support the cultural and historical heritage
- Increases educational level of the inhabitants
- Helps to develop the trade and prevents the disappearance of the culture and customs of a country
- Development of local culture and crafts

Positive impacts of Tourism

- Saves flora and fauna
- Conserves natural resources
- Environmental caretaking
- Infrastructure development

Tourism's role in a country's Image Enhancement

- Tourism helps in the enhancement of the country's image thereby making it more prominent in the world map.
- Economic advantages of tourism helps development of the society, thereby enhancing the image of the country.
- International recognition of a country is developed through tourism.

Tourism's role in a country's Image Enhancement

- Tourism preserves the socio-economic environment thereby enhancing a country's image.
- Tourism promotes peace & stability, thereby developing the image of a country as peaceful and secure.
- Tourism contributes to upgrading the overall status of a country, thus helping the country to maintain world class levels.
- Tourism upgrades the quality of life by activating cultural and sports events thus bringing recognition to a country.

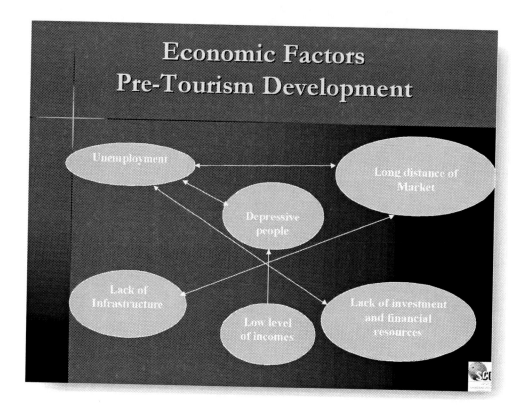

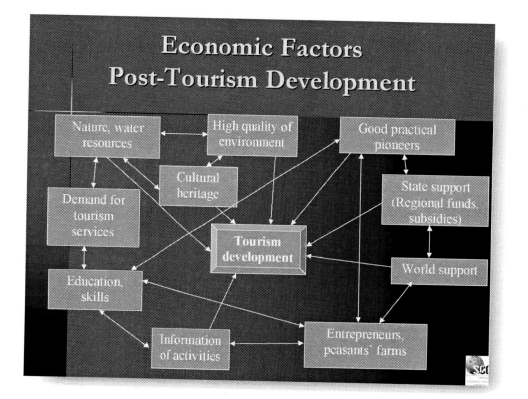

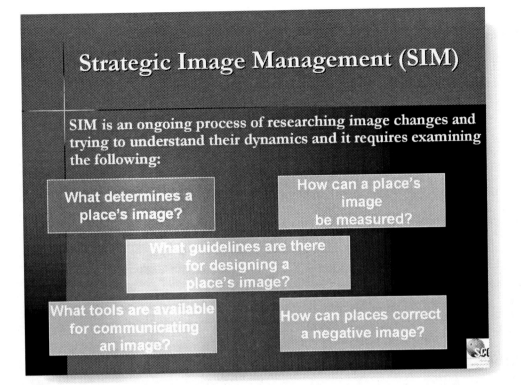

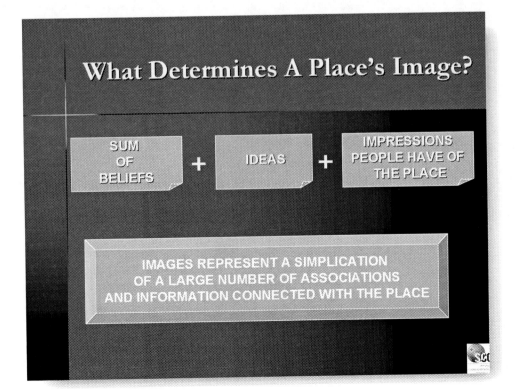

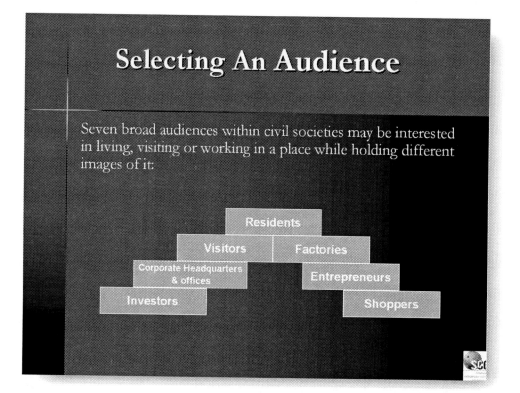

Measuring The Audience's Image

Familiarity – Favorability Measurement

Audience Awareness

Never heard of	Heard of	Know a little bit	Know a fair amount	Know very well

Audience Familiarity

Very unfavorable	Somewhat unfavorable	Indifferent	Somewhat favorable	Very favorable

Guidelines For Designing Place's Image

For an image to be effective it must meet the following criteria

IT MUST BE :

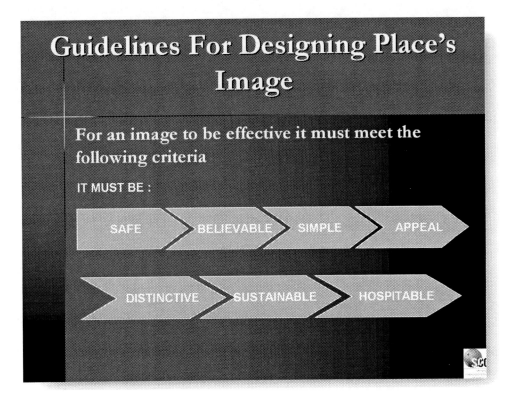

Tools For Communicating An Image

Place image makers can draw on three tools to implement an effective image of a place:

- Slogans , Themes & Positions

- Visual Symbols

- Events and Deeds

Slogans ,Themes & Positions

- Image makers develop a slogan to unify a specific campaign, and the slogan if successful is carried over many campaigns.
- A good slogan provides a platform from which the place's image can be further amplified.

PLACE CAMPAIGN SLOGANS	
Quebec	It feels so different
Pennsylvania	America starts here
Spain	Everything under the sun

Slogans ,Themes & Positions

IMAGE POSITIONING STATEMENTS	
Jordan	Jordan First
Berlin	Capital of New Europe
Costa Rica	Latin America's most stable democracy
Dubai	The city that cares/Forever Dubai

Visuals Symbols

Visual symbols have figured prominently in place marketing. Many landmark sites of places are permanently etched in the public's minds:

Big Ben   Eiffel Tower   Great Wall

The Statue of Liberty   Red Square   Burj Al Arab

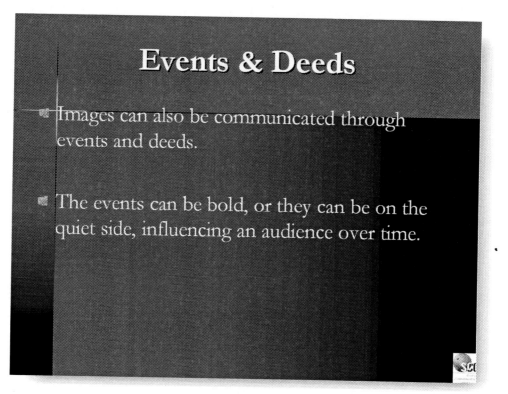

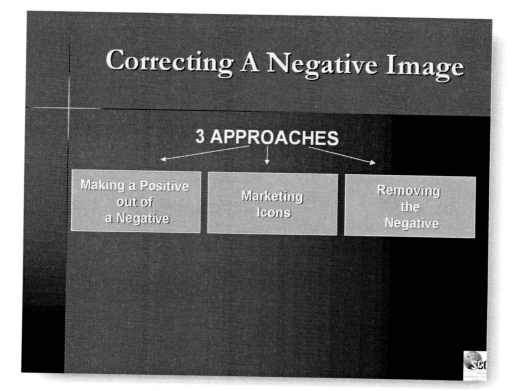

Making A Positive Out Of A Negative

ONE OPTION IS TO ADMIT THE PROBLEM AND
TURN THE NEGATIVE INTO A POSITIVE

EXAMPLE:

Wisconsin, turns reputation for harsh winters into much more

Emphasizes on good skiing, healthy dairy industry and natural features, i.e. great lakes

Shifts focus to inexpensive activities, lakeside cabins, fishing

Promotes friendly atmosphere by using the slogan
"Wisconsin You're Among Friends"

Removing The Negative

Image improvement is too often used as a quick–fix for a place's problems.

Leaders plagued by failing businesses or a drop in tourism are usually quick to demand a new image.

New York City, Post September 11 encouraged people to continue to live normally and for outsiders to visit by promoting a prideful, "no fear" confident attitude.

This was backed by Mayor Rudolph Giuliani who publicly stated, "We're going ahead with our lives."

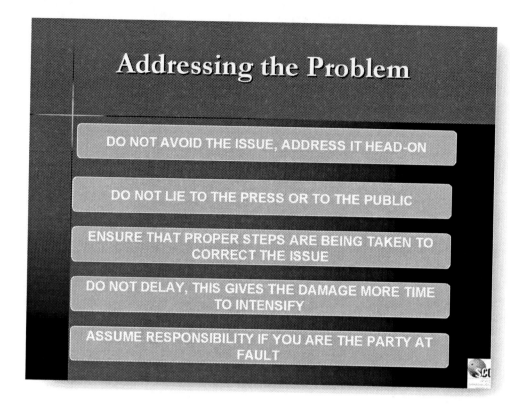

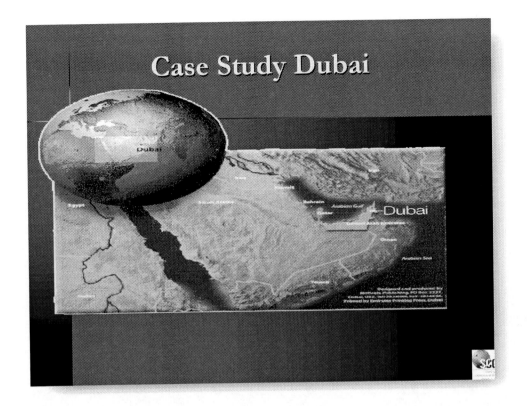

Case Study Dubai
"Dubai Facts"

- The second largest of the seven emirates which make up the United Arab Emirates, Dubai is located on the southern shore of the Arabian Gulf. It has an area of some 3,900 square kilometers.
- Outside the city itself, the emirate is sparsely inhabited and characterized by desert vegetation.

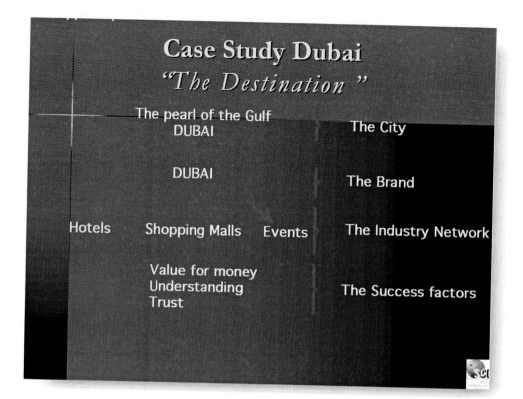

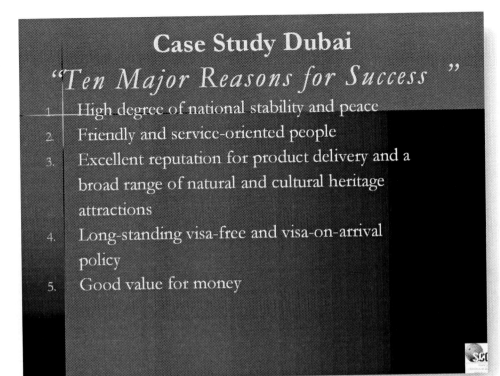

Case Study Dubai

"Ten Major Reasons for Success "

1. High degree of national stability and peace
2. Friendly and service-oriented people
3. Excellent reputation for product delivery and a broad range of natural and cultural heritage attractions
4. Long-standing visa-free and visa-on-arrival policy
5. Good value for money

Case Study Dubai

"Ten Major Reasons for Success "

6. Geographical advantage
7. Extensive airline and aviation access
8. Strong promotional campaigns
9. Excellent transportation, infrastructure, accommodation and restaurants
10. Strong regional tourism co-operation

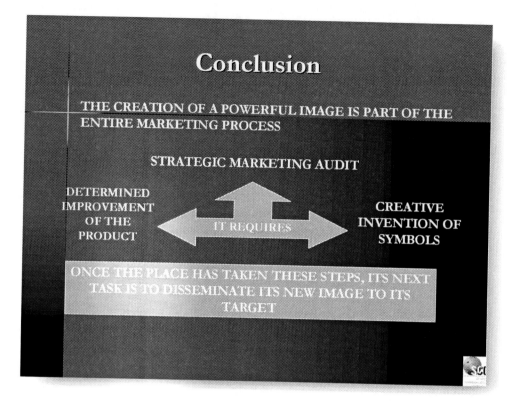

INFORMATION, COMMUNICATION AND TOURISM IN THE EUROPEAN UNION

MATHIEU HOEBRIGS

Principal Administrator - Tourism, European Commission

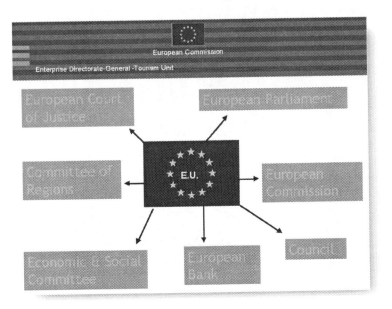

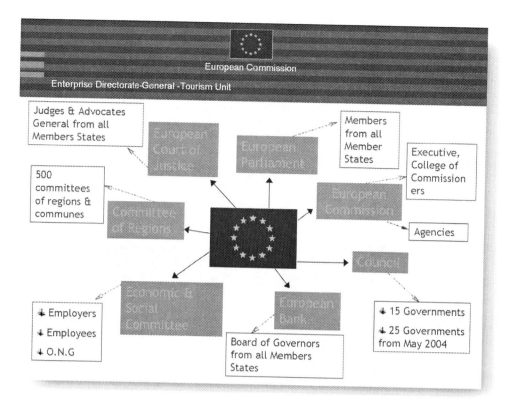

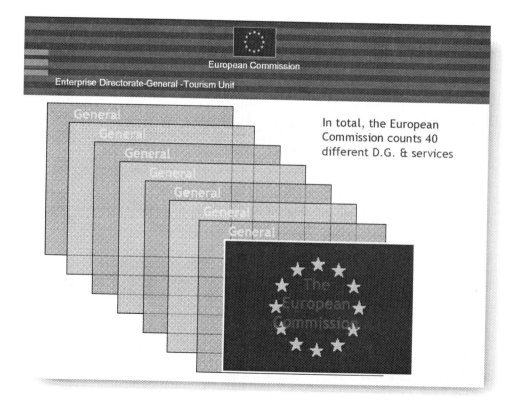

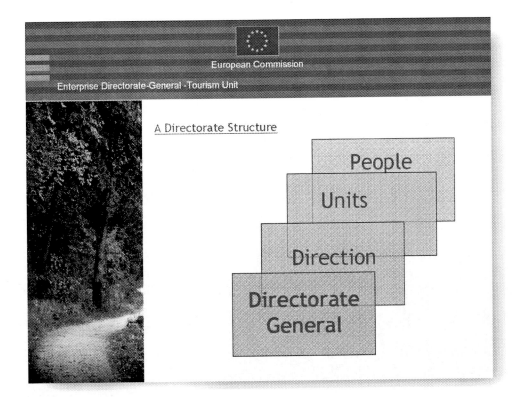

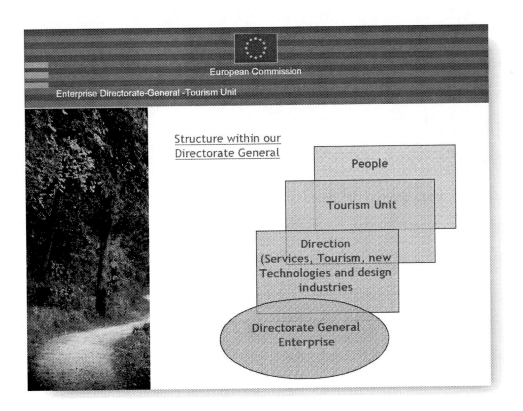

- Concept
  - *Objectives:

    To improve perceptions of the European Union, its institutions and their legitimacy by enhancing familiarity with and comprehension of its tasks, structure and achievements and establishing dialogue with the general public.

- Meaning

    *Translating into a simple and non-controversial communication terms the Union's main objectives as stemming from the Treaty on European Union (Articles 2 and 6).

- Central Thread

    *A thread woven round homogeneous general concepts profiling clearly the Union raison d'être and providing the institutions and the Member States with a reference framework within which to transmit coherent messages.

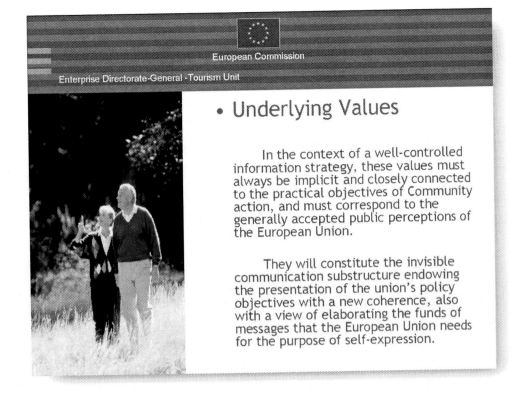

European Commission

Enterprise Directorate-General -Tourism Unit

- **Underlying Values**

In the context of a well-controlled information strategy, these values must always be implicit and closely connected to the practical objectives of Community action, and must correspond to the generally accepted public perceptions of the European Union.

They will constitute the invisible communication substructure endowing the presentation of the union's policy objectives with a new coherence, also with a view of elaborating the funds of messages that the European Union needs for the purpose of self-expression.

European Commission

Enterprise Directorate-General -Tourism Unit

- **Targeted Communication**
  - ❋ For each topic:
    - Formulate a strategy and messages geared to a public that is already informed ;
    - Formulate a strategy and messages geared to the general public.

- **Ensuring synergy**

  ❋Each institution should adapt its internal structures to reflect the requirements of this new strategy. It also invites each Member State to reflect on ways of improving synergy between its national information policy and the Union's communication strategy.***

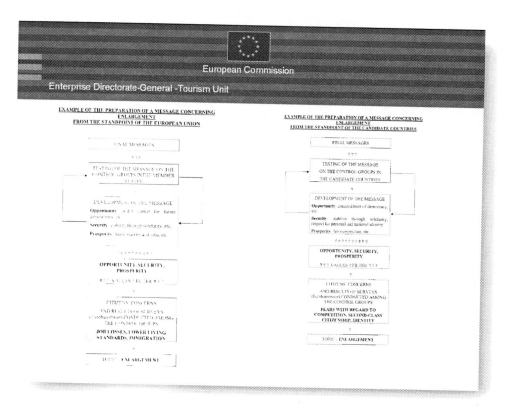

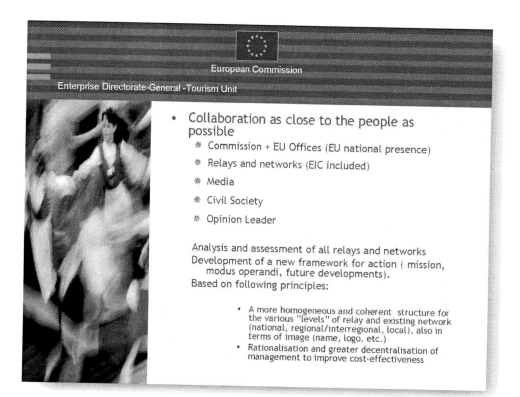

- **Communication, Information means...**

  - Oral Information (speeches, press interview, etc.)
  - Written information (legal texts, press releases, specific information and documentation, etc.)
  - Use of new technologies (Internet, Telephone, etc.)
  - Media services
  - Civil society dialogue (ensuring two ways communication flows)
  - EU offices & Relays & Networks

- **Means of Communication in Tourism**

  - Respect of framework as indicated
  - Add specific DG Enterprise and related policies issues (competitiveness, SME policy, etc.)
  - Add specific Tourism and related policies issues (depend of "policy" in tourism/related areas)

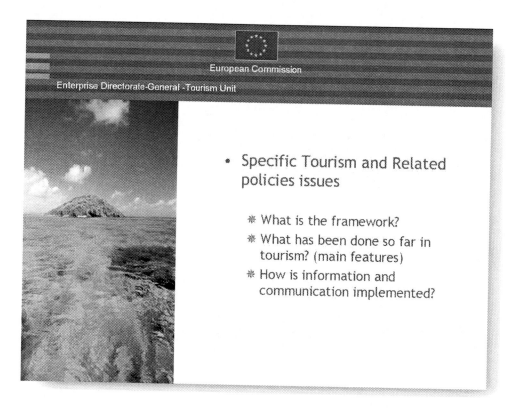

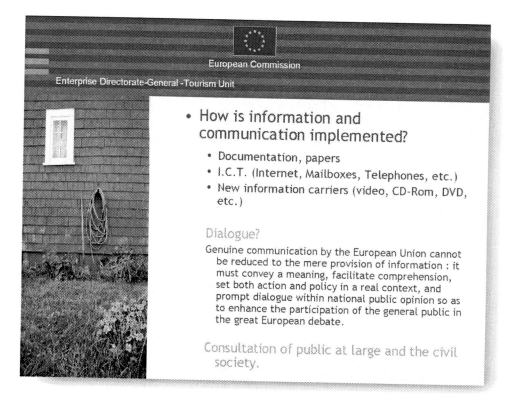

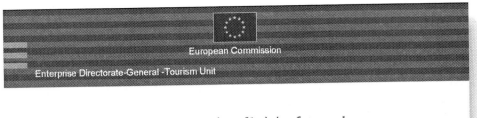

European Commission

Enterprise Directorate-General - Tourism Unit

- Any specific action the field of tourism concerning information and communication dialogue?

  ※ Studies (European Portal of Tourism Destinations with ETC), dissemination of information

  ※ European Tourism Forum 2004 (information, communication, dialogue and consultation), networking + interface

  ※ Tourism Advisory Committee (dialogue and consultation), permanent committee

  ※ Special meetings concerning accession countries

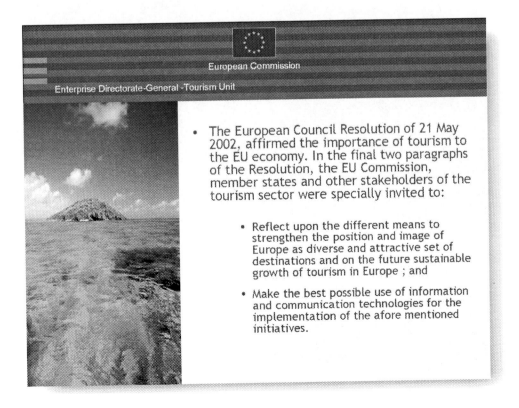

European Commission

Enterprise Directorate-General - Tourism Unit

- The European Council Resolution of 21 May 2002, affirmed the importance of tourism to the EU economy. In the final two paragraphs of the Resolution, the EU Commission, member states and other stakeholders of the tourism sector were specially invited to:

  - Reflect upon the different means to strengthen the position and image of Europe as diverse and attractive set of destinations and on the future sustainable growth of tourism in Europe ; and

  - Make the best possible use of information and communication technologies for the implementation of the afore mentioned initiatives.

European Commission

Enterprise Directorate-General -Tourism Unit

- Final Important Remark...

Dialogue on and describing and clarifying our activities in a positive way is of crucial importance....

Even important it is to indicate what we do not do!

... For reasons of limited competence for tourism the European Union does not have a task in initiating promotional tourism campaigns. This does not exclude that the general Europa Site does contain information for travellers in the European Union, as a consequence of the freedom to move within the E.U. territory.

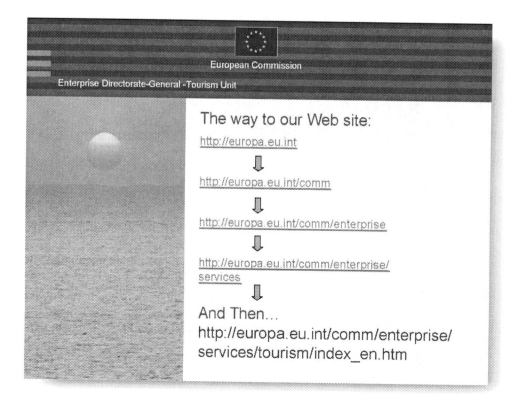

TOURISM BRANDING - CONTEMPORARY CHALLENGES FOR NATIONS, REGIONS AND CITIES

RICHARD TIBBOTT
Chairman, Locum Destinations

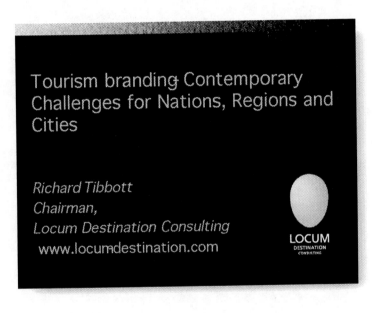

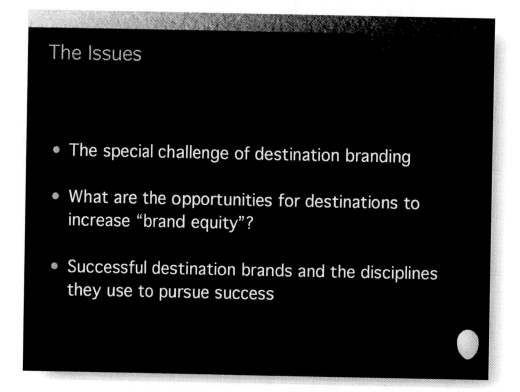

The Issues

- The special challenge of destination branding

- What are the opportunities for destinations to increase "brand equity"?

- Successful destination brands and the disciplines they use to pursue success

Underachieving Destination Branding

- Failure to manage the politics of place & "something for everyone"

- Lack of focus; no differentiation

- Not based on market evidence
- Not based on realistic view of destination assets

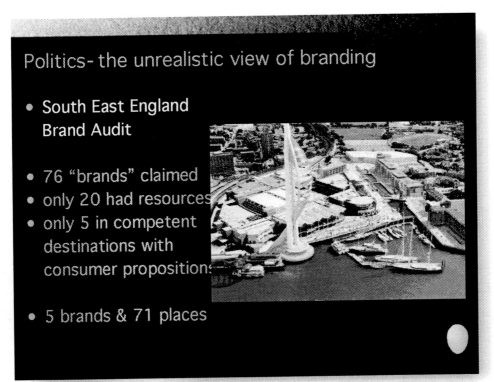

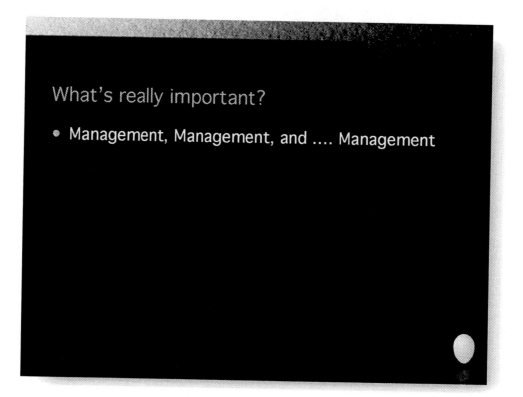

What's really important?

- Management, Management, and .... Management

What makes for success of destination branding?

- Wrapping the destination with "dreams"
- Connect with contemporary culture & Cities
- Delivering on the promise quality
- Partnerships for National brands
- Smart spending in use of new media

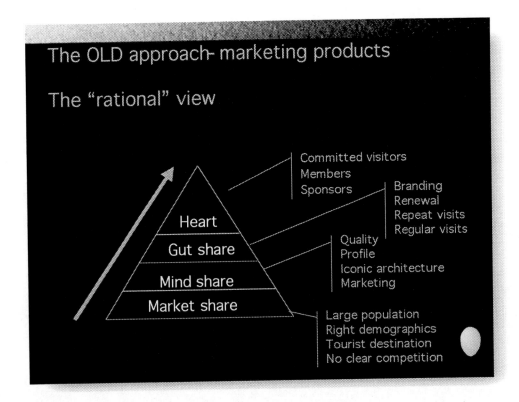

More Success factors

- Smart spending- use of nontraditional media
- The Quality promise has to be delivered
- Partnering essential

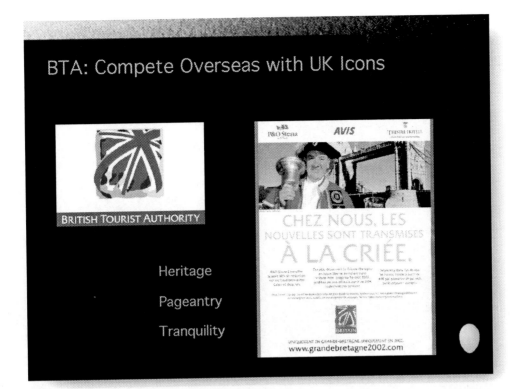

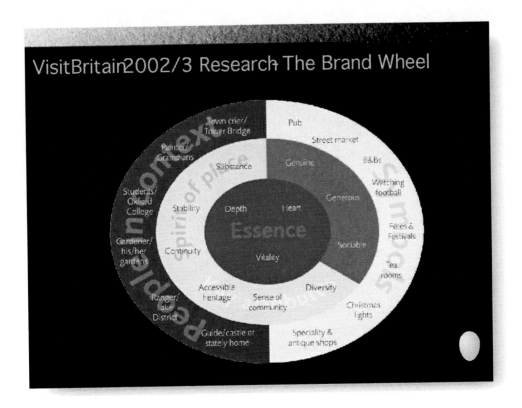

FROM "HIGH-TECH" TO "HIGH-TOUCH" – IMPORTANCE OF DIRECT COMMUNICATIONS, MEETING AND EXHIBITIONS INDUSTRY

STANISLAVA BLAGOEVA
President of ETTFA

Dear Ladies and Gentlemen,

It is my greatest pleasure to address this prestigious forum on behalf of one of the most talked about and the most controversial segments of our industry – the exhibitions.

Exhibitions is something most of us love to hate. In my professional career I have met both dedicated believers and fearsome critics of the event industry. It is very rare that a specialist in event management is invited to speak at international fora. And I would like to thank and congratulate our colleagues from WTO for the utmost courage displayed.

Meetings and exhibitions, as we all know, are and will be one of the most powerful marketing and communication tools in the industry of travel and tourism. I understand and realise the boldness of my statement. But if I didn't believe in that I wouldn't have agreed to speak today.

The word communication has its origin in the Latin *communicatio* – the act or fact of communicating, interchange of thoughts or opinions, by conference or other means.

Exhibitions are a communication tool, as is direct mail, sponsorship, corporate work-wear, body language, telephone marketing and trade journals are also important business-to-business communication tools. Exhibitions though are a more specialised and complicated form of communication.

The exhibitions industry has its deep roots in the human history. With the development of trade links between the nomadic tribes and later between states and continents the necessity of temporary or permanent meeting places provoked the birth of the first fairs and fair centres in the world. These were the places where people met to sell/exchange their produce. From the very first primitive gatherings during the medieval ages slowly emerged the first organised annual trade event in south of France.

Direct communication at its basic level was crucial. It was only and mainly during these annual events that people had the opportunity to meet and exchange goods and merchandise.

Today there are industrial trade centres of vast proportions. Major urban centres have become focal points for meetings and exhibitions. European city destinations such as Berlin, Frankfurt, Paris, London,

Madrid, Milan, etc. are the heart of the European exhibition industry. Events naturally increase the inbound traffic to the destination. They have a significant impact on the local economy not only through the traffic of business travel created, but through employing the local community to provide services to the event industry.

Exhibitions and events today are the places where most often the face-to-face communication between industry professionals takes place. When we attempt to discuss the hi-tech and high-touch approach we should be ready to address the issue at its every angle. With the boom of the latest communication technologies, the pool of possibilities that a marketing person can choose from, has widely diversified and multiplied.

Communication tools such as printed and digital media, various publications, increased Internet access and strong web presence, TV and other visual image translation methods send thousands of marketing messages per second. The consumer and the trade are bombarded with pre-packaged communications solutions.

Is the event industry ready to cope? There is no simple answer to that question.

Exhibitions and meetings are:

- time consuming – average of 8 months are spent on preparing for an event;
- effort consuming – to prepare and carry out a major project involves an average team of 10 – 20 coordinators;
- skills demanding – different skills are put together to achieve a positive result from an event.

Sense and sensibility: events are all about using all your senses to communicate properly the messages to all others around.

- the ultimate face-to-face communication. Face-to-face also stimulates two important neurotransmitters, dopamine, which enhances pleasure and serotonin to reduce worry.
- where the high touch of human interaction is the most important part of the project.

While any other communication tool offers a fairly simple and time and effort saving solution, exhibitions and meetings are still heavy on structure. Recently there has been an ongoing debate over virtual events vs. real events, online and on-ground exhibitions. More and more business people prefer the comfort of their own office, rather then the uncertainty of an exhibition environment.

Have we lost our human ability to create, connect and communicate with each other?

The threat to travel exhibition organisers from 'Virtual Trade Fairs' we believe is non-existent.

The European Tourism Trade Fairs Association commissioned and conducted a one-year study of both physical and virtual exhibitions. The findings show that Internet expos are up to seven times more cost effective, easy to access and free from the logistical headaches that face any traditional fair. But, while the market share for online fairs is increasing, the report shows clear evidence that their physical counterparts still outstrip them at the most fundamental level.

Exhibitors need the human touch and that's the one thing the Internet cannot offer. People prefer to negotiate face-to-face and read one another's body language. This is impossible online.

While maintaining a confident image, many exhibition organisers nevertheless have detailed knowledge of their high-tech competitors. Meanwhile, among show-goers, the aftershock of Sept 11th gave rise to uncertainty: might virtual fairs, safer, cheaper and more time-efficient to run and attend than real ones, soon become the better option? Certainly the spectrum of virtual shows has caused sleepless nights in the travel expo industry.

According to the findings published in the 2002 report, virtual fairs offer some tremendous advantages to visitors and exhibitors alike - attractions with which physical fairs cannot compete. Besides obvious savings in time and travel expenditure, the absence of materials means that exhibiting online costs a fraction of the 'real world' price. The scope for each exhibitor is seemingly limitless (and not measured in square metres); a single stand can hold seminars, competitions, product demos and conversations simultaneously. And the 24/7 nature of the Internet means that visitors who would be unable to attend a physical fair can visit online.

There are also fewer logistical problems.

The biggest advantage, however, is that a decentralised trade fair held in cyberspace is far more likely to ride out waves of economic uncertainty. Despite all of this, physical exhibition organisers remain confident that they will retain a comfortable lead - and their clients appear to agree.

Trevor Foley, Director General of the Association of Exhibition Organisers, concurs. "Organisers do not feel the need to go virtual because the human species needs human contact," he says. "Anyone who thinks that computers can replace this is dreaming."

With physical fairs enjoying steady growth and their virtual counterparts yet to mount a coherent offensive, it seems unlikely that any collision will take place in the foreseeable future. At ETTFA we believe that it is and will be a question of working together. The benefits offered by virtual fairs can never replace those of face-to-face dealings, but they can greatly enhance on-ground exhibitions. Outlining the Internet's ability to provide multi-lingual information day and night, hotel booking and car-rental online and image improvement. Organisers also use the internet to cut down on the time needed to input data, by posting online registration forms, online stand bookings, online payment and online badge booking for participants to fill out themselves. Real life exhibitions are looking on virtual fairs as the next enhancement of what they've already got.

Those organisers who take up the challenge of merging cyberspace with flesh and blood in one trade fair have everything to gain.

E-COMMUNICATION IN TOURISM – THE ROLE OF THE INTERNET, CHALLENGES AND OPPORTUNITIES FOR TOURISM

THOMAS STEINMETZ
Publisher, e-Turbo News

Ladies and gentlemen, distinguished members of the panel:

It is indeed a great honour to be speaking to you this afternoon, on this momentous occasion celebrating the significance of the advent of the Internet, here at the World Tourism Organization's TOURCOM Conference.

I am the publisher of eTurboNews, based in Haleiwa, Hawaii, USA. I can attest to the pivotal role the Internet has played not only in tourism, but on a general scale, including dissemination of information regarding conflicts, disease, and international affairs significant not only in the way of conduct business but in our lives altogether. And today, as we assess the significance of this technological breakthrough in the industry, we are reminded of the new role of the media and its responsibilities, which in recent months have been magnified through the Internet.

Through the Internet debates form in such a way that previously unheard voices are now given the forum to do so, which is one of the pillars of eTurbo News's existence.

In 1999 and 2000 my company was hired by the Indonesian Ministry of Tourism to represent Indonesia as a privatized tourism office to the USA and Canada.

Reports of unrest in Indonesia resulted in travel warnings devastating to the tourism community in that country. Hotel occupancies went dramatically down, airlines including Indonesia's very own Garuda cancelled flights from North America.

With the help of the industry in the ASEAN countries and large associations in North America we developed a contact database of key companies selling travel to Asia and started sending by email our own information to respond to and inform the travel industry about the travel warnings to Indonesia.

This was very effective. I remember one occasion where Arthur Frommer's reported about our side of the travel warnings and declared Indonesia as safe, despite the ongoing negative reporting in much of the mainstream media. Due to budget crisis in Indonesia we were unable to continue our representation but had a significant tool left: a database of 16,000 travel agents.

This was the birth of eTurboNews as a global travel trade online medium. eTurboNews started 1 April 2001 with 16,000 readers and now reaches 200,000 travel trade professionals and 3,200 journalists in more than 200 countries around the world five times a week. We have representatives and journalists giving us immediate information in 95 countries around the world.

With editors and a sales staff around the world we are the typical example of how a small company can operate with the help of the Internet on a global scale.

The Internet is a phenomenal tool for the industry. An excellent way of communicating for companies of any size to reach a much broader audience.

No longer would just around the corner companies be able to compete on a local scale, now consumers and travel agents can easily compare and buy land arrangements from a tour operator in Botswana.

A small hotel in Hong Kong can now advertise and reach consumers and trades in Europe for example.

Small online media like eTurboNews can now compete with the big media giants and generate independent information.

We developed a product Travel-Telegram where tourism offices, hotels, or tour operators can send their own information to readers who opted to receive promotional messages.

This is very effective and spontaneous. Companies are able to instantly change their promotions, tourism offices can send their own newsletter to a national or global audience. For this service our advertisers can choose the region they want to send their information to. Many tour operators send their own virtual brochures through links to a PDF Acrobat file.

eTurboNews also started TravelWireNews. TravelWireNews reaches the same readership as eTurboNews including 3,200 journalists, but all articles are press releases sponsored by the company posting them, while all articles in eTurboNews are non-advertorial and written by our own team members.

What is so wonderful about the electronic media, is that results can be measured in a way that is not possible with other media.

Every day we know how many editions of our newsletter or advertising send outs were delivered. We also know how many and who actually open and read the e-mail and we know how many and who read each article or click on links provided in the article or the advertising.

This allows us and of course our advertisers to change the content to the most effective way.

eTurboNews enjoys a very attractive average opening rate daily of about 35% and over a weeks time more than 70% of our readers actually opened and read at least one article. Readers are very active and participate. We receive an average of 1000 responses a day and in time of crisis like the bomb attack in Bali, the earthquake in Iran, this number or responses can easily increase tenfold.

One commercial sent out paid by the Hong Kong Tourism Board announcing the end of SARS had an 82 per cent opening rate.

The wealth of information would be beyond the imagination of a person living in the seventies. The more Internet users get access to broadband, the more possibilities there are. Online presentations, databases, movies, phone, to name a few - the possibilities seem infinite.

The percentage of broadband Internet users in the travel trade is one of the highest of any industries, because most of the airline reservation systems now use Internet broadband systems to provide their service.

There is no stopping. Internet as global communication along with wireless and cell technology has changed the way anyone can now operate in a global market-place

In time of crisis information is available from the source; therefore communication and help coordination can be established immediately.

Challenges:

- Spam is becoming a major nuisance and is hurting legitimate e-mail broadcasts.
- Spam can be kept under control very easily. A sophisticated spam control mechanism is available, but many consumers do not know how to effectively use it.
- Legitimate e-mails can end in a spam box and get lost. Legitimate contracts or travel confirmation can be erased, because they landed in a spam folder.
- Educating consumers on how to effectively use spam-blocking software is necessary and a challenge, but also a business opportunity for consulting company.

Another challenge is that consumers may not know who exactly the supplier may be. An entire business operation is likely to only be virtual, no physical office; which increases the danger of fraud. The danger of fraud and to get more information on business partners is a challenge and again an opportunity for organizations such as the Better Business Bureau or watchdog intelligence companies to get involved on a global scale. This is also a challenge for global media companies, like eTN, to fact check stories on the other side of the globe. We at eTN still feel it is important to have a representative and our own journalist in countries we frequently feature.

The time of faxes and the need for a personal visit may make the Internet impersonal.

The broadband technology of online meetings brings it back as to be a virtual personal market-place.

So, on the question as to whether the Internet is just a passing fad or a *bona fide* tool for the industry, the obvious answer is the latter. But to make certain that its features and its challenges are addressed, education must also be concomitantly enforced along with its use. That is why this gathering by the World Tourism Organization is commendable for it is directed at achieving just that. Conferences such as TOURCOM pave the way for the industry to share information and ultimately educate each other about today's various communication channels and how to address their growing demands.

Thank you.

OBSERVACIONES FINALES

La transformación de la OMT en organismo especializado de las Naciones Unidas – reconocimiento del papel del turismo en la comunidad internacional

FINAL REMARKS

WTO transformation into a specialized agency - a recognition of the role of tourism in the international community

REMARQUES FINALES

La transformation de l'OMT en institution spécialiséé des nations unies – reconnaissance du rôle du tourisme dans la communauté internationale

WTO - A NEW SPECIALIZED AGENCY
OF THE UNITED NATIONS

RAFEEUDDIN AHMED

Special Representative of WTO to United Nations

Ladies and Gentlemen,

It is no news to anyone that the United Nations General Assembly recently adopted a resolution by which the World Tourism Organization became a fully-fledged specialized agency of the UN. This happened on the 23rd of December 2003 and we actually did not know whether this was a Christmas gift from the United Nations to the tourism industry or – ours to the United Nations.

This is a big step forward for our Organization, but it is an even bigger one for the entire international tourism industry, as WTO's Secretary-General said yesterday. But in order to make the most out of this new status, the tourism sector, all 143 Member States and also non-members must understand what this conversion means and participate in our role of enhanced responsibility in leading the world's most important growth industry.

Allow me to just briefly recapitulate the history of our organization and our predecessors.

Tourism was a leisure activity practised by the privileged few from the latter half of the nineteenth century, but it was after the First World War that tourism first set out on the long road that was to endow it with its modern character we know today.

At its outset, tourism promotion was viewed by governments basically as an outgrowth of their information and communications dimensions. In the 1920s embryonic national tourism administrations, the first official offices abroad, and even local information bureaux in cities and at holiday resorts began to appear.

The first International Congress of Official Tourism Traffic Association was held in The Hague in 1925. Nine years later, the International Union of Official Tourist Propaganda Organizations was established and remained in existence until the Second World War.

Tourism activity and interchange began anew after the war and governments quickly understood their new-found importance.

Concurrently, government involvement began to grow and extended to all aspects of tourism policy.

On this same basis international cooperation also grew. This trend led to the establishment in 1947 of the International Union of Official Travel Organizations, or IUOTO, which was a direct forerunner of WTO.

The 1950s and 1960s saw a sea change in tourism with the rise in purchasing power in the developed countries, more free time, and lower transportation costs. The number of international tourists skyrocketed from 25 million in 1950 to 165 million in 1970 and the period was marked by the coming of age of the private automobile and the advent of the jet airplane in civil aviation.

The United Nations quickly realized the importance of these developments. In 1963, the UN convened a conference on international tourism in Rome, and 1967 was declared "The International Year of Tourism". But most importantly, in a resolution adopted in 1969, the General Assembly acknowledged, and I quote, "the vital contribution that international tourism is making to the economic, social, cultural and educational progress of mankind and in safeguarding world peace". It therefore called on the IUOTO to change into an intergovernmental organization.

The IUOTO answered this call and it decided to become an intergovernmental institution. The changeover was accomplished from 1970 to 1975, and the headquarters of the fledgling WTO was moved to Madrid. Two agreements were concluded, the first making the WTO an executing agency of the UNDP, the second giving the WTO the status of a related agency within the UN system.

Even as an intergovernmental organization in which decisions are taken solely by the representatives of States, the new WTO, like its predecessor, continued to cooperate with other tourism bodies, particularly those in the private sector.

Over the years the WTO has reflected and moved with these developments and our cooperation with the United Nations has grown ever closer. Some years ago the UN approved the WTO's work in the fields of statistics and measurement of the economic impact of tourism. The UN General Assembly has adopted the WTO Global Code of Ethics for Tourism and declared 2002 to be the "International Year of Ecotourism".

The last time an organization acquired the status of a UN specialized agency was in 1985, with the United Nations Industrial Development Organization.

In answering a question posed by a journalist as to why WTO wants to be a specialized agency of the UN, *while tourism does not represent a global problem*, we should first of all stress that the United Nations is not only about problems. But furthermore, tourism may be understood as one of the solutions for the problems of the world, including poverty alleviation. Global challenges - peace, poverty, sustainability and fair trade - will not disappear. New ones will emerge. They can only be dealt with by enlightened action of the world community. Our new status as a Specialized Agency will not change the nature of that action but it will help decision makers inside and outside the UN family better understand that tourism can play a constructive part in addressing these issues. That is why this transformation of our Organization is of real immediate and lasting importance.

In closing I would like to point out that, specifically, our new status will have no material implications for the United Nations itself, other than the contributions we can offer. The WTO is financially independent, supported by the contributions of its Members and by the income it generates itself. Its finances are in order, has no debt and even runs a modest surplus. It takes nothing from the United Nations. Regrettably for the staff of WTO, their salaries will not rise and nor do we plan to employ more people. WTO is one of the smallest intergovernmental organizations, with only some 100 employees, which makes it flexible and efficient.

The essence of the agreement lies elsewhere, in the visibility it will bring to us and in the recognition it will afford our sector. The WTO is a small agency with a large mission. By virtue of the agreement, the UN has signified that tourism will have equal footing with other principal activities of human society such as industry, agriculture, transport, education, culture, health, and labour, as stated yesterday by the WTO Secretary-General.

APÉNDICE I

La campaña "El turismo es riqueza" y la red TOURCOM de expertos en comunicaciones

ANNEX I

The "Tourism Enriches" campaign and the TOURCOM Network of Communications Experts

ANNEXE I

La campagne « Le tourisme, source d'enrichissement » et le réseau TOURCOM d'experts en communication

Campaña mundial sobre las comunicaciones en el turismo

A solicitud de los miembros de la Organización Mundial del Turismo, se preparó una campaña mundial para promover los efectos positivos del turismo, como parte de la I Conferencia Mundial sobre las Comunicaciones en el Turismo (TOURCOM) celebrada los días 29 y 30 de enero de 2004 en Madrid.

Los objetivos de la campaña "El turismo es riqueza" son:

- promover el turismo como un derecho humano fundamental y como una forma de vida que es fuente de riqueza para el individuo, para la familia, para la sociedad y para las naciones,
- fomentar la comunicación de los beneficios del turismo como la actividad económica más prometedora para las comunidades locales y los países,
- intensificar la cooperación de los destinos y del sector del turismo con los medios de comunicación locales, regionales e internacionales
- vincular a las entidades turísticas individuales con la comunidad más amplia del turismo internacional

Ámbito geográfico de la campaña:

Todos los destinos, empresas turísticas y medios de comunicación pueden tomar parte en la campaña, independientemente de su relación de afiliación con la Organización. Grupos a quienes se dirige: los sectores público y privado, las instancias decisorias, los profesionales del turismo, los líderes de opinión y también el público en general, a través de los medios de comunicación.

Componentes básicos:

La campaña consta de **cuatro componentes básicos** que pueden adaptarse o ampliarse según el empleo que quieran darle los Estados Miembros, los Miembros Afiliados de la OMT y el resto del sector en sus propias actividades de promoción del turismo y sensibilización:

El material de la campaña comprende:

1) El lema "El turismo es riqueza" ("Tourism enriches", "Le tourisme, source d'enrichissement", etc.) con la apostilla de "El turismo es riqueza para la persona, para la familia, para la comunidad y para el mundo entero". Más información sobre la campaña de sensibilización de la Organización Mundial del turismo en: **www.world-tourism.org.**

2) La imagen gráfica o logotipo de la campaña.

3) Un desplegable de seis páginas en tamaño A4 donde se resumen las consecuencias benefactoras del turismo, como son la generación de beneficios económicos, la contribución a la comprensión internacional, la creación de empleo en zonas rurales, la protección del medio ambiente, etc.

4) Un atractivo cartel que utiliza el mismo material gráfico.

Después de la presentación del material de la campaña en enero, la Red TOURCOM de Expertos en Comunicaciones (en proceso de creación) será responsable de poner en práctica la campaña en el contexto de sus actividades por el mundo.

Entre las actividades locales o nacionales que se sugieren figuran:

- Uso del lema y del logotipo en los folletos y en la publicidad de los destinos.
- Uso del lema, del logotipo y del material gráfico (cartel) en la prensa escrita.
- Uso del lema y del logotipo en los viajes de prensa.
- Anuncios en espacios gratuitos en emisoras de televisión (emisión gratuita del vídeo de la OMT).
- Publicación del folleto en idiomas locales.
- Inclusión de la campaña en las páginas web sobre turismo.
- Impresión de camisetas y carteleras con el lema y el logotipo.
- Sugerencias de temas de artículos basados en la campaña para los periodistas.
- Organización de un concurso para periodistas.
- Intercambio de ideas de promoción entre los miembros de la Red TOURCOM.

La Organización Mundial del Turismo acogerá con agradecimiento cualquier idea o proyecto que los Miembros o el resto del sector turístico deseen aportar. Las ideas y prácticas más destacadas se presentarán en la web de la OMT y en las *Noticias de la OMT*.

El turismo es riqueza, en muchos sentidos

Beneficios por exportaciones

El turismo internacional es el primer sector de exportaciones del mundo y un factor importante en la balanza de pagos de muchos países. Los ingresos de divisas procedentes del turismo internacional alcanzaron los 474.000 millones de dólares de los Estados Unidos en 2002, dejando atrás a los de los productos del petróleo, los vehículos de motor, los equipos de telecomunicaciones, los textiles o cualquier otro producto o servicio.

Empleo

El turismo es un importante generador de empleo, que da trabajo a millones de personas en el mundo. La gran mayoría de los empleos del turismo están en empresas familiares de pequeño o mediano tamaño. Las investigaciones demuestran que la creación de empleo en el sector turístico es 1,5 veces más rápida que en cualquier otro sector industrial.

Oportunidades para las zonas rurales

Los puestos de trabajo y las empresas de turismo se crean normalmente en las regiones menos desarrolladas, lo que ayuda a equiparar las oportunidades económicas a lo largo y ancho del país e incentiva a los habitantes a permanecer en las zonas rurales, en lugar de emigrar a ciudades ya superpobladas.

Inversión en infraestructuras

Los viajes y el turismo fomentan enormes inversiones en nuevas infraestructuras, la mayoría de las cuales ayudan a mejorar las condiciones de vida de los residentes locales, al mismo tiempo que las de los turistas. Los proyectos de desarrollo turístico a menudo incluyen aeropuertos, carreteras, puertos deportivos, sistemas de alcantarillado, plantas de tratamiento de aguas, restauración de monumentos culturales, museos y centros de interpretación de la naturaleza.

Impuestos y producto interior bruto (PIB)

La actividad turística proporciona a los gobiernos cientos de millones de dólares a través de los impuestos que pagan los alojamientos y restaurantes, las tasas de aeropuerto, los impuestos sobre las ventas, las entradas a los parques, los impuestos de los empleados y otros muchos instrumentos fiscales. El turismo internacional y el turismo interno generaron, entre los dos, hasta el 10% del producto interior bruto (PIB), cuota considerablemente superior en muchas naciones pequeñas y en países en desarrollo.

La riqueza no es sólo económica...

El medio ambiente y la cultura local se promueven cuando las autoridades restauran monumentos, abren museos y crean parques naturales para atraer a los visitantes. Al tiempo que aumenta el turismo, aumenta también la necesidad de los destinos de mejorar su infraestructura para atender esa afluencia. Entonces nacen nuevos aeropuertos, carreteras, puertos deportivos, plantas de tratamiento de aguas residuales, potabilizadoras de agua y decenas de otros adelantos, que aportan una mejora sustancial a la vida de los residentes locales, desde el acceso al agua potable hasta unas comunicaciones más rápidas.

Lo más importante: El turismo concierne al ser humano... enriquece a través de la cultura y de la sensibilización medioambiental y social, promueve la abertura y la amistad, ayuda a los familiares a pasar tiempo juntos, ya sea por ocio o por trabajo. El turismo promueve la paz y la cooperación entre las naciones y tiende puentes.

El turismo es riqueza para la persona, para la familia, para la comunidad y para el mundo entero

* * *

Red TOURCOM de expertos en comunicaciones en el turismo

Tal como sugirieron los delegados que asistieron a la I Conferencia Mundial sobre las Comunicaciones en el Turismo, la Organización Mundial del Turismo comenzó los preparativos para la creación de una red de expertos en comunicaciones en el turismo ("Red TOURCOM").

La Red de Comunicaciones en el Turismo (TOURCOM) no es un órgano de la OMT, sino un grupo consultivo informal que aspira a incrementar los conocimientos específicos de los miembros de la OMT en un campo de importancia creciente como es el de las comunicaciones. Como pedía el programa de trabajo de la OMT para 2004 y 2005, pretende también ayudar a la Organización en su doble objetivo de hacer comprender la importancia del turismo y mitigar los efectos nocivos de la actividad turística, además de constituir un centro neurálgico para la asistencia a los Miembros en comunicaciones de crisis, relaciones mediáticas, creación de marcas y otras técnicas de promoción.

Finalidades y objetivos:

- coordinar las actividades conjuntas de comunicación en nombre del sector turístico,
- definir los mejores métodos de comunicación en momentos de crisis,
- compartir recursos y técnicas de comunicación,
- fomentar la profesionalidad de las comunicaciones en el turismo,
- apoyar las actividades de comunicación de la OMT y fijar prioridades.

Entre las actividades de la Red TOURCOM figurarán:

- apoyar la campaña mundial sobre las comunicaciones en el turismo "El turismo es riqueza",
- organizar seminarios y talleres locales y regionales y conferencias mundiales sobre las comunicaciones en el turismo bajo el nombre de "TOURCOM",

- apoyar las actividades de los periodistas y escritores especializados en los viajes, en general en todo el mundo, y más concretamente en África, Latinoamérica y Asia,
- respaldar los esfuerzos en materia de comunicación de los Miembros de la OMT,
- elaborar unos "Principios TOURCOM", una enumeración de las prácticas idóneas en unas comunicaciones integrales en el campo del turismo,
- promover la diversificación lingüística y cultural de las comunicaciones relativas al turismo internacional,
- promover cuestiones tales como la liberalización del comercio, el proyecto ST-EP y los Objetivos de Desarrollo de las Naciones Unidas para el Milenio mediante unas comunicaciones eficaces en el contexto del turismo,
- abordar y promover las partes del Código Ético Mundial para el Turismo que hacen referencia a las relaciones con los medios de comunicación,
- publicar artículos o prospectos sobre las comunicaciones de crisis, elaborar páginas web para los destinos, preparar boletines, etc.

Miembros:

La Red no tiene una función decisoria, aunque sí formulará recomendaciones y asesorá en cuestiones técnicas al Departamento de Comunicaciones de la OMT. La afiliación no está restringida a los Miembros de la OMT. Además, no habrá cuota de afiliación para sus integrantes. Podrán ser miembros de la Red únicamente las personas que ejerzan una responsabilidad directa en materia de comunicación para sus organizaciones.

Ventajas de pertenecer a la red TOURCOM:

- Boletín TOURCOM (carta de información mensual sobre comunicación turística)
- publicación de artículos y de documentos en el Boletín TOURCOM y en la colección de buenas prácticas de comunicación
- recepción inmediata de las obras sobre comunicación en el campo del turismo en cuanto se publiquen
- información privilegiada de la OMT e invitaciones a las reuniones comunes

Conferencias y Talleres TOURCOM Sobre las Comunicaciones en el Turismo

En vista del éxito de la I Conferencia Mundial sobre las Comunicaciones en el Turismo (TOURCOM), celebrada los días 29 y 30 de enero de 2004 en Madrid, la OMT propondrá al Consejo Ejecutivo la integración de una serie de conferencias regionales y talleres locales sobre las comunicaciones en el turismo en el programa de trabajo de la Organización.

Los programas se adaptarán en función de las preocupaciones locales o regionales en lo que se refiere a las comunicaciones en el turismo. Como parte de ese tipo de eventos, podría añadirse una formación básica sobre relaciones públicas, comunicaciones electrónicas, comunicaciones de crisis, publicidad, etc. Los hallazgos de esas conferencias locales y regionales sobre las comunicaciones en el turismo se debatirán posteriormente en una segunda edición de la Conferencia Mundial sobre las Comunicaciones en el Turismo.

A Global Communications Campaign for Tourism*

As requested by Members of the World Tourism Organization, a global campaign promoting the positive impacts of tourism was prepared as part of the First World Conference on Tourism Communications (TOURCOM) held on 29-30 January 2004 in Madrid.

The aims of TOURISM ENRICHES campaign are:

- to promote tourism as a basic human right and way of life, which enriches individuals, family, societies and nations
- to stimulate communication about the benefits of tourism as the most prospective economic activity for the local communities and countries
- to enhance cooperation between destinations and the tourism industry with the local, regional and international media
- to link individual tourism entities to the larger community of international tourism

Geographical scope of the campaign:

Participation in the Campaign will be offered to all destinations, tourist companies and the media, unconditionally with membership status in the WTO. Target groups: public and private sectors, decision makers, tourism professionals, opinion leaders, but also general public through the media.

Basic components:

The campaign features four basic components that can be adapted and expanded for use by Member States, Affiliate Members of the WTO and the rest of the tourism industry in their own tourism promotion and awareness building activities.

Materials include:

1) Slogan "Tourism Enriches" (Turismo es riqueza, Le tourisme, source d'enrichissement etc.) Tag line: Tourism enriches individuals, families, communities and all the world. Awareness campaign of the World Tourism Organization: more information at **www.world-tourism.org**

2) A graphic image or logo of the campaign

3) Six-page A4 size flyer outlining positive impacts of tourism, such as economic benefits, increased international understanding, rural jobs, environmental protection, etc.

4) Attractive poster using the same artwork

Suggested local or national activities might include:

- using the slogan and logo on destination brochures and advertising;
- using the slogan and logo and artwork (poster) in the print media;
- using the slogan and logo on press familiarization trips;
- public service announcements on TV stations (free airing of the WTO video)
- publishing the flyer in local languages;
- adding the campaign to tourism websites;
- printing T shirts or billboards with the slogan and logo;
- providing journalists with story ideas based on the campaign;
- conducting a contest for journalists;
- exchange of promotion ideas among TOURCOM Network members.

World Tourism Organization will highly appreciate ideas and projects received from the Members and the rest of the tourism sector.

Tourism enriches in many ways...

Export Earnings

International tourism is the world's largest export earner and an important factor in the balance of payments of many countries. Foreign currency receipts from international tourism reached US dollars 474 billion in 2002, outstripping exports of petroleum products, motor vehicles, telecommunications equipment, textiles or any other product or service.

Employment

Tourism is an important job creator, employing millions of people around the world. The vast majority of tourism jobs are in small or medium-sized, family-owned enterprises. Research shows that job creation in tourism is growing 1 1/2 times faster than any other industrial sector. Tourism jobs and enterprises are usually created in the most underdeveloped regions, helping to equalize economic opportunities throughout the country.

Rural Opportunities

Tourism jobs and businesses are usually created in the most underdeveloped regions of a country, helping to equalize economic opportunities throughout a nation and providing an incentive for residents to remain in rural areas rather than move to overcrowded cities.

Infrastructure Investment

Travel and tourism stimulates enormous investments in new infrastructure, most of which helps to improve the living conditions of local residents as well as tourists. Tourism development projects often include airports, roads, marinas, sewage systems, water treatment plants, restoration of cultural monuments, museums and nature interpretation centres.

Tax Revenues and Gross Domestic Product (GDP)

The tourism industry provides governments with hundreds of millions of dollars in tax revenues each year through accommodation and restaurant taxes, airport users' fees, sales taxes, park entrance fees, employee income tax and many other fiscal measures. International and domestic tourism combined generate up to 10 per cent of the world's Gross Domestic Product (GDP) and a considerably higher share in many small nations and developing countries.

Enrichment is not just economic...

The environment and local culture receive a boost when authorities restore monuments, open museums and establish natural parks to lure visitors. As tourism increases, so does a destination's need to improve infrastructure to handle the influx. New airports, roads, marinas, sewage and water treatment plants and dozens of other projects are the result, providing a substantial improvement in the residents' own lives from cleaner drinking water to speedier communications.

But most important of all: tourism is a human story... it enriches with culture, environmental and social awareness, brings openness and friendliness, helps families to spend time together, be it on leisure or work. Tourism promotes peace and cooperation among nations and builds bridges.

Tourism enriches individuals, families, communities and all the world.

* * *

TOURCOM Network of Communication Experts

As suggested by the delegates at the 15th Session of the WTO General Assembly in Beijing and by the delegates of the First World Conference on Tourism Communications, the World Tourism Organization established a network of tourism communication experts – TOURCOM, in the following text referred as "TOURCOM Network".

The Tourism Communications Network (TOURCOM) is not a WTO body but an informal consultative group, which aims to enhance the expertise of WTO Members in the increasingly important field of communications. As called for in the 2004-2005 WTO Programme of Work, it also aims to support the Organization in its goals of communicating the importance of tourism, mitigating the undesirable impacts of tourism activity and serve as a backbone for assistance to Members in crisis communications, media relations, advertising, branding and other techniques. The Network does not have a decision-making role but will provide recommendations and expertise to the WTO Communications Department.

Aims and objectives:

- to encourage professionalism in tourism communications;
- to coordinate joint communications actions on behalf of the tourism industry;
- to identify the best methods of crisis communications;
- to share communications resources and techniques;
- to support and set priorities for WTO communications activities.

Activities of the TOURCOM Network include:

- support for the global tourism communications campaign "Tourism Enriches";
- organization of local, regional seminars, workshops and world conferences on tourism communications under "TOURCOM" brand (upon consent of the WTO Executive Council, July 2004)
- support for activities of travel journalists and writers, in the world in general and in Africa, Latin America and Asia specifically
- support for the communications efforts of WTO Members
- establishment of "TOURCOM Principles" – a breakdown of best practices in integral tourism communications
- pursuing linguistic and cultural diversification in international tourism communications
- promoting issues like trade liberalization, ST-EP, UN Millennium Development Goals through effective tourism communications
- addressing and promoting the parts of the World Code of Ethics in Tourism, referring to the media relations
- publication of articles or brochures on crisis communications, destination websites, newsletters, etc.
- publication of Good Communication Practices series (first, on the global level, to be published by the end of 2004).

Membership:

Membership will not limited to WTO Members. There will be no membership fee for the Network members. Membership in the network will be limited to individuals with direct responsibility for communications within their organizations.

Benefits of membership:

- regular monthly newsletter on tourism communications TOURCOM Bulletin;
- publication of the articles and papers in TOURCOM Bulletin and the Good Communication Practices series;
- immediate receipt of the books on tourism communications on publication;
- insider information from the WTO and invitations to attend the meetings.

TOURCOM conferences and workshops on tourism communications

In view of the success of the First World Conference on Tourism Communications (TOURCOM) held on 29-30 January 2004 in Madrid, the World Tourism Organization will suggest the Executive Council to integrate to the Programme of Work of the Organization regional conferences and local workshops on tourism communications.

The programmes will be adapted to the local or regional issues related to tourism communications. Basic education on public relations, e-communications, crisis communications, advertising etc., can be added as a part of such an event. Findings of local and regional tourism communications conferences will be discussed at the next edition of the World Conference on Tourism Communications.

Campagne « le Tourisme, Source d'Enrichissement »

Comme l'avaient demandé les États Membres, l'OMT a lancé la campagne mondiale « Le tourisme, source d'enrichissement », qui met en relief les effets positifs de cette branche d'activité.

Les objectifs de cette campagne sont les suivants :

- encourager le tourisme en tant que droit et activité fondamentaux de l'être humain, source d'enrichissement pour les personnes, les familles, les sociétés et les nations;
- stimuler la communication au sujet des avantages du tourisme en tant qu'activité économique la plus prometteuse pour les communautés locales et les pays ;
- développer la coopération entre destinations et professionnels du tourisme à l'aide des médias locaux, régionaux et internationaux ; et
- relier les divers acteurs du secteur à la grande communauté du tourisme international.

Portée géographique

Les destinations, les entreprises touristiques et les médias sont tous invités à participer à la campagne, indépendamment de leur appartenance ou non à l'OMT. Les cibles de la campagne sont les secteurs public et privé, les décideurs, les professionnels du tourisme et les prescripteurs, sans oublier le grand public grâce aux médias.

Éléments essentiels

La campagne se compose d'éléments essentiels pouvant être adaptés et développés pour servir aux États membres et aux Membres affiliés de l'OMT ainsi qu'au reste du secteur touristique dans leurs propres activités de promotion du tourisme et de sensibilisation à son intérêt.

Ces éléments sont les suivants :

1) le slogan « Le tourisme, source d'enrichissement ». Formule complémentaire : « Le tourisme, source d'enrichissement pour les personnes, les familles, les communautés et le monde entier ». Campagne de sensibilisation de (par ex. votre Administration nationale du tourisme) en coopération avec l'Organisation mondiale du tourisme ;

2) le signe distinctif – image ou logo – de la campagne ;

3) le dépliant en format A4 de six pages exposant succinctement les effets positifs du tourisme tels que ses avantages économiques, une meilleure entente internationale, la création d'emplois dans les zones rurales et la protection de l'environnement, et

4) l'affiche attrayante qui utilise la même maquette.

À l'échelon local ou national, la **participation à la campagne** pourrait se traduire comme suit :

- utilisation du slogan et du logo dans les brochures et la publicité de la destination,
- utilisation du slogan, du logo et de l'affiche dans la presse écrite,
- utilisation du slogan et du logo lors des voyages d'information pour la presse,
- message d'intérêt public sur les chaînes de télévision,
- publication du dépliant dans les langues locales,
- incorporation de la campagne aux sites touristiques de la Toile,
- impression du slogan et du logo sur des tee-shirts ou sur des panneaux d'affichage grand format,
- suggestion aux journalistes d'idées d'articles sur le thème de la campagne,
- organisation d'un concours pour les journalistes et
- échange d'idées de promotion entre les membres du réseau TOURCOM.

D'avance, l'Organisation mondiale du tourisme remercie vivement ses États membres qui voudront bien lui faire part de leurs idées et projets concernant la campagne. Les traductions du slogan, les idées les plus originales et les meilleures pratiques seront présentées sur le site de l'OMT sur la Toile et dans les *Nouvelles de l'OMT*.

Le tourisme est source d'enrichissement de diverses manières...

Bénéfices à l'exportation

Le tourisme international est le plus gros secteur exportateur du monde et un poste important dans la balance des paiements de beaucoup de pays. En 2002, les recettes en devises qu'a rapportées le tourisme international ont atteint 474 milliards de $EU, devançant les exportations de produits pétroliers, de véhicules automobiles, de matériel de télécommunications, de textiles ou de n'importe quel autre produit ou service.

Emploi

Le tourisme crée de nombreux emplois. Il représente des millions de salariés de par le monde. La grande majorité des emplois du tourisme se trouvent dans de petites ou moyennes entreprises familiales. Des études montrent que la création d'emplois dans le tourisme progresse 1,5 fois plus vite que dans toute autre branche d'activité.

Possibilités d'emploi dans les zones rurales

Généralement, les emplois et les entreprises touristiques sont créés dans les régions les plus défavorisées d'un pays, ce qui, sous l'angle économique, contribue à garantir l'égalité des chances sur toute l'étendue du territoire national. L'activité touristique incite les habitants des zones rurales à y rester au lieu de migrer vers les villes surpeuplées.

Investissements d'infrastructure

Le tourisme encourage d'énormes investissements d'infrastructure. Outre le fait de rendre plus agréable le séjour des touristes, la plupart des nouveaux équipements contribuent à améliorer les conditions de vie de la population locale. Les projets de mise en valeur touristique comprennent souvent des aéroports, des routes, des marinas, des réseaux d'égouts, des stations de traitement des eaux de distribution et d'épuration des eaux usées, la restauration de monuments culturels, des musées et des centres d'interprétation de la nature.

Recettes fiscales et produit intérieur brut (PIB)

Le secteur touristique rapporte chaque année aux États des centaines de millions de dollars de recettes fiscales sous forme de taxes sur les services d'hébergement et de restauration, de taxes d'aéroport, d'impôt sur le chiffre d'affaires, de droits d'entrée dans les parcs, d'impôt sur le revenu des salariés, etc. Ensemble, le tourisme international et le tourisme interne représentent jusqu'à 10 % du produit intérieur brut (PIB) mondial et un pourcentage nettement plus élevé dans beaucoup de petites nations et de pays en développement.

L'enrichissement n'est pas qu'économique...

L'environnement et la culture locale sont mis en valeur quand l'État restaure les monuments, ouvre des musées et crée des parcs naturels pour attirer les visiteurs. Au fur et à mesure que le tourisme se développe, il faut améliorer l'infrastructure de la destination pour gérer l'afflux des visiteurs. C'est ainsi qu'on construit de nouveaux aéroports, des routes, des marinas et des stations de traitement des eaux et que des dizaines d'autres projets voient le jour, ce qui se traduit par un mieux-être évident pour les habitants (eau potable de meilleure qualité, communications plus rapides, etc.).

Le plus important de tout, c'est l'aspect humain de cette activité... Le tourisme enrichit l'esprit en faisant découvrir d'autres cultures, il sensibilise aux problèmes écologiques et sociaux, il permet de cultiver la gentillesse et la tolérance et il réunit les familles, que ce soit pour les vacances ou pour travailler ensemble dans une petite entreprise touristique. En créant des liens, le tourisme favorise la paix et la coopération entre les peuples.

Le tourisme est source d'enrichissement pour les personnes, les familles, les communautés et le monde entier

***

Réseau *TOURCOM* d'Experts en Communication

Comme l'ont suggéré les délégués à la quinzième session de l'Assemblée générale de l'OMT à Beijing, puis les participants de la Première Conférence mondiale sur la communication dans le domaine du tourisme, le Secrétariat de l'Organisation a commencé à préparer la constitution d'un réseau TOURCOM d'experts en communication spécialistes du tourisme, dénommé ci-après « réseau TOURCOM ».

Le réseau TOURCOM est inscrit au programme de travail de l'Organisation pour la période 2004-2005, dans sa section 8-A Communication, objectif 1 – Information : renforcement du rôle de l'OMT comme institution de premier plan dans le domaine du tourisme et comme pôle d'information sur ce secteur, point 3.4.

Le réseau TOURCOM n'est pas un organe de l'OMT mais un groupe consultatif informel dont le but est d'étendre les connaissances spécialisées des Membres de l'OMT dans le domaine de plus en plus important de la communication. Comme prévu dans le programme de travail de l'OMT pour la période 2004-2005, il vise aussi à soutenir l'Organisation dans son double but de faire prendre davantage conscience de l'importance du tourisme en atténuant les effets indésirables de cette activité et de servir de base d'assistance à ses Membres pour ce qui est des techniques de communication en temps de crise, de relations avec les médias et de choix d'une marque et d'autres techniques de promotion.

Mission

- Coordonner des actions communes de communication en faveur du secteur touristique
- Recenser les meilleures méthodes de communication en cas de crise
- Partager les ressource et les techniques de communication
- Encourager le professionnalisme de la communication dans le domaine du tourisme
- Aider l'OMT à fixer ses priorités pour ses activités de communication et appuyer ces dernières

Les activités du réseau TOURCOM comprendront :

- le soutien de la campagne mondiale de communication sur le tourisme qui a pour slogan « Le tourisme, source d'enrichissement » ;
- l'organisation de séminaires et d'ateliers locaux et régionaux et de conférences mondiales sur la communication dans le domaine du tourisme sous la marque « TOURCOM » ;
- le soutien des activités des journalistes et écrivains du tourisme dans le monde en général et, plus particulièrement, en Afrique, en Amérique latine et en Asie ;
- le soutien des efforts des Membres de l'OMT en matière de communication ;
- la définition de « principes TOURCOM » s'inspirant des meilleures pratiques de communication intégrale en matière de tourisme ;
- la recherche de la diversification linguistique et culturelle de la communication internationale en matière de tourisme ;
- des actions de communication efficace visant à faire mieux connaître, entre autres, la problématique de la libéralisation du commerce, le programme ST-EP (Le tourisme durable, instrument d'élimination de la pauvreté) et les objectifs de développement de la Déclaration du Millénaire des Nations Unies ;

- des actions visant à faire mieux connaître et à appliquer les dispositions du Code mondial d'éthique du tourisme qui ont trait aux relations avec les médias, et
- la publication d'articles ou de brochures sur la communication par temps de crise, sur les sites *web* des destinations, sur leurs bulletins d'information, etc.

Composition

Le réseau, qui n'a pas à prendre de décisions, soumettra des recommandations et des avis de spécialistes au département Communication de l'OMT. Pour en faire partie, il n'est pas nécessaire d'être ressortissant ou représentant de Membres de l'Organisation. Les membres du réseau ne devront pas payer de cotisation. La qualité de membre du réseau ne sera accordée qu'à des personnes physiques ayant une responsabilité directe en matière de communication au sein de leur organisation.

Avantages d'appartenir au réseau TOURCOM:

- Bulletin TOURCOM (lettre d'information mensuelle sur la communication touristique)
- publication d'articles et de documents dans le Bulletin TOURCOM et dans la collection des bonnes pratiques de communication
- réception immédiate des ouvrages sur la communication dans le domaine du tourisme dès parution
- informations privilégiées de l'OMT et invitations aux réunions communes

Conférences et Ateliers *TOURCOM* sur la Communication dans le Domaine du Tourisme

Vu le succès de la Première Conférence mondiale sur la communication dans le domaine du tourisme (TOURCOM), qui a eu lieu les 29 et 30 janvier 2004 à Madrid, le Secrétariat de l'OMT proposera au Conseil exécutif d'incorporer au programme de travail de l'Organisation des conférences régionales et des ateliers locaux sur le même thème.

Leurs programmes seront adaptés aux problèmes régionaux ou locaux en matière de communication dans le domaine du tourisme. Ils pourront être assortis d'une formation de base en relations publiques, en communication par voie électronique, en communication par temps de crise, en publicité, etc. Les résultats des conférences régionales et des ateliers locaux seront discutés à la Deuxième Conférence mondiale sur la communication dans le domaine du tourisme.

APÉNDICE II

**Currículo vitae
(siguiendo el orden del programa de TOURCOM)**

ANNEX II

**Bios
(in order of the TOURCOM programme)**

ANNEXE II

**Résumés de carrière des Intervenants
(dans l'ordre du programme)**

CV para TOURCOM, convocada por la OMT

(siguiendo el orden del programa de TOURCOM)

Francesco Frangialli
Secretario General, Organización Mundial del Turismo

Nacido en París, el Sr. Frangialli es licenciado por el Instituto de Estudios Políticos de París y posee un título en Ciencias Económicas, además de diplomas de postgrado en Ciencias Económicas y en Derecho Público. Estudió también en la Escuela Nacional de Administración francesa y en la Escuela de la Comisaría de Marina. Su carrera profesional empezó con su trabajo como oficial de intendencia a bordo del buque escolta "Dupetit-Thouars" de la Marina francesa, después de lo cual se convirtió en un joven magistrado del Tribunal de Cuentas y en profesor del Instituto de Estudios Políticos de París y del Instituto Internacional de Administración Pública.

El primer cargo del Sr. Frangialli en el sector turístico fue el de consejero técnico del gabinete del Ministro de Juventud, Deporte y Ocio hasta que, en 1980, fue nombrado asesor del Consejo Superior de Turismo de Francia. Un año después se convirtió en miembro del Consejo Nacional de Turismo. Otros hitos de su carrera turística son su labor como Director de Turismo en el Ministerio de Turismo, como miembro del Consejo de Administración de Air France, en la administración pública de Marne-la-Vallée, en la Agencia Nacional para Cheques de Vacaciones y en ACTIM.

En 1990, el Sr. Frangialli fue nombrado Secretario General Adunto de la Organización Mundial del Turismo y en 1997 fue elegido Secretario General para el periodo 1998-2001. Al final de ese mandato, fue reelegido para el periodo 2002-2005. Entre sus libros y publicaciones figuran La France dans le tourisme mondial (1991, Éditions Economica), Tourisme et loisirs – Une question sociale (coautor, 1997, Éditions Bayard), Consideraciones sobre el turismo internacional (1999 y 2000, Organización Mundial del Turismo) y International Tourism: The Great Tourning Point, Texts and documents 2001 - 2003 (2004, Organización Mundial del Turismo).

Entre las condecoraciones y premios recibidos por el Sr. Frangialli cabe mencionar el nombramiento de Chevalier des Palmes académiques, así como de Caballero del Mérito Nacional y Caballero de la Legión de Honor. Además, ha recibido condecoraciones de la República de San Marino, la República Togolesa y la Autoridad Palestina.

Debbie Hindle
Directora general, BGB & Associates

En 1991, la Sra. Hindle ayudó a fundar BGB & Associates, actualmente considerada la empresa de relaciones públicas en materia de viajes y estilo de vida más importante del Reino Unido, cuyos clientes abarcan desde la Comisión Turística Australiana hasta Travelbag. Tiene más de 13 años de experiencia en la industria de viajes y de ocio. Ha organizado y dirigido campañas de relaciones públicas para organizaciones como juntas de turismo, hoteles, agencias de viajes, tour operadores, GDS, atracciones, vacaciones en el Reino Unido, compañías aéreas, la industria de cruceros y transbordadores para pasajeros. La Sra. Hindle también ha dirigido campañas de presión política y de investigación. Durante muchos años representó al tour operador Lunn Poly y actualmente dirige equipos para clientes como la *Passenger Shipping Association y la Caribbean Tourism Organization*.

Su carrera también ha incluido la creación de una revista sobre comercio regional en la región central de Inglaterra y su trabajo para el departamento de relaciones públicas de *McCann Erikson*, donde llevó la contabilidad de bienes y servicios como equipo de entrenamiento físico, refrescos y seguros, y para una serie de empresas pertenecientes a las industrias inmobiliaria y de la construcción.

Becky Anderson

Presentadora de Business International en la CNN

Becky Anderson ha presentado el programa de negocios internacionales "Business International" de la CNN, emitido dos veces al día, desde su lanzamiento en febrero de 2001. Como presentadora de este programa tan agitado y llenos de continuos cambios, Anderson proporciona información sobre la coyuntura de la jornada comercial en todo el mundo, inclusive Asia, Europa y Estados Unidos, y evalúa los efectos de los mercados y de las noticias comerciales en Europa. Durante el programa, se pone en contacto con los corresponsales de la CNN en todo el mundo para conocer las últimas noticias en el mundo de los negocios.

Desde el lanzamiento de "Business International," Anderson ha entrevistado a muy diversas personalidades del mundo de las finanzas, la política y la industria, entre ellas el Sr. Gordon Brown, Ministro de Economía y Hacienda del Reino Unido; Jean-Claude Trichet, Gobernador del Banco de Francia; Sir John Browne, Director Ejecutivo de *BP Amoco*, y Alí Rodríguez, Secretario General de la OPEC. Anderson también presenta el programa de vela de la CNN "Inside Sailing", un análisis mensual de los principales eventos en el mundo de la navegación.

Anderson se incorporó a la CNN en mayo de 1999 como primera presentadora del programa matinal sobre negocios "World Business This Morning," un paso clave en el inicio de la estrategia de regionalización continua de la CNN consistente en llevar programas de producción local al mercado europeo. Anderson participó en la primera fase en que algunos programas matinales en directo salieron del centro de producción de Londres de la CNN.

Desde que entró en la CNN, Anderson ha realizado presentaciones en directo desde lugares lejanos para muchas misiones en el extranjero de gran importancia, y ha entrevistado a personalidades del mundo de los negocios en eventos como la Feria de Tecnología CeBIT de 2000 y 2001, el Foro Global de Fortuna y Telecom 1999.

Anderson tiene una gran experiencia en periodismo de negocios, ámbito en el que trabajó para las empresas británicas *Channel 5*, *CNBC Europe* y *Bloomberg*. Comenzó su carrera periodística colaborando para varias publicaciones sobre negocios en Arizona, tras cursar un Master en Comunicación de Masas en la Escuela de Periodismo Walter Cronkite en la Universidad Estatal de Arizona, en 1992.

Anderson es británica y vive en Londres. Se licenció con honores en Económicas y Francés por la Universidad de Sussex.

Anderson is British and lives in London. She has a BA (Hons) degree in Economics and French from Sussex University.

Thierry Baudier

Director General de Maison de la France

Después de muchos años de trabajo en actividades de gobierno y turismo, Thierry Baudier fue nombrado Director General de la Maison de la France el pasado mayo. El Sr. Baudier sustituyó a Jean-Philippe Pérol, que había ocupado el cargo desde agosto de 1999 y que es hoy Director de la representación de la Maison de la France para América.

Titulado superior en Derecho y Sociología, y antiguo profesor del Instituto de Altos Estudios de la Defensa Nacional, Thierry Baudier forma parte de la agrupación de interés económico Maison de la France desde 1997. Su primer cargo fue el de Director de Mercados Exteriores. A continuación, y hasta su reciente nombramiento, fue Director de Marketing y Asociaciones y, como tal, coordinó las actividades de marketing y comunicación de la sede y de las diversas oficinas. De 1995 a 1997, Thierry Baudier fue Agregado Parlamentario del Primer Ministro, habiendo trabajado antes como ayudante especial del presidente de una formación política en la Asamblea Nacional de Francia. Thierry Baudier inició su trayectoria profesional en la Compagnie Générale du Bâtiment donde, de 1989 a 1993, participó en diversos proyectos, entre los que destaca la construcción de hoteles en la Europa central y oriental.

Marc Meister

Presidente y Director Gerente, Sergat España

El Sr. Meister es el fundador, Presidente y Director Gerente de *Sergat España S.L.*, la principal agencia de márketing y comunicaciones de España especializada en turismo y en las industrias hotelera y de la aviación. Su formación académica incluye un Master en Ciencias de Márketing, un Diploma en Gestión Hotelera por Lucerna y un Diploma en Estudios de Comunicación e Información por el Instituto Drexler.

Miembro fundador del capítulo sobre España de *PATA* y *Visit US*, el Sr. Meister también ha desempeñado cargos importantes en gestión de márketing en Suiza, Estados Unidos y España, en tour operadores y empresas hoteleras importantes. Habla español, alemán, francés e ingles y tiene el título de piloto privado.

Javier Piñanes

Director de Turespaña

Licenciado en Derecho por la Universidad Autónoma de Madrid y doctor en Derecho por la Complutense, Javier Piñanes pertenece al Cuerpo Superior de Administradores Civiles del Estado.

En la Administración Pública, ha ocupado diversos cargos en los Ministerios de Industria y Energía y Transportes, Turismo y Comunicaciones, y ha sido subdirector general de Estudios en la Secretaría General Técnica del Ministerio de Justicia e Interior.

En el ámbito de la Administración de Turismo ha sido director adjunto de la Oficina Española de Turismo en Frankfurt y director de la Oficina Española de Turismo en Berlín. También ha sido subdirector general de Medios de Promoción del Instituto de Turismo de España (Turespaña). Desde el pasado mes de marzo es director de Turespaña.

Christopher Brown

Director Gerente y Director Ejecutivo de TTF, Australia

El Sr. Brown es actualmente Director Gerente y Director Ejecutivo de *Tourism Task Force (TTF)*, organismo que defiende y promueve los intereses del turismo en Australia. Se trata de una entidad independiente a la que pertenecen los directores ejecutivos de las 200 principales instituciones activas en el sector del turismo, el transporte, el ocio y la infraestructura conexa en Australia. El *TTF* se ha propuesto influir en las decisiones políticas y en materia de inversiones en una de las principales ramas de la actividad económica del país. Antes de acceder, en 1992, al cargo que desempeña en la actualidad, el Sr. Brown fue Director de Relaciones Públicas de *JMA* y asesor político de varios miembros del Parlamento. Anteriormente desempeñó funciones en la empresa de publicidad *Ogilvy y Mather*. Estudió Economía y Derecho en la Universidad de Sydney. El Sr. Brown, que se describe como "fanático del deporte", participó en el concurso que se celebró para elegir la Sede de los Juegos Olímpicos de 2000 en Sydney. Fue Embajador Nacional en los Juegos Paraolímpicos de 2000 (Sydney) y Agregado Honorario de Bostwana en los mismos. En estos diez últimos años ha sido Director Ejecutivo de Turismo y de la Fundación que otorga becas a las jóvenes promesas del deporte. Además de las actividades mencionadas anteriormente en torno al *TTF*, es Presidente del *Authentic Outback Experiences Pty Ltd.*, empresa asociada con el fabricante de utensilios de acampada *RM Williams* y con la empresa rural AACo, que organiza campamentos y safaris en el interior de Australia. También es miembro del Consejo de *Best Western Australia* (Lo mejor del Oeste australiano), iniciativa en que participan empresas turísticas del sector público y privado, y Director de *See Australia Ltd* (Visite Australia Ltda.), iniciativa –también mixta– destinada a promover el turismo. El Sr. Brown es el portavoz entusiasta del Grupo Asesor en Rugby y Turismo, y del Foro Nacional para el Turismo y la Exportación de Vinos; miembro del Consejo para la Promoción del Turismo de la Confederación de Australia, miembro del Grupo Directivo en materia de turismo; Medalla de Oro para los que se distinguen en la elaboración de estrategias encaminadas a integrar a los deportistas con discapacidades, otorgada por el Primer Ministro de Australia, y miembro de la Mesa redonda para la promoción del turismo. En la actualidad es el Vicepresidente del Consejo Empresarial de la Organización Mundial del Turismo, organismo afiliado a la Naciones Unidas, y representante regional del prestigioso Consejo Mundial de Viajes y Turismo.

Thomas J. Wallace

Director de la revista Condé Nast Traveler

En 1990, el Sr. Wallace empezó a dirigir la prestigiosa revista norteamericana especializada en viajes *Condé Nast Traveler*. Desde su lanzamiento, la revista se ha distinguido por la calidad de sus artículos periodísticos, por lo que ha sido nominada candidata a premios nacionales de periodismo en 16 ocasiones, seis de ellas en la categoría "excelencia general". Hasta la fecha ha recibido cinco premios: en 1998 y 1999 en la categoría "interés especial"; en 1991 recibió un premio en la categoría "dibujo" y otro en "excelencia general", y en 1999 en la categoría "excelencia general". Entre las publicaciones especializadas en viajes, es la única que ha obtenido el Premio Nacional de artículos de revistas.

Además de ser la única publicación especializada en viajes del Grupo *Condé Nast*, es la única que ha producido series televisivas, la *Condé Nast Traveler: Insider's Guide*, cuyo 260 episodio corresponde a octubre de 2002, fecha que coincide con el 15o aniversario de la revista.

Bajo la dirección del Sr. Wallace, dicha revista fue la primera que pudo consultarse en línea, en junio de 1955, y contó con un ambicioso sitio Web precursor de un nuevo tipo de interacción con el cliente, conocido ahora con la denominación "concierge.com." El Sr. Wallace se ha destacado por su firmeza en la promoción de un turismo responsable de sus efectos en el medio ambiente. En este marco, en 1990 la revista creó el Premio Anual del Medio Ambiente, destinado a alentar las iniciativas de empresas independientes. Con el propósito de impulsar esta idea creó un Premio de Ecoturismo, para recompensar las iniciativas emprendidas a este respecto en la industria del turismo.

Antes de incorporarse al equipo de Condé Nast, ocupó cargos destacados en los diarios más importantes de Estados Unidos, como *The New York Times*, *Newsday y Stamford Advocate*, donde, en calidad de redactor, tuvo que supervisar e hacer investigaciones sobre las series que obtuvieron el Premio Pulitzer en 1979. El Sr. Wallace es licenciado por la Universidad de Harvard.

Gary Wardrope

Director Comercial del canal "Travel Channel"

El Sr. Wardrope se encarga de la publicidad y el patrocinio a escala mundial del canal Travel Channel, que se ha propuesto ampliar sus actividades a Oriente Medio y otras regiones. Actualmente ha iniciado la prestación de servicios de agencias de viajes en los Países Escandinavos y Sudáfrica.

Otrora esquiador de competición, empezó trabajando como monitor de esquí y gerente de sitios turísticos en Canadá -su tierra natal-, Francia, Suiza y Austria, y posteriormente fue Jefe de Ventas y Márketing en *Neilson Ski*. En el decenio de 1990 dirigió la División de servicios de turismo por vía aérea, que mueve fondos que ascienden a 250 millones de libras esterlinas y se especializa en apoyar a empresas incipientes, incluidas cuatro empresas de cruceros, y el programa *Escapades* y salidas de esquí, destinados a los jóvenes.

En 2000, el Sr. Wardrope fue Director Comercial del canal Travel Channel, donde supervisó el establecimiento de *Travel Deals Direct*, programa televisivo que funciona 18 horas diarias como agencia de viajes, que consultan 8 millones de hogares y gracias al cual viajan al Reino Unido más de 30.000 personas cada año. Estuvo también al frente del primer servicio de vídeo de banda ancha con BT, disponible para los usuarios que lo soliciten.

Geoffrey Lipman

Asesor Especial del Secretario General de la Organización Mundial del Turismo sobre el comercio de servicios turísticos, la liberalización de rostro humano y la iniciativa ST-EP

El Sr. Lipman es Presidente de Green Globe 21, la organización mundial de certificaciones de turismo sostenible, y de GTREX, una empresa de desarrollo de Internet de cuarta generación. Ha sido también Consejero de la Great Canadian Railway Company y de AIA Communications. De 1990 a 1999, fue Presidente del Consejo Mundial de Viajes y Turismo y, bajo su mandato, el número de miembros pasó de diez a cien, mientras el turismo se convertía en el sector de más rápido crecimiento del mundo.

Geoffrey Lipman pasó 20 años con la Asociación de Transporte Aéreo Internacional (IATA), de la que fue Jefe de Personal y Director de Asuntos Gubernamentales. Más tarde, fue Director Ejecutivo de IFAPA, una fundación que representa los intereses de los pasajeros de líneas aéreas. Fue también socio de Global Aviation Associates, una consultoría estratégica de líneas aéreas especializada en cuestiones de regulación y de competencia.

El Sr. Lipman ha escrito y presentado ponencias en todo el mundo sobre estrategia turística y liberalización de líneas aéreas. Ha sido miembro de dos comisiones de alto nivel de la Unión Europea sobre liberalización de líneas aéreas y empleo en turismo, de la Mesa Redonda sobre Desarrollo Sostenible del Reino Unido y del Consejo Asesor de Royal Jordanian Airlines. Actualmente, es miembro de la Tourism Society y de la Australian Tourism Research Association, así como "Embajador de Buena Voluntad" de la Organización de Turismo del Océano Índico y miembro del Consejo de Asesoramiento Empresarial del Presidente de Zambia.

Donald E. Hawkins

Profesor titular de la cátedra Eisenhower de Política Turística, Universidad George Washington

Junto con su labor de investigación y docente, el Dr. Hawkins promueve la colaboración activa entre la industria turística e instituciones internacionales como Naciones Unidas, el Banco Mundial, el Banco Interamericano de Desarrollo y la Organización Mundial del Turismo. Entre las actividades realizadas en relación con esta última, cabe citar su labor docente en el CICATUR en la ciudad de México, sus servicios como delegado de los Estados Unidos en las Asambleas Generales de la OMT celebradas en Roma y Nueva Delhi, su labor pionera como investigador sobre TEDQUAL, numerosas intervenciones públicas y otros servicios prestados en algunos de los Comités más importantes de la OMT. En 2003, fue el primer galardonado con el Premio Ulises de la OMT, en recompensa por su labor de investigación y difusión de conocimientos en el ámbito de la política y gestión turísticas.

Entre sus logros académicos cabe citar su labor como profesor en el primer curso sobre Turismo (1979) que ofreció la Universidad George Washington, una de las primeras en ofrecer un Master en Gestión Turística, y cuya primera promoción se licenció en 1974. El programa de estudios se centra en el turismo internacional y aborda tanto los aspectos profesionales como el trabajo de investigación sobre las industrias turística y hotelera.

El Dr. Hawkins desempeñó hasta 1999 el cargo de Director del Instituto Internacional de Estudios Turísticos, creado en 1988, que fue el primer centro educativo establecido en colaboración con la OMT. En 1994 fue nombrado profesor titular de la cátedra Dwight Eisenhower de Política Turística.

También es autor o ha dirigido unas 100 publicaciones sobre aspectos actuales de política y estrategias turísticas. Asimismo, ha trabajado como consultor en proyectos y estudios sobre turismo en numerosos países, como Honduras, Jordania, Egipto, Bermudas, St. Kitts y Nevis, y Palestina. Recientemente ha participado en el estudio realizado con el apoyo financiero de las Naciones Unidas sobre la relación estratégica entre desarrollo del turismo, conservación de la diversidad biológica y utilización sostenible de la energía y los recursos hídricos.

Mariano López

Decano de la Cámara de Periodistas y Comunicadores de Turismo

Mariano López es el Decano de la Cámara de Periodistas y Comunicadores de Turismo, una organización profesional que reúne a responsables de medios de comunicación especializados en viajes y directores de comunicación de empresas del sector. Es, también, director de la revista Viajar, del Grupo Zeta, la primera revista de viajes que nació en España y que acaba de cumplir su 25 aniversario.

Richard D. Lewis

Presidente de Richard Lewis Communications

El Sr. Lewis, que habla diez idiomas europeos y dos asiáticos, es Presidente de *Richard Lewis Communications*, instituto internacional de enseñanza de lenguas y transculturalismo, con oficinas establecidas en unos 12 países. En 1989 fundó la revista de publicación trimestral *Cross Cultura*, y su libro *When Cultures Collide* se considera un clásico entre las obras que abordan las cuestiones interculturales. En primavera de 1997 esta obra fue seleccionada como "libro del mes" por el Club del Libro estadounidense.

Activo durante más de 35 años en el ámbito de la lingüística antropológica y aplicada, trabajo también como periodista en Alemania, donde escribía textos para Konrad Adenauer. En 1961 creó la primera serie televisiva del mundo en inglés sobre turismo en Finlandia. En 1962 volvió a trabajar como guionista para la serie *Walter y Connie* que presentaba la BBC.

Ha vivido y trabajado en varios países europeos y entre sus clientes figuran ABB, Allianz, Banco de España, Banque de France, Deutsche Bank, Ericsson, Fiat, Gillette, IBM, Mercedes Benz, Nestlé, Nokia, Saab y Volvo. Durante los cinco años que vivió en Japón fue tutor de la emperatriz Michiko y de otros miembros de la familia imperial nipona. Trabajó también para las empresas Nomura, Mitsubishi, Hitachi, Sanyo, Mitsui y Nippon Steel. En los últimos años ha colaborado activamente en el campo del interculturalismo y ha fundado empresas especializadas en técnicas de comunicación en Francia, Alemania, España, Italia, Brasil, Finlandia, Suecia, Reino Unido y Estados Unidos.

En 1999, la Asociación *Pacific Asia Travel* eligió al Sr. Lewis "Personalidad del Año" por su "profunda dedicación y extraordinaria labor en el ámbito de la comunicación transcultural, y por su comprensión y profunda sensibilidad por las culturas de la región de Asia y el Pacifico". En 1997, el Sr. Ahtisaari, Presidente de Finlandia, le nombró "caballero" en reconocimiento de sus servicios en el ámbito de los programas de formación en materia de transculturalismo, destinados a los ministerios finlandeses y que han sido pioneros, incluso si se comparan con los aplicados en los países de la Unión Europea.

Rolf Jensen

Jefe de Imaginación en Dream Company Ltd.

El Sr. Jensen, autor danés especializado en obras futuristas, es el Jefe de Imaginación en *Dream Company Ltd.*, cargo que creó en 2001 y que ha servido de inspiración a las principales empresas mundiales de la industria turística para que interpreten los desafíos presentes y futuros que plantea la transformación de un modo de producción en otro, proporcionando a las empresas del sector los instrumentos que les permitan hacer frente a los profundos cambios que tienen lugar.

En 1999 publicó, primero en los Estados Unidos y luego en Dinamarca, un libro titulado *The Dream Society: From Information to Imagination*, que ha tenido un gran éxito de ventas y se ha traducido a seis idiomas. Viajero apasionado, es miembro de la *Royal Geographic Society* de Londres. Entre los viajes que más le impresionaron figura el que hizo al corazón de las selvas de Borneo, donde fue testigo directo de una sociedad en transición de la etapa de caza y recolección a la etapa de sedentarización apoyada en la agricultura.

En 1970, el Sr. Jensen cursó un Master en Ciencias Políticas en la Universidad de Aarhus, y trabajó posteriormente en los Ministerios de Defensa y Pesca, y Relaciones Exteriores. En 1983 ingresó en el Instituto de Estudios Futuristas (Institute for Future Studies (CISF)), que pasó a dirigir cinco años después.

Scott Wayne

Director de SW Associates

Como Director de *SW Associates*, el Sr. Wayne ha administrado y participado en una amplia gama de programas y proyectos de desarrollo turístico, inclusive programas de desarrollo económico a través del turismo, promoción de las inversiones, estrategia de comunicación y organizativa, administración, y establecimiento de asociaciones y relaciones internacionales. Entre sus trabajos más recientes como consultor cabe citar el estudio que realizó para el Banco Mundial sobre la competencia los países en lo que respecta a la industria turística; una clasificación de los hoteles y la elaboración de un sistema de control de calidad para el Gobierno de Barhein; la elaboración de una estrategia ecológica para la industria de los cruceros; un estudio preliminar de factibilidad de la infraestructura turística en Marruecos y una evaluación rápida de las condiciones que brinda Croacia para invertir en turismo. Ha creado además una sociedad de inversiones en turismo, varias organizaciones nacionales y provinciales de turismo, y es autor de una estrategia de desarrollo de servicios turísticos y comunicaciones. También es Profesor Adjunto de Planificación y Turismo en la universidad *George Washington*.

En virtud de su cargo en *SW Associates*, fue Director de la oficina que mantiene en Washington D.C. la sección norteamericana del Consejo Mundial de Viajes y Turismo, y ha dirigido varios de sus proyectos y programas financiados con ayuda de instituciones financieras multilaterales, varios gobiernos estatales y el gobierno central. Ha ocupado también el cargo de Vicepresidente de Desarrollo Internacional en *Vivid Travel Network*, una nueva empresa que ofrece sus servicios por Internet, filial de *Vivid Studios*, conocida en el mundo entero.

El Sr. Wayne fue también Jefe de Comunicaciones de la Organización Mundial del Turismo donde asesoró al Secretario General en materia de comunicaciones estratégicas, en la creación de asociaciones con mandantes gubernamentales y no gubernamentales, y en el establecimiento de programas de publicaciones y de relaciones con el público y con los medios de comunicación.

También es autor de siete libros de viajes para el club *Sierra* y para *Lonely Planet* sobre Egipto, Sudán, los países del Magreb (Argelia, Marruecos y Túnez), México, el Estado de Baja California y numerosos artículos en periódicos y revistas.

Dawid de Villiers

Secretario General Adjunto, Organización Mundial del Turismo

El Sr. de Villiers fue nombrado Secretario General Adjunto de la OMT en 1998 después de haber sido Ministro de Medio Ambiente y Turismo de Sudáfrica bajo la presidencia de Nelson Mandela. Es licenciado en psicología, filosofía y teología por la Universidad de Stellenbosch, cursó un máster en filosofía en la Ran Afrikaans University y obtuvo el doctorado en filosofía por la Universidad de Stellenbosch.

Su experiencia profesional abarca su labor docente como profesor universitario de filosofía, su trabajo como ministro de la Iglesia Reformada Holandesa y su labor como parlamentario y Embajador de Sudáfrica en Londres. A su regreso a Sudáfrica, el Sr. de Villiers fue nombrado Ministro de Comercio, Industria y Turismo, cargo que desempeñó durante seis años, para convertirse posteriormente en Ministro de Presupuesto y Bienestar, Ministro de Administración y Privatización y Ministro de Recursos Mineros y Energéticos y de Empresas Públicas.

En 1991, el Sr. de Villiers participó intensamente en el proceso de negociaciones que desembocó en una nueva Constitución y la convocatoria de las primeras elecciones democráticas de Sudáfrica y, en 1994, fue Presidente del Consejo Ejecutivo de Transición que había de conducir y supervisar el proceso de gobierno durante la transición política del país hacia la democracia.

El Sr. de Villiers ha sido Gobernador del Banco de Desarrollo de Sudáfrica y consejero de diversas empresas públicas tales como el Banco de Johannesburgo, el Santam Bank, Triomf Fertiliser y Landbou-Chemiese Beleggings (inversiones agroquímicas). Gran deportista, el Sr. de Villiers representó a Sudáfrica en el equipo de rugby en competiciones internacionales contra Inglaterra, Irlanda, Gales, Australia, Nueva Zelandia, Francia y Argentina. Además, fue capitán del equipo sudafricano en 23 partidos, una cifra récord.

Diego Cordovez

Candidato a la presidencia del Comité Mundial de Ética del Turismo

Diego Cordovez es el presidente del Centro Andino de Estudios Internacionales de la Universidad Andina Simón Bolívar de Quito (Ecuador), cargo que asumió después de haber sido funcionario de las Naciones Unidas durante 25 años, primero en el sector económico y después en el sector político. En sus primeros años de funcionario fue director de la Secretaría del Consejo Económico y Social y subsecretario general a cargo de los servicios de la Secretaría para asuntos económicos y sociales. Fue el principal asesor de una comisión especial encargada de la reestructuración de todo el sistema de las Naciones Unidas para el desarrollo y actuó como secretario de la Comisión Económica y Financiera de la Asamblea General durante ocho períodos de sesiones. En 1972 y 1992 fue asesor especial del secretario general de las conferencias de las Naciones Unidas sobre medio ambiente. En 1981 fue designado secretario general adjunto de asuntos políticos. Como mediador en el conflicto afgano negoció los Acuerdos de Ginebra, en virtud de los cuales la Unión Soviética retiró todas sus tropas de Afganistán. Fue nominado para el Premio Nobel de la Paz de 1988, año en que el premio recayó en las Naciones Unidas. Cumplió misiones especiales en la República de Corea, la República Popular Democrática de Corea, la República Dominicana, Granada, Irán, Iraq y Pakistán y fue el principal asesor de Olof Palme, mediador de las Naciones Unidas en el conflicto entre Irán e Iraq. En 1988 fue designado ministro de Relaciones Exteriores y, cuatro años más tarde, se incorporó a LeBoeuf, Lamb, Greene and MacRae, un estudio jurídico internacional con sede en Nueva York. De 1992 a 1996, fue Diplomático Residente en la Facultad de Estudios Internacionales de la Universidad de Columbia. En 1996, fue además candidato a la vicepresidencia de la República de Ecuador.

Anil Kumarsingh Gayan

Ministro de Turismo y Ocio de Mauricio

El Sr. Anil Kumarsingh Gayan fue nombrado Ministro de Asuntos Exteriores y de Cooperación Regional el 16 de septiembre de 2000. Había ocupado el mismo puesto entre 1983 y 1986, cuando este Ministerio se llamaba Ministerio de Asuntos Exteriores, Turismo y Emigración. Recientemente ha sido nombrado Ministro de Turismo y Ocio, cargo que desempeña desde el 23 de diciembre de 2003. Nacido en Port Louis el 22 de octubre de 1948, el Sr. Gayan fue a la escuela primaria en Triolet, el pueblo de su infancia, y en Port Louis. En 1968 concluyó sus estudios secundarios, por los que fue galardonado, en el Royal College de Port Luis. Estudió Derecho en la *London School of Economics* de 1969 a 1972, y entró en el Colegio de Abogados o barristers en Inner Temple, Londres, en 1972. En 1973 hizo un Master en la *University of London,* especializándose en Derecho Internacional y Derecho del Mar.

Después de trabajar durante un tiempo por cuenta propia, se incorporó en 1974 a la Oficina del Fiscal General (*Attorney General's Office*) en calidad de Asesor de la Corona. Entre 1974 y 1982 se encargó particularmente de la Conferencia de las Naciones Unidas sobre el Derecho del Mar y, como delegado de Mauricio, participó en todas sus reuniones y en otras conferencias conexas en todo el mundo. En 1982 firmó la Convención sobre el Derecho del Mar en Montego Bay. En 1982, el Sr. Gayan decidió trabajar nuevamente por cuenta propia y entró en el mundo de la política. Fue elegido miembro del Parlamento y del Consejo Municipal de Curepipe. En 1983, fue reelegido miembro del Parlamento y nombrado Ministro de Asuntos Exteriores, Turismo y Emigración. Ese mismo año fue nombrado también Presidente del Consejo de la Universidad de Mauricio. En 1986, volvió a ejercer como abogado colegiado. Fue Presidente del Consejo de los Colegios de Abogados en 1989-90. En 1995 fue nombrado Asesor Principal. El Sr. Gayan ha trabajado como consultor en el Centro de Derechos Humanos, en Ginebra, y ha ejercido como tal en Bután, Mongolia, Armenia y Togo.

Jonathan B. Tourtellot

Director de Turismo Sostenible en la National Geographic Society, Redactor Jefe de Geotourism y de la revista National Geographic Traveler

Como Director de Turismo Sostenible en la *National Geographic Society* y Redactor jefe de *Geotourism* y de *National Geographic Traveler,* el Sr. Tourtellot escribe en esta última revista una columna titulada *Travel Watch* donde trata del estado de conservación de los destinos turísticos, y escribe y revisa artículos sobre temas de interés turístico. Actualmente trabaja en el Sondeo y Panorama General que realiza la *National Geographic Society* sobre la sostenibilidad de algunos destinos turísticos muy conocidos; en un libro sobre geoturismo, y en el programa de desarrollo turístico sostenible de la *National Geographic Society,* que incluye una participación en "Mundo Maya. Alianza para un turismo sostenible", en el Foro Mundial del Turismo para la Paz y el Desarrollo Sostenible, y en el lanzamiento del sitio Web de la iniciativa *World Heritage* para la protección del medio ambiente.

En 1979 el Sr. Tourtellot se incorporó a la *National Geographic Society* y un año después ocupó el cargo de Redactor Principal. In 2001 fue el primer Director del programa titulado Turismo Sostenible, en cuyo marco elaboró el concepto de "geoturismo" que ha definido como "aquel turismo que conserva o amplía el carácter de un determinado lugar geográfico –el entorno físico, la cultura, la estética, el patrimonio heredado y el bienestar de sus residentes."

El Sr. Tourtellot es coautor de la primera investigación que utilizó dicho término, a saber, "Estudio sobre Geoturismo" (*Geotourism Study*) y del primer sondeo sobre la conducta y las actitudes de los viajeros estadounidenses, la sostenibilidad y la situación en que se encuentran los destinos turísticos patrocinado por la *Travel Association of America* entre 2001 y 2003. Contribuyó a instituir el Premio *World Legacy* de turismo sostenible en los ámbitos de los viajes de observación de la naturaleza, del patrimonio cultural, de los hoteles y complejos turísticos, y de la conservación de los sitios turísticos, premio presentado al público por primera vez en enero de 2003 por la reina Noor de Jordania en nombre de *National Geographic Traveler* y de *Conservation International.*

Deborah Luhrman

Consultora de la OMT en materia de comunicaciones

Hasta 2001 la Sra. Luhrman fue Jefa de Comunicaciones de la Organización Mundial del Turismo, donde se encargaba de las relaciones con los medios de comunicación, de las Noticias de la OMT, de ferias comerciales y del sitio Web de la Organización. Actualmente sigue colaborando con la OMT en proyectos relacionados con las comunicaciones y la gestión de crisis. Es miembro del equipo de la OMT encargado de la gestión de crisis.

Esta periodista de vocación, nacida en Estados Unidos, trabajó para la televisión de California, donde obtuvo el Premio Emmy. Llegó a España en 1989 y trabajó como redactora de noticias para la Agencia española de noticias EFE y como productora para la red de televisión alemana ZDF. Comenzó a cubrir las noticias relativas al turismo en España para varias publicaciones de carácter comercial, entre ellas *Travel Trade Gazette* y *Hotel & Motel Management*. Es coautora de varias de las guías de viajes Fodor, entre otras, las relativas a España, Francia y Portugal. Colaboró también en la producción de las emisiones de televisión correspondientes a cuatro sesiones de los Juegos Olímpicos de Verano, a saber, las de Los Ángeles (1984), Barcelona (1992), Atlanta (1996) y Sydney (2000).

Dexter Koehl

Vicepresidente de Relaciones Públicas y Comunicaciones en la TIA

Desde su nombramiento en marzo de 1992 como Vicepresidente de Relaciones Públicas y Comunicaciones en la *Travel Industry Association of America (TIA)*, organización que cuenta con 2.100 organizaciones afiliadas, el Sr. Koehl se ha encargado de las relaciones con los medios de comunicación nacionales e internacionales en apoyo de la misión de la TIA de promover y facilitar la realización de viajes dentro y hacia los Estados Unidos; de utilizar las comunicaciones para sensibilizar al público sobre los efectos económicos, sociales y culturales del turismo y los viajes en el país, y de gestionar el contenido del sitio Web de la TIA.

El Sr. Koehl tiene una gran experiencia en relaciones públicas, comunicaciones, márketing y desarrollo de la industria de los viajes. Antes de incorporarse a la TIA fue Director de Relaciones Públicas en la agencia de viajes *Carlson Travel Group de Miniápolis* (1986 a 1992) y como tal se encargó de todas las actividades en materia de relaciones públicas de una agencia de viajes cuyo volumen de negocios ascendía a 7.000 millones de dólares en todo el mundo. Fue también Vicepresidente de Márketing y Desarrollo en *Hershey Entertainment and Resort Co.*, Director de Desarrollo de Mercados en Sea Pines Co., Director de Márketing del Balneario Palmas del Mar (Puerto Rico) y Gerente de Planes de Viajes de los Pasajeros, en American Airlines.

Se licenció en Estudios del Lejano Oriente por la Universidad de Berkeley, California. Tras estudiar japonés en el Instituto de Lenguas de la Defensa, en Monterrey, California, trabajó dos años como traductor para la Agencia Nacional de Seguridad.

Sandra Lee

Secretaria Permanente para cuestiones laborales y de desarrollo económico del Gobierno de la Región Administrativa Especial de Hong-Kong

La Sra. Lee fue nombrada Secretaria Permanente para cuestiones laborales y de desarrollo económico en 2002. En el desempeño de sus funciones, se encarga de diversos ámbitos, como los servicios aéreos, marítimos y portuarios; la logística del desarrollo; el turismo; la energía; los servicios de correos y de meteorología; la política en materia de competencia y la protección de los consumidores. Desde que se incorporó a las labores de gobierno en 1974, en calidad de funcionaria ejecutiva, ha trabajado en varios departamentos gubernamentales ocupándose de la elaboración de políticas y de los recursos, tanto en Hong-Kong como en el extranjero. Entre sus actividades en el extranjero cabe mencionar su labor en la Oficina de Economía y Comercio de Hong-Kong en Washington D.C., donde prestó servicios de asesoramiento entre 1985 a 1988 y luego entre 1993 y 1995. Fue Directora Adjunta del Ministerio del Interior entre 1995 y 1996, Secretaria Adjunta del Servicio Civil de 1996 a 1999, Directora General de la Oficina de Economía y Comercio de Hong-Kong en Londres de 1999 a 2000, y Secretaria de Servicios Económicos de 2000 a 2002.

Dr. Osmane Aïdi

Presidente Honorario de la Asociación Internacional de Hoteles y Restaurantes

El Dr. Aïdi es actualmente el Presidente Honorario de la Asociación Internacional de Hoteles y Restaurantes, cargo para el que fue reelegido en 2000. Desde su fundación en 1947, ha sido el único caso de reelección para un segundo mandato en toda la historia de la Asociación. También es Presidente de *Irrifrance*, importante empresa europea líder en el ámbito de los equipos de irrigación. Durante su larga y distinguida carrera en el gobierno y en el sector privado, ha prestado servicios en varias comisiones del Gobierno de Siria en materia de irrigación y energía, y ha realizado actividades en los ámbitos editorial y bancario. Dirige una fundación que lleva su nombre destinada a preservar el rico patrimonio cultural de su país.

Durante muchos años, trabajó en los Consejos de diversas empresas que actúan en las industrias turística y hotelera en Europa, Estados Unidos y Oriente Medio. Fue Presidente de la Unión Interárabe de Hoteles y Turismo, y de la Organización Euromediterránea de Turismo. Ha sido galardonado con varios premios en reconocimiento de su labor, entre otros, por los gobiernos de Francia, Bulgaria y el Líbano.

Steve Dunne

Director Ejecutivo del Grupo Brighter

El Sr. Dunne es uno de los Directores Ejecutivos del Grupo Brighter y Director Gerente de su filial *Brighter PR*, empresa de relaciones públicas cuyo ritmo de crecimiento es el más elevado en el Reino Unido. Especialista en relaciones públicas, con más de 20 años de experiencia en el ámbito de las comunicaciones empresariales, ha desempeñado varios cargos de alto rango en algunas de las empresas más importantes completamente privatizadas. Fue Jefe de Relaciones Públicas en *British Telecom* durante el período de ebullición que acompañó la liberación del mercado financiero en el Reino Unido en 1987, y estuvo al frente de las relaciones públicas de British Telecom durante la contienda con los sindicatos de fines del decenio de 1980. En 1990 formó parte de un equipo de profesionales de las relaciones públicas que consiguió revertir la pésima reputación del Banco Midland en Gran Bretaña.

A mediados del decenio de 1990, fue nombrado Jefe de Comunicaciones con *Europa de South African Airways*, donde supervisó las negociaciones entre la empresa y el Gobierno sudafricano, ambos interesados en promover a Sudáfrica como destino turístico en toda Europa. En 1997 fue nombrado Director Gerente de *Affinity Consulting*, una de las empresas de publicidad en materia de viajes y turismo más importantes de Gran Bretaña. Dirigió las operaciones de fusión de dicha agencia con *Countrywide Porter Novelli*, empresa que en 2000 figuraba en el cuarto lugar entre las más importantes empresas inglesas en el ámbito de las relaciones públicas. Como Director de *Countrywide*, estuvo a la cabeza de la galardonada División de los Consumidores. En 2002 se incorporó al Consejo del Grupo Brighter.

Christian Nielsen

Autor y Director de European Service Network

El Sr. Nielsen tiene una vasta experiencia académica y comercial en el ámbito del turismo y los medios de comunicación. Ha publicado un libro y varios artículos sobre este tema. Se licenció en Gestión Turística por la Universidad de Victoria en Melbourne (Australia). A continuación cursó un Master en Administración de Empresas en la Universidad Libre de Bruselas, especializándose en turismo, industrias locales y desarrollo. Durante su labor como profesor asociado en una universidad belga, publicó varios artículos sobre turismo y desarrollo urbano. Tras obtener un diploma en periodismo prosiguió su carrera en este campo, lo que le llevó, entre otras cosas, a trabajar como redactor para el periódico *Wall Street Journal Europe*.

En 2001 fue nombrado Director de *European Service Network*, empresa que produce varias revistas y otras publicaciones para la Comisión Europea en Bruselas. Ha escrito también para *Europemedia.net*, y para varias otras publicaciones en línea sobre temas muy variados, como turismo y tecnología de la información, y ha realizado estudios sobre los mismos para la Unión Europea. El año pasado cursó un Master en Política Internacional y ha previsto escribir un libro sobre el tema de las comunicaciones en el turismo.

William J. Gaillard

Director de Comunicaciones, IATA

El Sr. Gaillard ha ocupado desde 1994 el cargo de Director de Comunicaciones en la Asociación Internacional de Transporte Aéreo (IATA). Nació en París en 1959 y se interesó por las ciencias políticas. Cursó estudios en el Instituto de Estudios Políticos de París, en Italia, Suiza y en la universidad de Harvard (Estados Unidos), donde comenzó su carrera como profesor universitario. Antes de incorporarse a la IATA desempeñó diversas funciones de gestión en el ámbito de las relaciones públicas y las relaciones exteriores para la Comisión Europea y la Naciones Unidas en Europa, Oriente Medio y Estados Unidos.

Mustapha Elalaoui

Presidente y Director Ejecutivo, Strategic Communications Group

El Sr. Elalaoui es actualmente Presidente y Director Ejecutivo de *Strategic Communications Group*, establecido en la Ciudad de los Medios de Comunicación de Dubai (*Dubai Media City*) en los Emiratos Árabes Unidos. El Grupo actúa como caja de resonancia de las instituciones del sector público y privado, y como gabinete estratégico para las autoridades decisorias de alto nivel. Antes de desempeñar su cargo actual, fue Director Ejecutivo de *Sunco International Corporation*, empresa establecida en el Estado de Michigan en Estados Unidos y dedicada a las inversiones, el comercio y la promoción del turismo. Ha ocupado varios cargos importantes en la industria de defensa de los Estados Unidos y fue Subsecretario del Ministro de Inversiones Exteriores, Comercio Exterior y Turismo; Presidente y Director Ejecutivo de la *National Coal Trade Company*; Director del Gabinete del Ministro de Energía y Minas, y desempeñó otros cargos gubernamentales importantes. Asimismo, ha trabajado para las Juntas Directivas de la *National Railway Company*, *Royal Air Maroc*, *National Airport Authority*, *National Company for Agadir Bay Development*, *Capital Time Corporation*, *Talkomatic Corporation* y la *Middle East & Mediterranean Tourism and Travel Association*. También ha sido autor de algunas publicaciones sobre turismo, administración pública y buen gobierno en los países en desarrollo.

Mathieu Hoebrigs

Administrador Principal – Turismo, Comisión Europea

Antes de entrar en la Comisión Europea, el Sr. Hoebrigs, jurista y economista de formación, trabajó como investigador y profesor en la Universidad de Nimègue (Nijmegen – Países Bajos). En esta ciudad trabajó como colaborador asociado de un bufete de abogados, consultores especializados en asuntos europeos, y fue asesor de la Asociación Europea de Municipios.

Desde 1983, Mathieu Hoebrigs ha trabajado en la Comisión Europea, sucesivamente, en los siguientes ámbitos:

- El servicio financiero de la Dirección General XXV (Instituciones Financieras y Derecho de las Sociedades).
- La Dirección General IV (Competencia), en la División de Servicios, incluidos servicios financieros.
- La Dirección General XII (Ciencia, Investigación y Desarrollo), primero en la División de Política y Gestión de Contratos, y luego en el marco de la colaboración con países terceros y las organizaciones internacionales; fue miembro del Grupo de Trabajo Peco Copernicus.
- La Dirección General X (Información, Comunicación, Cultura y Sector Audiovisual), encargándose de la gestión del deporte con miras a la creación de la División de Deporte de la Comisión Europea.
- La Dirección General Educación y Cultura, encargándose de representaciones: campañas de información y redes.
- La Dirección General de Prensa y la Dirección de Relaciones Interinstitucionales, Política de Información, Representaciones y Redes (*Team Europe, Groupe Euro, Carrefour, Info. Europe, Urban Forums for Sustainable Development*).
- Por último, la Dirección General de Empresas, en la División de Turismo y Relaciones Exteriores.

Richard Tibbott

Consultor especializado en industria turística

Richard Tibbott ha sido reconocido como una de las principales autoridades del Reino Unido en gestión turística y de destinos. En 1979, cursó el primer Master en Ocio y Turismo del Reino Unido. En mayo de 2002, fue nombrado por sus homólogos "principal profesional del turismo" en un artículo publicado en el *Independent on Sunday*. En la actualidad es Presidente de *Locum Destination Consulting*, que ofrece asesoramiento estratégico, en el terreno y financiero a organizaciones que desarrollan y gestionan destinos. *Locum* proporciona asesoramiento comercial adaptado a las necesidades de destinos culturales, turísticos y de ocio, y a proyectos inmobiliarios y de regeneración.

Richard Tibbott está especializado en ofrecer asesoramiento estratégico sobre economía y turismo para las ciudades, regiones y países, y sobre importantes proyectos para el desarrollo de destinos en el Reino Unido y Europa, inclusive atracciones turísticas, hoteles, centros turísticos, museos y destinos de interés múltiple. Trabajó como asesor en materia de estrategia turística en Polonia durante cinco años, y también para otros ministerios de turismo en países de Europa Central y del Este, cuando se interesaron por la economía de mercado.

Recientemente, el Sr. Tibbott ha desempeñado un papel clave en la definición de la estrategia turística inglesa y británica. Los equipos que trabajan en su proyecto han elaborado estrategias para las regiones inglesa, galesa y escocesa, y para regiones urbanas como Londres, Manchester, Liverpool, Cardiff y Belfast. Tiene una gran experiencia como consultor, que adquirió trabajando como defensor acérrimo de muy diversos intereses comerciales, inclusive para el hotel de lujo Royal Scotsman galardonado con el Premio Queen, *Continental Waterways* –una importante empresa establecida en Francia que promueve hoteles de lujo, y *Windsor Royal Arcade* –fomentando la venta de sus artículos.

Stanislava Nikolova Blagoeva

Presidenta de la Asociación Europea de Ferias de Turismo

La Sra. Blagoeva es actualmente Presidenta de la Asociación Europea de Ferias de Turismo (ETTFA), y Directora de Operaciones de la empresa británica *ITE Group Plc.*, prestigiosa empresa organizadora de exposiciones en los mercados emergentes. Tiene un Master en Lingüística y Psicología, y su carrera profesional empezó en 1984 en la Academia Búlgara de las Ciencias, donde fue Directora de Ventas, Márketing y Exposiciones de la Editorial. En 1994, la Sra. Blagoeva se incorporó al equipo de *ITE Ltd.* con sede en Londres, y ha tomado parte en el lanzamiento y establecimiento de algunas de las ferias comerciales más importantes de Europa Central y del Este, como la Feria Internacional de Turismo de Moscú, el Salón del Automóvil de Moscú, la Feria Internacional de Deportes de Moscú, Feria Internacional de Barcos de Moscú, la Semana Rusa de la Construcción, la Feria Internacional del Petróleo de Moscú, y eventos destacados en Ucrania, Kazajstán, Azerbaiyán, Turquía, Bulgaria y la República Checa. Con frecuencia, asiste en calidad de ponente a conferencias internacionales, y aborda asuntos específicos de la industria turística en los mercados emergentes.

Thomas Steinmetz

Presidente y Editor de eTurbo News

El Sr. Steinmetz es el Presidente y Editor de *eTurbo News*, una innovadora publicación en línea con noticias de turismo, y una de las primeras en imprimir digitalmente y atendiendo las exigencias del cliente. Supervisa todo el proceso, inclusive la publicación, la comercialización, la venta, la difusión y el servicio al cliente de la publicación, que aparece de lunes a viernes, excepto los principales días festivos del Reino Unido. En la actualidad, ofrece *Travel-Telegram* para poner anuncios y *Travel Wire News* para comunicados de prensa. Con 192.000 abonados en todo el mundo, es la publicación de noticias turísticas más importante, lo que el Sr. Steinmetz ha conseguido en menos de tres años. En 2003, *eTurbo News* fue la publicación oficial de la Conferencia Internacional sobre la Paz a través del Turismo, celebrada en Ginebra.

Antes de crear eTurbo News, fue Especialista en Comunicaciones en *Bloody Good Stuff Marketing*, el Representante Turístico en América del Norte para la República de Indonesia, Director Ejecutivo de *Unique Destination Asia* y copropietario de *Horizon Travel* en Alemania, donde se convirtió en una de las primeras y más importantes compañías aéreas fusionadas antes de establecerse en Estados Unidos.

Rafeeuddin Ahmed

Representante Especial de la Organización Mundial del Turismo ante las Naciones Unidas

El Sr. Ahmed es el Representante Especial de la OMT ante las Naciones Unidas en Nueva York, y también Asesor Especial del Director Ejecutivo del Fondo de Desarrollo de las Naciones Unidas para la Mujer (UNIFEM). De febrero a julio de 2000, fue Asesor Especial sobre Irak del Secretario General de las Naciones Unidas. Educado en la Universidad de Punjab en Lahore, (Pakistán) y en la *Fletcher School of Law and Diplomacy* en Estados Unidos, el Sr. Ahmed entró en el Servicio Exterior de Pakistán y desempeñó cargos en Beijing, Cairo, Ottawa, Nueva York e Islamabad. Durante su larga carrera en las Naciones Unidas, el Sr. Ahmed ha sido Secretario del Consejo Económico y Social de las Naciones Unidas; Director del Departamento de Asuntos Económicos y Sociales; Asistente Ejecutivo y Jefe de Gabinete del Secretario General; Subsecretario General de Asuntos Políticos y Descolonización, y Subsecretario General de Asuntos Internacionales Económicos y Sociales, entre otros cargos principales.

Martin Brackenbury

Presidente de la Federación Internacional de Tour Operadores

El Sr. Brackenbury es el Presidente de la Federación Internacional de Tour Operadores (IFTO); Presidente de la Federación de Tour Operadores (Reino Unido); Director de *Classic Collection Holidays* y Profesor Especial en la Universidad de Nottingham. También es socio gestor de *Brankenbury & Partners;* colaborador asociado de la empresa de gestión ambiental *Travelwatch,* y miembro de la *Royal Geographical Society.* El Sr. Brackenbury estudió en la Universidad de Cambridge y, tras ejercer durante un cierto tiempo en los sectores de la industria, los medios de comunicación y bancario, se incorporó a una empresa de gestión comercial, de la que llegó a ser socio principal. En 1980, trabajó como director de *Thompson Holidays* y, en 1989, entró en la Junta Directiva de *Thompson Travel Group,* la principal organización de viajes del Reino Unido. Empresa innovadora y un gigante del turismo emisor, se convirtió en un grupo integrado de agencias de viajes, tour operadores, compañías aéreas, hoteles, cruceros y negociantes en el terreno. El Sr. Brackenbury trabajó para su Junta Directiva hasta que la empresa se cotizó en Bolsa en 1998.

Ese año fue nombrado Presidente de *Panorama Holiday Group,* que posteriormente se vendió a *Airtours Plc,* donde trabajó tres años en calidad de director. Fue Presidente de la empresa de viajes de aventura *Exodus Holiday.* En 1998 se le invitó a que fuera el primer Director del *Christel De Haan Research Institute in Travel & Tourism* en la Universidad de Nottingham, centrado en los efectos económicos del turismo. El Sr. Brackenbury también ha sido Vicepresidente y más tarde Presidente de la Federación de Tour Operadores del Reino Unido. Fue nombrado Presidente de la IFTO en 1990, y ha trabajado seis años en la Junta Directiva de ABTA y ocho años como Presidente de los Miembros Afiliados de la Organización Mundial del Turismo. Ha llevado a cabo misiones en más de 40 países en los últimos 25 años.

Rok V. Klancnik

Jefe del Comité Organizador de TOURCOM

El Sr. Klancnik se incorporó a la Organización Mundial del Turismo como Jefe de Comunicaciones en junio de 2002, y se ha encargado y encarga de lanzar campañas de comunicaciones para la 15ª Asamblea General de la OMT en Beijing, del proyecto "El turismo es riqueza" y de la transformación de la OMT en organismo especializado de las Naciones Unidas. También ha preparado la tercera edición del manual "Shining in the Media Spotlight" y ha participado como Jefe y supervisor de la Conferencia TOURCOM.

El Sr. Klancnik es esloveno y colaboró con la Junta de Turismo de Eslovenia tras su creación en 1996. Como Director de Comunicaciones en la Junta, lanzó campañas de comunicaciones para representaciones de ferias comerciales y en importantes eventos internacionales como la Expo 1998 de Lisboa, los Juegos Olímpicos de Sydney, la Copa Mundial en Corea del Sur y la primera Cumbre entre el Presidente estadounidense, George Bush, y el Presidente ruso, Vladimir Putin, en Eslovenia. Como orador y organizador, participó en conferencias y eventos promocionales en unos 40 países de Europa, Oriente Medio, Asia y Australia.

El Sr. Klancnik es licenciado en Ciencias Políticas y Relaciones Internacionales, y trabajó como periodista para el diario "Delo" y para la Agencia Eslovena de Prensa. Se especializó en periodismo y comunicaciones en la Universidad de Tennessee y ha tomado parte en numerosos seminarios y cursos sobre comunicaciones, periodismo, gestión y márketing en Eslovenia, así como en instituciones internacionales como el Consejo de Europa. En el ejercicio de sus funciones como periodista, es Editor Jefe de "Noticias de la OMT" y publica regularmente artículos sobre temas relativos al turismo internacional, las relaciones públicas, el márketing y las marcas.

BIOS

(in order of the TOURCOM programme)

Francesco Frangialli

Secretary-General, World Tourism Organization

Born in Paris, Mr. Frangialli is a graduate of the Paris Institute of Political Studies, has a degree in Economics and postgraduate degrees in Economics and Public Law. He has also studied at France's National School of Administration and the Naval Supply Service School. His professional career has included stints as a supply officer aboard the French Navy escort ship "Dupetit-Thouars", as a junior court magistrate and as a lecturer at both the Paris Institute of Political Studies and the International Institute of Public Administration.

Mr. Frangialli's first post in the tourism sector was as a technical advisor with the Office of the Minister for Youth, Sports and Leisure and in 1980 he was named to advise France's Tourism Governing Board before being appointed a year later to the National Tourism Board. Other highlights of his tourism career include his role as Director of Tourism Industry within the Ministry of Tourism, member of the boards of Air France, the Public Administration of Marne la Vallée, the National Agency for Holiday Vouchers and ACTIM. In 1990, Mr. Frangialli was named World Tourism Organization Deputy Secretary-General and in 1997 was elected Secretary-General for the period 1998-2001. At the end of that term, he was re-elected for the 2002-2005 period. His books and publications include "La France dans le tourisme mondial (1991, Economica), "Tourisme et loisirs-Une question sociale" (co-author,1997, Bayard) "Observations on International Tourism (1999 and 2001, the World Tourism Organization) and International Tourism: The Great Turning Point, Texts and documents 2001 - 2003 (2004, World Tourism Organization).

Mr. Frangialli's decorations and awards include France's Chevalier des Palmes académiqies, National Order of Merit and Knight of the Legion of Merit, and decorations bestowed by the Republic of San Marino, the Togolese Republic and the Palestinian Authority.

Debbie Hindle

Managing Director

Debbie Hindle helped to found BGB & associates in 1991 and has more than 13 years' experience in leisure and travel. She has managed and directed public relations campaigns for organisations such as tourist boards, hotels, travel agents, tour operators, GDS, attractions, UK holidays, airlines, the cruise industry and ferries. Debbie has also led political lobbying and research-led campaigns. Debbie represented Lunn Poly for many years and now heads up teams for clients including Passenger Shipping Association and The Caribbean Tourism Organisation. Debbie previously set up a regional business magazine in the Midlands and worked for McCann Erikson PR handling accounts including fitness equipment, soft drinks, insurance and a range of companies in the building, construction and property industry. BGB & associates is now the UK's leading travel and lifestyle public relations company with clients ranging from the Australian Tourist Commission to Travelbag.

Becky Anderson

Anchor, Business International, CNN

Becky Anderson has anchored CNN's twice-daily international business programme "Business International" since its launch in February 2001. As anchor of this pacy and fast moving programme, Anderson taps into the key junctures of the global market day, from Asia, Europe and the USA, assessing the impact of the markets and business news on Europe. Throughout the programme, she links up with CNN reporters around the world for the latest developments and news breaking in the business world.

Since the launch of "Business International," Anderson has interviewed a wide range of top names from the world of finance, politics and industry. These have included the UK Chancellor of the Exchequer, Gordon Brown MP, the Governor of the Bank of France, Jean-Claude Trichet, BP Amoco s CEO, Sir John Browne and Ali Rodriguez, the Secretary General of OPEC. Anderson also presents for CNN's sailing programme, "Inside Sailing," a monthly look at news and events in the world of yachting.

Anderson joined CNN in May 1999 as the launch anchor for CNN's breakfast business show "World Business This Morning," a key step in the inception of CNN's ongoing regionalisation strategy to bring locally-produced programming to the European market place. She was part of the first phase of live morning programming to come out of CNN's London production centre.

Since joining CNN, Anderson has carried out live remote anchoring for numerous high profile foreign assignments and has interviewed a number of high profile business people at events such as the CeBIT Technology Fair 2000 and 2001, Fortune Global Forum and Telecom 1999.

Anderson has extensive business journalism experience including posts with the UK's Channel 5, CNBC Europe and Bloomberg. She began her career in journalism as a print reporter with various business publications in Arizona after gaining a Master of Mass Communication from the Walter Cronkite School of Journalism at Arizona State University in 1992.

Anderson is British and lives in London. She has a BA (Hons) degree in Economics and French from Sussex University.

Thierry Baudier

Director-General of Maison de la France

Following many years of involvement in government and tourism, Mr. Baudier was appointed director-general of the French Tourism Office, Maison de la France, last May. He replaced Jean Philippe Pérol, who had occupied the post since 1999 and who is now the director of Maison de la France's operations in the Americas.

Mr. Baudier holds degrees in law and sociology and is a former scholar at the Institut des Hautes Etudes de Défense Nationale. He joined the Groupement d'intérêt economique (GIE) Maison de la France in 1997 as Director of Foreign Markets, then served as Director of Marketing and Partnerships and was in charge of marketing and communications between the head office and the organization's branches until his recent appointment as director-general.

Between 1995 and 1997, Mr. Baudier worked as a parliamentary attaché for the Prime Minister and before that he had worked as a special assistant to the president of a political group in France's National Assembly. He began his professional career at the Compagnie Générale du Bâtiment where between 1989 and 1993 he was involved in hotel construction in Central and Eastern Europe, among other projects.

Marc Meister

President and Managing Director, Sergat Spain

Mr. Meister is the Founder, President and Managing Director of Sergat España S.L., the premier communications and marketing agency in Spain specialized in tourism and the hotel and aviation industries. His educational accomplishments include a Master's Degree in Marketing Sciences, a Hotel Management Diploma from Lucerne and a diploma in Communications and Information Studies from the Drexler Institute.

A founding member of the Spain chapter of PATA and Visit US, Mr. Meister has also held senior marketing management positions in Switzerland, the United States and Spain with major tour operating and hotel companies. He speaks Spanish, German, French and English and is a licensed private pilot.

Javier Piñanes

Director of Turespaña

Javier Piñanes holds a law degree from the Universidad Autónoma de Madrid and a doctorate in law from the Universidad Complutense de Madrid. He is a member of the Corps of Senior Civil State Administrators.

He has occupied various government posts including functions in the Ministries of Industry and Energy and Transport, Tourism and Communications, and served as Deputy General Director for Research at the Technical General Secretariat of the Ministry of Justice and the Interior.

In the area of tourism administration, he has served as deputy director of the Spanish tourism office in Frankfurt and director of the Spanish tourism office in Berlin. He was also Deputy General Director for Promotion at the Spanish Institute of Tourism (Turespaña). He was named Director of Turespaña last March.

Christopher Brown

Managing Director & CEO, Tourism Task Force

Mr. Brown is the Managing Director & CEO of Australia's national lobby group, TTF. A private, non-partisan organization, TTF comprises the CEO's of the 200 major institutions involved in the tourism, transport, leisure and infrastructure sectors. TTF provides influence over the political and investment environment affecting Australia's largest industry sector. Before taking up the TTF post in 1992, Mr. Brown was Managing Director of JMA Public Affairs, he worked as a Political Advisor to Members of Parliament and trained with Ogilvy & Mather Advertising. He also studied Economics and Law at Sydney University.

A self-proclaimed "sports nut", Mr. Brown was involved in the bid and industry liaison for the Sydney 2000 Olympic Games. He served as National Ambassador for the Sydney 2000 Paralympics and was Honorary Olympic Attaché for Botswana at the 2000 Olympic Games. For the past ten years, Mr. Brown has been the Executive Director of the Sport & Tourism Youth Scholarship Foundation.

Along with his activities at TTF, Mr. Brown is Chairman of Authentic Outback Experiences Pty Ltd, a joint venture company of bush outfitter RM Williams and pastoral company AACo, to develop Outback safari bush camps. He also sits on the Board of Best Western Australia. He is also Director of See Australia Ltd, the government and private sector domestic tourism initiative.

Mr. Brown is the conveyor of the Rugby Tourism Advisory Group and the National Tourism & Wine Export Forum and is a Member of the Commonwealth Tourism Forecasting Council, the Indigenous Tourism Leadership Group, the Prime Minister's Gold Medal Disability Access Strategy Group and the Tourism Export Roundtable.

He is currently a Vice-President of the UN-affiliated World Tourism Organization Business Council and the regional representative for the prestigious World Travel & Tourism Council.

Thomas J. Wallace

Editor-in-chief, Condé Nast Traveler

Mr. Wallace became editor-in-chief of the prestigious U.S. travel magazine in 1990. Since its launch, "Condé Nast Traveler" has been distinguished by its award-winning journalism and been nominated for 16 National Magazine Awards, six of which were in the General Excellence category. It has won five awards: in 1998 and 1999 for Special Interest; in 1991, one for Design and one for General Excellence; and in 1999 for General Excellence. Among travel publications, "Condé Nast Traveler" is the only one to win a National Magazine Award.

It is also the only travel publication, and the only magazine in the Condé Nast group, to have a regular television series, "Condé Nast Traveler: Insider's Guide", a 26-episode series for U.S. public television that was launched in October, 2002, to coincide with the magazine's 15th anniversary.

During Mr. Wallace's time at the helm of the publication, it was the first Condé Nast magazine to go online, in June, 1995, with an ambitious website, heralding the beginning of another type of interactive relationship. It is now known as concierge.com. He has been a staunch proponent of environmentally responsible travel and in 1990 the magazine founded an annual Environmental Award to honor independent crusaders. Mr. Wallace took the idea a step further with the creation of an Ecotourism Award which recognizes innovative efforts of the travel industry.

Before joining Condé Nast, Mr. Wallace held senior positions at top U.S. newspapers, including "The New York Times", "Newsday" and the "Stamford Advocate" where as city editor he supervised an investigative series which won a Pulitzer Prize in 1979. He is a graduate of Harvard University.

Gary Wardrope

Commercial Director, Travel Channel

Mr. Wardrope is responsible for worldwide advertising and sponsorship for the Travel Channel and involved in the global expansion of the channel into the Middle East and other regions. He is also currently looking at the launch of travel agency services in Scandinavia and South Africa.

A one-time competitive skier, Mr. Wardrope worked as a ski instructor and resort manager during the 1980s in his native Canada, France, Switzerland and Austria, after which he was chief of sales and marketing at Neilson Ski. In the 1990s, he headed up Airtours Specialist Products Division responsible for a 250 million pound sterling division which included four cruise ships, a youth program called Escapades and skiing, all of which were start ups.

In 2000, Mr. Wardrope started as Commercial Director at the Travel Channel where he oversaw the establishment of Travel Deals Direct, an 18-hour-per-day virtual television travel agency which is received in 8 million homes and carries over 30,000 people year in the United Kingdom. He was also responsible for launching the first broadband video on demand services with BT.

Geoffrey Lipman

Special Advisor to the Secretary-General of the World Tourism Organization for Trade, Liberalization with a Human Face and the ST-EP initiative.

Mr. Lipman is the Chairman of Green Globe 21, the worldwide sustainable tourism certification organization and GTREX, a fourth-generation Internet development company. He is also a Member of the Board of the Great Canadian Railway Company and AIA Communications. Between 1990 and 1999, Mr. Lipman served as President of the World Travel & Tourism Council and oversaw the organization's growth from ten to 100 members and the positioning of travel and tourism as the world's largest and leading growth industry.

For 20 years, Mr. Lipman worked at the International Air Transport Association (IATA) as Chief of Staff and Head of Government Affairs before being named as Executive Director of IFAPA, a foundation representing the interests of airline passengers. He was also a partner in Global Aviation Associates, a strategic airline consultancy specializing in regulatory and competition issues.

Mr. Lipman has written and lectured around the world on tourism strategy and airline liberalization. He was a member of the European Union High Level Commissions on Airline Liberalization and on Tourism Employment, the UK Roundtable on Sustainable Development and the Advisory Board of Royal Jordanian Airlines. He is currently a Fellow of the Tourism Society and the Australian Tourism Research Association, the "Goodwill Ambassador" for the Indian Ocean Tourism Organization and Member of the Business Advisory Council to the President of Zambia.

Prof. Donald E. Hawkins

Eisenhower Professor of Tourism Policy, George Washington University

Along with his research and teaching activities, Dr. Hawkins facilitates active collaboration between the tourism industry and international institutions such as the United Nations, the World Bank, the Inter-American Development Bank and the World Tourism Organization. His work with the WTO has included teaching at the organization's CICATUR in Mexico City, serving on the U.S. delegation to the WTO General Assemblies in Rome and New Delhi, conducting early research on TEDQUAL and numerous speaking engagements and service on key WTO committees. In 2003, Dr. Hawkins received the first WTO Ulysses Prize for individual accomplishment in research and dissemination of knowledge in the area of tourism policy and management.

His academic achievements include teaching the first course offered by George Washington University in 1970. The university was one of the first in the world to offer a master's degree in Tourism Administration and graduated its first students in 1974. The degree is an internationally-oriented program focused on the professional and research aspects of the tourism and hospitality field.

Until 1999, Dr. Hawkins served as the Director of the International Institute of Tourism Studies which was initiated in 1988 as the first education center established in collaboration with the World Tourism Organization. He was appointed as the Dwight D. Eisenhower Professor of Tourism Policy, an endowed chair, in 1994.

Dr. Hawkins has also authored or edited around 100 publications on contemporary aspects of tourism policy and strategy, and worked as a consultant on tourism projects and studies in countries around the world including Honduras, Jordan, Egypt, Bermuda, St. Kitts and Nevis and Palestine. More recently, he has been involved in a United Nations-funded study of the strategic relationship of tourism development to biodiversity conservation and the sustainable use of energy and water resources.

Mariano López

Dean, Chamber of Journalists and Communicators in Tourism

Mr. Lopez heads the Cámara de Periodistas y Comunicadores de Turismo, a professional association that brings together managers of travel media and communications directors of tourism enterprises. He is also the director of "Viajar", a publication of the Grupo Zeta media group, which recently celebrated the 25th anniversary of its launch as the first Spanish-produced travel magazine.

Richard D. Lewis

Chairman of Richard Lewis Communications plc

Mr. Lewis, who speaks ten European and two Asian languages, is chairman of Richard Lewis Communications plc, an international institute of language and cross-cultural training with offices in over a dozen countries. He founded the quarterly magazine "Cross Culture" in 1989 and his book "When Cultures Collide" is regarded as the classic work on intercultural issues. It was the main spring selection of the U.S. Book of the Month Club in 1997.

Active in the fields of applied and anthropological linguistics for more than 35 years, Mr. Lewis has worked as a broadcast journalist in Germany, where he was also a scriptwriter for Dr. Konrad Adenauer, and in 1961 pioneered the world's first English by television series in Finland. He was also a scriptwriter for the BBC series "Walter and Connie" in 1962.

He has lived and worked in a number of European countries where his clients included ABB, Allianz, Banco de España, Banque de France, Deutsche Bank, Ericsson, Fiat, Gillette, IBM, Mercedes Benz, Nestlé, Nokia, Saab and Volvo. During five years spent in Japan, Mr. Lewis was a tutor to Empress Michiko and other members of the Japanese Imperial Family. He also worked with such companies as Nomura, Mitsubishi, Hitachi, Sanyo, Mitsui and Nippon Steel. More recently, he has been heavily involved in the intercultural field, founding companies in France, Germany, Spain, Italy and Brazil, teaching communication skills in these countries as well as Finland, Sweden, the United Kingdom and the United States.

Mr. Lewis was chosen as the Personality of the Year 1999 by the Pacific Asia Travel Association for his "dedicated and extraordinary work carried out in the area of cross-cultural communication, having clear understanding and sensitivity for the cultures of in the Asia-Pacific region". He was knighted by Finnish President Ahtisaari in 1997 in recognition of his services in the cross-cultural field related to training programs for Finnish ministries ahead of the country's European Union membership.

Rolf Jensen

Chief Imagination Officer, Dream Company Ltd

Mr. Jensen, a Danish futurist and author, is the Chief Imagination Officer at Dream Company Ltd which he founded in 2001 and which aims to inspire the majority of leading global companies to interpret present and future challenges at the transformation from one societal type to another, providing these businesses with the tools to deal with profound change.

In 1999, Mr. Jensen published his book "The Dream Society: From Information to Imagination", first in the United States and then in Denmark. It became a best-seller and has since been translated into six other languages. A dedicated traveller, he is a Fellow of the Royal Geographic Society in London. One of his most inspiring journeys was a trip deep into the heart of Borneo where he had a first-hand look at one society's transition from hunter-gatherers to agriculture.

Mr. Jensen obtained a master's degree in political science from the University of Aarhus in 1970 and then entered government service to work for the Danish Ministries of Defense and Fisheries and the Foreign Office. In 1983, he joined the Copenhagen Institute for Future Studies, or CISF, of which he became director five years later.

Scott Wayne

Principal, SW Associates

As Principal of SW Associates, Mr. Wayne has managed and participated in a broad range of tourism development programs and projects. These include economic development through tourism, investment promotion, communications and organizational strategy, issues management, coalition building and international relations. His most recent consulting experience includes a multi-country tourism competitiveness study for the World Bank, a hotel classification and quality standards system for the Government of Bahrain, cruise industry environmental strategy for Conservation International, a tourism infrastructure pre-feasibility study in Morocco and a rapid assessment of tourism investment conditions in Croatia.

Other relevant experience includes the establishment of a tourism investment association, establishment of national and provincial-level tourism organizations and product development and communications strategy. Mr. Wayne is also an Adjunct Professor of Tourism Planning at George Washington University.

Through SW Associates, he directed the World Travel & Tourism Council's North American office in Washington, D.C. and managed projects and programs for them with multilateral financial institutions and several national and state governments. During his career, Mr. Wayne was also the Vice President for International Development of an Internet start up company, Vivid Travel Network, a subsidiary of the world-renowned web development firm, Vivid Studios.

He also served as Chief of Communications for the World Tourism Organization and was responsible for advising the Secretary-General on strategic communications issues, developing alliances with governmental and non-governmental constituencies and developing the organization's publishing, media and public relations programs.

Mr. Wayne authored seven travel books for Sierra Club books and Lonely Planet covering Egypt and Sudan, the countries of the Maghreb (Algeria, Morocco and Tunisia) and Mexico and the State of Baja California, as well as numerous articles for newspapers and magazines.

Dawid de Villiers

Deputy Secretary-General, World Tourism Organization

Mr. De Villiers was named Deputy Secretary-General of the WTO in 1998 after serving as the South African Minister of Environmental Affairs and Tourism under President Nelson Mandela. He has undergraduate degrees in psychology, philosophy and, theology from the University of Stellenbosch, a master's degree in philosophy from Rand Afrikaans University and a doctorate in philosophy from the University of Stellenbosch.

His work experience has included university lectureships in philosophy, a ministry in the Dutch Reformed Church, a member of parliament and South African Ambassador to London. On his return to South Africa, Mr. De Villiers was appointed Minister of Trade, Industries and Tourism, a post he held for six years, and then became Minister of Budget and Welfare, Minister for Administration and Privatisation and Minister of Mineral and Energy Affairs and Public Enterprises.

In 1991, Mr. De Villiers became deeply involved in the negotiating process which led to a new constitution and the first democratic elections in South Africa and in 1994, he was the Chairman of the Transitional Executive Council that guided and oversaw the process of government during the country's political transition to majority rule.

Mr. De Villiers has served as the Governor of the Development Bank of South Africa and on the Boards of such public companies as Bank of Johannesburg, Santam Bank, Triomf Fertiliser and Landbou-Chemiese Beleggings (Agro-Chemical Investments). A keen sportsman, Mr. De Villiers represented South Africa in rugby-football in international matches against England, Ireland, Wales, Australia, New Zealand, France and Argentina. He captained the South African team in a record 23 matches.

Diego Cordovez

Candidate for the first Chairman of the World Committee on Ethics in Tourism

Mr. Cordovez is the president of the Centro Andino de Estudios Internacionales of the Universidad Andina Simón Bolivar in Quito, Ecuador, a post he took up after working for the United Nations for 25 years. He initially served in the organization's economic sector before becoming involved in political work. Mr. Cordovez' early appointments in the United Nations included Director of the Secretariat of the Economic and Social Council and Assistant Secretary-General for Secretariat Services for Economic and Social Affairs. He was the principal adviser of a special commission in charge of restructuring the entire United Nations system for development and served as the Secretary of the Economic and Financial Committee of the General Assembly during eight sessions. In 1972 and 1992, Mr. Cordovez was Special Adviser of the Secretary-General for United Nations conferences on the environment. In 1981, he was designated Under Secretary-General for Special Political Affairs and as mediator in the Afghan conflict, he negotiated the Geneva Accords under which the Soviet Union withdrew its troops from Afghanistan. Mr. Cordovez was nominated for the 1988 Nobel Peace Prize and that year it was awarded to the United Nations. He carried out special missions in Korea, the Dominican Republic, Grenada, Iran, Iraq and Pakistan and was the principal advisor of Olof Palme, the United Nations mediator in the Iran-Iraq war. Mr. Cordovez was named as Ecuadorean Foreign Minister in 1988 and four years later he joined the New York-based international law firm of LeBoeuf, Lamb, Greene and MacRae. In 1992 he was Diplomat-in-Residence at Colombia University's School of International and Public Affairs and was a vice-presidential candidate in the 1996 Ecuadorean elections. He was graduated from the Faculty of Social and Juridicial Sciences of the Universidad de Chile and took his oath as a lawyer before the Supreme Court. Mr. Cordovez has authored a memoir on the Afghan war, "Out of Afghanistan", and another on the territorial dispute between Ecudor and Peru, as well as number of essays and press articles.

Hon. Anil Kumarsingh Gayan

Minister of Tourism and Leisure, Mauritius

Hon. Anil Kumarsingh GAYAN, M.P. was sworn in as Minister of Foreign Affairs and Regional Cooperation on 16 September, 2000. He had occupied the same post between 1983 and 1986 when the Ministry was styled Ministry of External Affairs, Tourism and Emigration. Hon. Anil Kumarsingh GAYAN, M.P. has been appointed as Minister of Tourism & Leisure with effect from 23 December 2003. Born in Port Louis on the 22nd October 1948, Hon. Gayan attended primary school in Triolet, the village of his childhood, and in Port Louis. He completed his secondary school at the Royal College of Port Louis as a Laureate in 1968. He read law at the London School of Economics from 1969 to 1972 and was called to the Bar at the Inner Temple, London in 1972. He earned his Master's degree at the University of London in 1973 specialising in International Law and the Law of the Sea. After a brief period of private practice, he joined the Attorney General's Office as Crown Counsel in 1974. Between 1974 and 1982 he held special responsibility for the United Nations Conference on the Law of the Sea and as delegate of Mauritius, he participated in all its sessions and other related conferences around the world. He signed the Convention on the Law of the Sea in Montego Bay in 1982. In 1982, Hon. Gayan resumed private practice and entered politics. He was elected to Parliament and to the Municipal Council of Curepipe. In 1983, he was re-elected to Parliament and became Minister of External Affairs, Tourism and Emigration. In the same year he became Chairman of the Council of the University of Mauritius. In 1986, he resumed practice at the Bar. He served as Chairman of the Bar Council in 1989-90. In 1995 he was appointed Senior Counsel. Hon. Gayan has been a consultant to the Geneva-Based Centre for Human Rights and has done consultancy work in Bhutan, Mongolia, Armenia and Togo. He has been Chairperson of the Council of the University of Mauritius in the mid 1980s.

Jonathan B. Tourtellot

Director of Sustainable Tourism, National Geographic Society and Geotourism Editor, National Geographic Traveler magazine

As Director for Sustainable Tourism at the National Geographic Society and Geotourism Editor for "National Geographic Traveler", Mr. Tourtellot writes the magazine's "TravelWatch" column on destination stewardship and develops and edits feature articles on tourism issues. He is currently working on the National Geographic Destination Outlook Survey on the sustainability of well-known tourist destinations, a book on geotourism and the ongoing development of the National Geographic Society's sustainable tourism program which includes participation in the Mundo Maya Sustainable Tourism Alliance, the World Tourism Forum for Peace and Sustainable development and the inauguration of a World Heritage Site conservation initiative. Mr. Tourtellot joined the staff of the National Geographic Society in 1979 and was promoted to senior editor a year later. In 2001, he became the Society's first Director of Sustainable Tourism. He originated the concept and the term "geotourism" which is defined as "tourism that sustains or enhances the geographical character of a place - its environment, culture, aesthetics, heritage and the well-being of its residents." Mr. Tourtellot co-developed the research bearing the first published use of that term, the Geotourism Study, and the first major survey of U.S. traveller behavior and attitudes about sustainability and destination stewardship conducted by the Travel Association of America from 2001 to 2003. He also co-developed the new World Legacy Awards for sustainable tourism - in Nature Travel, Heritage Tourism, Hotels/Resorts and Destination Stewardship - first presented by Queen Noor of Jordan on behalf of "National Geographic Traveler" and Conservation International in January 2003.

Deborah Luhrman

WTO Communications Consultant

Ms. Luhrman was the Chief of Communications of the World Tourism Organization until 2001 with responsibility for media relations, the WTO News, trade fairs and the WTO website. She continues to collaborate with the organization in projects related to communications and crisis management, and she is a member of the WTO's Crisis Action Team. Ms. Luhrman is a life-long journalist from the United States and worked as a television news reporter in California where she won an Emmy Award. After moving to Spain in 1989, she worked as an editor at the Spanish news agency EFE and as a producer for the German television network ZDF. Ms. Luhrman covered the Spanish tourism sector for a number of trade publications, among them "Travel Trade Gazette" and "Hotel & Motel Management", coauthored several of Fodor's travel guide books, including those on Spain, France and Portugal. Ms. Luhrman has also helped produce television broadcasts of four sessions of the Summer Olympic Games in Los Angeles (1984), Barcelona (1992), Atlanta (1996) and Sydney (2000).

Dexter Koehl

Vice President, Public Relations and Communications, TIA

Since his appointment as Vice President, Public Relations and Communications for the Travel Industry Association of America (TIA) in March 1992, Mr. Koehl has been responsible for communications to the TIA's 2,100 member organizations and to the domestic and international media in support of the Association's mission to promote and facilitate increased travel to and within the United States. He also provides communications support in raising awareness of the economic, social and cultural impact of travel and tourism on the nation, and is in charge of managing content of the TIA website.

Mr. Koehl has an extensive background in public relations, communications, marketing and development in the travel industry. Prior to joining TIA, he was Director of Public Relations for Carlson Travel Group in Minneapolis from 1986 to 1992, responsible for all public relations activities of the then $7 billion worldwide retail travel agency. Mr. Koehl also served as Vice President Marketing and Development for Hershey Entertainment and Resort Company, Director of Market Development for Sea Pines Company, Director of Resort Marketing for the Palmas del Mar resort in Puerto Rico and Corporate Manager of Passenger Market Plans at American Airlines.

He graduated from the University of California, Berkeley with a B.A. in Far Eastern Studies. Following the study of Japanese at the Defense Language Institute in Monterey, California, Mr. Koehl worked for two years as a Japanese translator at the National Security Agency.

Sandra Lee

Permanent Secretary for Economic Development and Labour of the Government of the Hong Kong Special Administrative Region

Ms. Lee was appointed Permanent Secretary for Economic Development and Labour in 2002 and her policy portfolio covers air services, port and maritime services, logistics development, tourism, energy, postal services, meteorological services, competition policy and consumer protection. Since joining the Hong Kong Government in 1974 as an executive officer, Ms. Lee has worked in a number of government policy and resource departments in Hong Kong and overseas, including the Hong Kong Economic and Trade Office in Washington, D.C. as Counsellor from 1985 to 1988 and from 1993 to 1995. She was Deputy Director of Home Affairs from 1995 to 1996, Deputy Secretary for the Civil Service from 1996 to 1999, Director-General of the Hong Kong Economic and Trade Office in London from 1999 to 2000, and Secretary for Economic Services from 2000 to 2002.

Dr. Osmane Aïdi

President, International Hotels & Restaurants Association

Dr. Aïdi is President of the International Hotels & Restaurants Association to which he was re-elected in 2000, the only president to be given a second mandate in the history of the Association since its founding in 1947. He is also President of Irrifrance, a leading European manufacturer of irrigation equipment. In a long and distinguished career in government and the private sector, Mr. Aidi has served on a number of Syrian government committees on irrigation and energy, been involved in banking and publishing and heads a foundation in his name devoted to the preservation of Syria's rich cultural heritage.

For many years, he has served on the Boards of several companies operating in the hospitality and tourism industries in Europe, the United States and the Middle East, and was President of the Inter-Arab Union for Hotels and Tourism and President of the Euro-Mediterranean Tourism Organization. Mr. Aidi has won various awards for achievement from the French, Bulgarian and Lebanese governments, among other citations and decorations.

Steve Dunne

Executive Director, Brighter Group

Mr. Dunne is an Executive Director of the Brighter Group and Managing Director of its subsidiary, Brighter PR which is the fastest growing travel pubic relations company in the United Kingdom. A public relations professional with over 20 years experience in the corporate communications field, he has worked in a variety of senior management posts within leading blue-chip companies. Mr. Dunne was head of public relations at British Telecom during the "Big Bang" deregulation of the United Kingdom financial market in 1987 and led British Telecom's public relations campaign during the industrial strife of the late 1980s. In 1990, he was one of a team of public relations professionals brought together to successfully combat Midland Bank's then reputation as the most disliked bank in Britain.

In the mid-1990s, Mr. Dunne was Head of Corporate Communications (Europe) for South African Airways and oversaw the huge interest in the airline and worked closely with the South African Government to promote the country across Europe. He became Managing Director of Affinity Consulting, one of Britain's leading travel and tourism public relations agencies , in 1997 and managed the agency's merger with Countrywide Porter Novelli, the fourth largest public relations agency in Britain, in 2000. As a director of Countrywide, Mr. Dunne headed up the award-winning Consumer Division. He joined the Board of Brighter Group in 2002.

Christian Nielsen

Editor and author, European Service Network

Mr. Nielsen has wide academic and commercial experience in tourism and the media and has published a book and a number of articles on the subject. He received an undergraduate degree in tourism management from Victoria University in Melbourne, Australia, which led to an MBA specializing in tourism and industrial locations and development from Free University Brussels. While working as an associate professor in a Belgian university, Mr. Nielsen published several articles on tourism and urban development. With a journalism diploma under his belt, he pursued a career in the field which included a stint as copy editor for the Wall Street Journal Europe.

In 2001, Mr. Nielsen took up a position as an editor at European Service Network which produces a variety of magazines and publications for the European Commission in Brussels. He has also written for Europemedia.net and for various web publications on a range of topics including tourism, information technology and research in the European Union. Last year, he completed a masters in international politics and has plans for a new book expanding on the theme of tourism communication.

William J. Gaillard

Director for Corporate Communications, IATA

Mr. Gaillard has been Director for Corporate Communications at the International Air Transport Association since 1994. A political scientist by training, he was born in Paris in 1950 and was educated in France (Institut d'Etudes Politiques, Paris) , Italy, Switzerland and the United States (Harvard University), where he began his career as a university professor. Before joining IATA, Mr. Gaillard spent 16 years in external relations and public information management positions for the European Commission and the United Nations in Europe, the Middle East and the United States.

Mustapha Elalaoui

President and CEO, Strategic Communications Group

Mr. Elalaoui is President and CEO of the Strategic Communications Group which is based at Dubai Media City in the United Arab Emirates. The group acts as a sounding board for private and public sector institutions, and plays the role of a think tank for high-level policy makers. Prior to his current position, he was CEO of Sunco International Corporation based in the U.S. state of Michigan and which deals with investments, trade and tourism promotion.

He has held several senior posts in the U.S defense industry and was Undersecretary to the Ministry of Foreign Investments, Foreign Trade and Tourism, President and CEO of the National Coal Trade Company, Director of the Cabinet for the Minister of Energy and Mines and several other senior government positions. Mr. Elalaoui has also served on the Boards of Directors of National Railway Company, Royal Air Maroc, National Airport Authority, National Company for Agadir Bay Development, Capital Time Corporation, Talkomatic Corporation and the Middle East & Mediterranean Tourism and Travel Association. He has also authored several publications on tourism, public administration and governance in developing countries.

Mathieu Hoebrigs

Principal Administrator - Tourism, European Commission

With degrees in law and economics, Mathieu Hoeberigs was a research fellow and course director at the University of Nijmegen (Netherlands) before joining the European Commission.

At Nijmegen, he was also a partner at a law firm providing consultancy in European affairs, and a councillor in the European Association of Municipalities.

Since 1983, Mathieu Hoeberigs has been working in the European Commission, where he has occupied posts in various areas:

- The finance service at the Directorate-General XV (Financial Institutions and Company Law).
- Directorate-General IV (Competition), services unit, including financial services.
- Directorate-General XII (Science, Research & Development), initially in the contract policy and management, then in the area of collaboration with third parties and international organizations, members of the Peco/Copernicus Task Force.
- Directorate-General X (Audiovisual Media, Information, Communication and Culture), management of the sports sector, leading to the creation of the Sports Unit in the European Commission.
- The Directorate-General for Education and Culture, Representations: Information Campaigns, Relays and Networks The Directorate-General Press and Communication, Interinstitutional Relations, Information Policy, Representations, Relays and Networks (Team Europe, Euro Group, Carrefour, Info. Europe, Urban Forums for sustainable development).
- And finally, Directorate-General Enterprise, Tourism Unit, external relations.

Richard Tibbott

Chairman, Locum Destination Consulting

Richard Tibbott is recognised as one of the UK's foremost authorities on tourism and destination management. Richard Tibbott obtained the first post-graduate Masters degree in Leisure & Tourism in the UK in 1970. In May 2002, he was named as the UK's leading tourism professional by his peers in a feature published by the Independent on Sunday. He is the Chairman of Locum Destination Consulting, which delivers strategic, operational and financial advice to organisations that develop and manage destinations. Locum provide business consulting tailored to the needs of cultural, heritage, tourism, and leisure destinations and property & real estate and regeneration projects.

Richard Tibbott specialises in delivering strategic economic and tourism advice for cities, regions and countries and in advising major destination development projects in the UK and Europe including attractions, hotels, resorts, museums and mixed-use destinations. Richard Tibbott advised on Poland's tourism strategy over a 5-year period and several other tourism ministries in Central & Eastern European states, as they emerged into the market economy.

Recently, Richard Tibbott has had a key role in defining the English and British Tourism strategy. His project teams have undertaken tourism strategies for English, Welsh and Scottish Regions, and for city regions such as London, Manchester, Liverpool, Cardiff, and Belfast.

Richard's consulting activity is informed by a wealth of experience gained as the highly successful operator of a broad portfolio of entrepreneurial interests, including the Queen's Award-winning Royal Scotsman luxury hotel train, Continental Waterways - a leading luxury hotel barge company in France, and the Windsor Royal Arcade specialty shopping development.

Stanislava Nikolova Blagoeva

President of the European Travel Trade Fairs Association

Ms. Blagoeva is President of the European Travel Trade Fairs Association and Operations Director of the British-owned company, ITE Group Plc, the renowned exhibition organizer in emerging markets. She holds an MA in Linguistics and Psychology and her professional career began in 1984 at the Bulgarian Academy of Sciences where she was Sales, Marketing and Exhibitions Director of the Publishing House. In 1994, Ms. Blagoeva joined the team of ITE Ltd at their headquarters in London and has taken part in launching and establishing some of today's largest trade fairs in Central and Eastern Europe such as the Moscow International Travel and Tourism Exhibition, the Moscow International Motor Show, the Moscow International Sports Show/ Moscow International Boats Show, Russia Building Week, the Moscow International Oil and Gas Exhibition as well as leading events in Ukraine, Kazakhstan, Azerbaijan, Turkey, Bulgaria and the Czech Republic. She is a frequent guest speaker at international conferences, discussing issues and specifics of the exhibition industry in emerging markets.

Thomas Steinmetz

Chairman and Publisher, eTurbo News

Mr. Steinmetz is the Chairman and Publisher of eTurbo News, an innovative online travel trade news publication and one of the first to print digitally and to customer demand. He oversees the entire operation, including editorial, marketing and sales, circulation and customer service for the publication that appears Monday through Friday except major U.S. holidays. eTurbo News currently offers Travel-Telegram for advertising messages and Travel Wire News for press releases. With 192,000 subscribers worldwide, eTurbo News is the leading travel trade publication and this was achieved in less than three years. In 2003, eTurbo News was the official publication of the International Peace through Tourism conference held in Geneva.

Before establishing eTurbo News, Mr. Steinmetz was a Communication Specialist at Bloody Good Stuff Marketing, the Tourism Representative in North America for the Republic of Indonesia, Chief Executive Officer for Unique Destination Asia and co-owner of Horizon Travel in Germany where it became one of the first and largest airline consolidators before the company moved to the United States.

Rafeeuddin Ahmed

Special Representative of the World Tourism Organization to the United Nations

Mr. Ahmed is the Special Representative of the WTO to the United Nations at its headquarters in New York and is also Special Adviser to the Executive Director of the United Nations Development Fund for Women. From February to July 2000, he was Special Adviser to the U.N. Secretary-General on Iraq. Educated at the Univerity of the Punjab in Lahore, Pakistan, and the Fletcher School of Law and Diplomacy in the United States, Mr. Ahmed joined the Pakistan Foreign Service and held posts in Beijing, Cairo, Ottawa, New York and Islamabad. In his long United Nations career, Mr. Ahmed has been Secretary of the UN Economic and Social Council and Director, Department of Economic and Social Affairs; Executive Assistant and Chef de Cabinet to the U.N. Secretary General; Under-Secretary-General for Political Affairs, Trusteeship and Decolonization; Under-Secretary-General for International Economic and Social Affairs and served in other senior positions.

Martin Brackenbury

President of the International Federation of Tour Operators

Mr. Brackenbury is President of the International Federation of Tour Operators (IFTO); Chairman of the Federation of Tour Operators (UK); Director, Classic Collection Holidays and Special Professor at Nottingham University. He is also Managing Partner of Brankenbury & Partners; an associate of the environmental management company, Travelwatch, and a fellow of the Royal Geographical Society. Mr. Brackenbury was educated at Cambridge University and after a period spent in industry, the media and banking, joined a management consultancy where he became a senior partner. In 1980, he went to work at Thompson Holidays as a director and in 1989 was promoted to the Board of the Thompson Travel Group, the United Kingdom's leading travel organization. An innovator and giant in outbound tourism, it became an integrated group of travel agents, tour operators, airline, hotels, cruise ships and ground handlers. He served on the Board until the company was floated in 1998.

That year, Mr. Brackenbury became Chairman of the Panorama Holiday Group which was subsequently sold to Airtours Plc where he served as a Director for three years. He served as Chairman of the adventure travel company Exodus Holiday. In 1998, he was invited to become the first Director of the Christel De Haan Research Institute in Travel & Tourism at Nottingham University focussing on the economic impact of tourism. Mr. Brackenbury has also served as Vice Chairman and subsequently Chairman of the United Kingdom Federation of Tour Operators. He was named as Chairman of the IFTO in 1990 and has served six years on the Board of ABTA and for eight years as the Chairman of Affiliate Members of the World Tourism Organization. Mr. Brackenbury has carried out missions in more than 40 countries over the past 25 years.

Rok V. Klancnik

Chief of the TOURCOM Organizing Committee

Mr. Klancnik joined the World Tourism Organization as Chief of Communications in June 2002 and was/is in charge of communications campaigns for the 15th WTO General Assembly in Beijing, the Tourism Enriches project and the transformation of the WTO into a United Nations specialized agency. He has also edited the third edition of the "Shining in the Media Spotlight" handbook and has been involved as Chief and supervisor of the TOURCOM Conference.

A native of Slovenia, Mr. Klancnik worked with the Slovenian Tourist Board following its creation in 1996. As Director of Communications at the Board, he implemented communications campaigns for trade fair representations and at important international events such as the 1998 Expo in Lisbon, the Sydney Olympic Games, the World Cup in South Korea and the first summit between U.S. President George W. Bush and Russian President Vladimir Putin in Slovenia. As a speaker and organizer, he was involved in conferences and promotional events in some 40 countries in Europe, the Middle East, the United States, Asia and Australia. Mr. Klancnik has a university degree in political science and international relations and worked as a journalist for the daily newspaper "Delo" and for the Slovenian Press Agency. He specialized in journalism and communications at the University of Tennessee and has taken part in numerous seminars and courses on communications, journalism, management and marketing in Slovenia and at international institutions as the Council of Europe and such. In his journalistic work, he is Chief Editor of the "WTO News" and regularly contributes articles to print media on subjects relating to international tourism, public relations, marketing and branding.

RÉSUMÉS DE CARRIÈRE DES INTERVENANTS

(dans l'ordre du programme)

Francesco Frangialli

Secrétaire général, Organisation mondiale du tourisme

Né à Paris, M. Frangialli est diplômé de l'Institut d'études politiques de la capitale française et titulaire d'une licence en économie. Il a également deux diplômes d'études supérieures en sciences économiques et en droit public. Il a aussi suivi les cours de l'École nationale d'administration et de l'École du Commissariat de la marine. Sa carrière professionnelle comprend des fonctions de commissaire de l'escorteur « Dupetit-Thouars » de la marine française, de jeune magistrat à la Cour des comptes et de maître de conférences à la fois à l'Institut d'études politiques de Paris et à l'Institut international d'administration publique.

Dans le domaine du tourisme, le premier poste de M. Frangialli est celui de conseiller technique au cabinet du ministre de la Jeunesse, des Sports et des Loisirs. En 1980, il est nommé conseiller technique auprès du Conseil supérieur du tourisme de France et, un an plus tard, il devient membre du Conseil national du tourisme. Les autres temps forts de sa carrière dans ce domaine comprennent son rôle en qualité de directeur de l'industrie touristique au ministère du Tourisme et de membre des conseils d'administration d'Air France, de l'Établissement public de Marne-la-Vallée, de l'Agence nationale pour le chèque-vacances et de l'ACTIM.

En 1990, il rejoint l'Organisation mondiale du tourisme comme Secrétaire général adjoint et en 1997, il en est élu Secrétaire général pour la période 1998-2001. Au terme de ce mandat, il est réélu pour la période 2002-2005. Ses livres et publications comprennent « La France dans le tourisme mondial » (1991, Éditions Economica), « Tourisme et loisirs – Une question sociale » (coauteur, 1997, Bayard Éditions) « Considérations sur le tourisme international » (1999 et 2001, Organisation mondiale du tourisme) et Tourisme International : Le Grand Tournant, Textes et documents 2001 - 2003 (2004, Organisation mondiale du tourisme).

Pour ce qui est des distinctions, M. Frangialli est chevalier des Palmes académiques, chevalier du Mérite national et chevalier de la Légion d'honneur et il s'est vu décerner des décorations nationales de la République de Saint-Marin, de la République togolaise et de l'Autorité palestinienne.

Debbie Hindle

Présidente-Directrice générale, BGB & Associates

En 1991, Mme Hindle participe à la fondation de BGB & Associates, qui est aujourd'hui la première entreprise de relations publiques en matière de mode de vie et de voyage du Royaume-Uni, avec une clientèle allant de la Commission australienne du tourisme à Travelbag. Elle a plus de treize ans d'expérience dans le secteur des loisirs et du tourisme. Elle gère et dirige des campagnes de relations publiques pour des organisations comme des conseils de tourisme, des hôtels, des agences de voyages, des voyagistes, des systèmes mondiaux de distribution (SMD), des centres d'intérêt, des entreprises britanniques de vacances, des compagnies aériennes, des sociétés de croisières et des entreprises de ferrys. Mme Hindle mène aussi des campagnes d'études et de lobbying politiques. Elle a représenté pendant de nombreuses années le voyagiste Lunn Poly et actuellement, elle dirige des équipes pour des clients comme la Passenger Shipping Association et la Caribbean Tourism Organization.

Au cours de sa carrière, elle a également créé une revue professionnelle régionale dans les Midlands (centre de l'Angleterre) et travaillé pour McCann Erikson PR en s'y occupant des comptes pour des biens et des services comme le matériel de culture physique, les boissons non alcoolisées, les assurances et tout un éventail d'entreprises du bâtiment et de l'immobilier.

Becky Anderson

Présentateur, Business International, CNN

Depuis son lancement en février 2001, Becky Anderson présente deux fois par jour l'émission Business International de CNN sur l'activité économique dans le monde. Avec ce programme au rythme enlevé, Mme Anderson dévoile les éléments essentiels de la conjoncture quotidienne en Asie, aux États-Unis et en Europe et elle évalue les répercussions en Europe de l'état des marchés et des nouvelles du monde des affaires. Tout au long de l'émission, elle est en liaison avec les journalistes de CNN qui, des quatre coins de la planète, lui font part immédiatement des derniers faits nouveaux concernant les entreprises.

Depuis que Business International existe, Mme Anderson s'est entretenue avec un large éventail de personnalités du monde des finances, de la politique et de l'économie, dont le chancelier de l'Échiquier du gouvernement britannique, Gordon Brown, le gouverneur de la Banque de France, Jean-Claude Trichet, le président-directeur général de BP Amoco, John Browne, et le secrétaire général de l'OPEP, Ali Rodriguez. Mme Anderson présente également sur CNN l'émission mensuelle Inside Sailing sur l'actualité du monde de la navigation de plaisance.

Mme Anderson est entrée chez CNN en mai 1999 comme présentatrice de la nouvelle émission World Business This Morning diffusée à l'heure du petit déjeuner. Cette émission a été une étape décisive lors du démarrage de la mise en œuvre de la stratégie de régionalisation de la chaîne pour offrir le matin au marché européen une programmation locale en direct à partir du centre de production de Londres.

Depuis ses débuts à CNN, Mme Anderson s'est vu confier de nombreuses et importantes missions à l'étranger pour des reportages en direct et elle a interrogé plusieurs personnalités de premier plan du monde des affaires lors de manifestation comme le salon CeBIT Technology Fair (éditions 2000 et 2001), le forum mondial de Fortune et Telecom 1999.

Ayant occupé des postes à la chaîne britannique Channel 5, à CNBC Europe et chez Bloomberg, Mme Anderson a une longue expérience du journalisme économique. Elle a commencé sa carrière dans la presse écrite en étant journaliste de plusieurs publications économiques de l'Arizona après avoir obtenu en 1992 une maîtrise de communication de masse à l'École de journalisme Walter Cronkite à l'Université de l'État de l'Arizona. Britannique, Mme Anderson vit à Londres. Elle est titulaire d'une licence d'économie et de français de l'Université du Sussex qui lui a été décernée avec mention.

Thierry Baudier

Directeur général de Maison de la France

En mai 2003, après de nombreuses années consacrées à la politique et au tourisme, M. Baudier est nommé directeur général de Maison de la France. Il succède à Jean-Philippe Pérol qui occupait le poste depuis 1999 et qui est aujourd'hui directeur de la représentation de Maison de la France pour les Amériques. Diplômé d'études supérieures en droit et en sociologie et ancien auditeur de l'Institut des hautes études de défense nationale, il intègre en 1997 le groupe d'intérêt économique (GIE) Maison de la France. Il y est successivement directeur des marchés extérieurs et directeur du marketing et du partenariat. À ce titre, jusqu'à sa récente nomination, il coordonne les actions de marketing et de communication menées par le siège et les bureaux de Maison de la France. De 1995 à 1997, M. Baudier est attaché parlementaire auprès du premier ministre. Auparavant, il travaille comme chargé de mission auprès du président d'une formation politique à l'Assemblée nationale.

M. Baudier débute sa carrière à la Compagnie générale du bâtiment où, de 1989 à 1993, il participe notamment à la construction d'hôtels en Europe centrale et orientale.

Marc Meister

Président-Directeur général, Sergat España

M. Meister est le fondateur et le président-directeur général de Sergat España, S.L., premier cabinet espagnol de communication et de marketing spécialisé dans le tourisme, l'hôtellerie et le transport aérien. Ses études lui ont permis d'obtenir une maîtrise de science du marketing, un diplôme de gestion hôtelière à Lucerne et un diplôme en sciences de la communication et de l'information à l'Institut Drexler.

Membre fondateur de la branche espagnole de la PATA et de Visit US, M. Meister a également occupé des postes de cadre supérieur en marketing en Suisse, aux États-Unis et en Espagne chez de grands voyagistes et dans de grandes entreprises hôtelières. Il parle l'espagnol, l'allemand, le français et l'anglais et il a un brevet de pilote d'avion privé.

Javier Piñanes

Directeur, Turespaña

Licencié en droit de l'Université autonome de Madrid et docteur en droit de l'Université Complutense, Javier Piñanes appartient au corps supérieur des administrateurs civils de l'État.

Dans l'Administration publique, il a occupé plusieurs fonctions au ministère de l'Industrie et de l'Énergie et au ministère des Transports, du Tourisme et des Communications. Il a été sous-directeur général chargé des études au secrétariat général technique du ministère de la Justice et de l'Intérieur.

Dans l'Administration du tourisme, il a été directeur adjoint de l'Office espagnol du tourisme à Francfort et directeur de l'Office espagnol du tourisme à Berlin. Il a aussi été sous-directeur général chargé des moyens de promotion à l'Instituto de Turismo de España (Turespaña). Il est directeur de Turespaña depuis le mois de mars 2003.

Christopher Brown

Président-Directeur général, Tourism Task Force (TTF)

M. Brown est président-directeur général du groupe de pression australien TTF. Groupe privé indépendant des partis, le TTF rassemble les PDG de deux cents grandes sociétés des secteurs du tourisme, des transports, des loisirs et de l'infrastructure. Le TTF exerce son influence sur l'environnement politique et financier de la plus grosse branche d'activité de l'Australie. Avant d'occuper son poste au TTF en 1992, M. Brown a été président-directeur général de JMA Public Affairs et conseiller politique de plusieurs députés après avoir fait un stage chez Ogilvy & Mather Advertising. Il a fait des études d'économie et de droit à l'Université de Sydney.

Se traitant lui-même de « fou de sports », M. Brown s'est occupé de la candidature de Sydney pour les Jeux olympiques de 2000 et, en cette occasion, il a été l'agent de liaison du secteur touristique. Il a été ambassadeur national des Jeux paralympiques de 2000 à Sydney et attaché olympique honoraire du Botswana aux Jeux olympiques de la même année. Depuis dix ans, M. Brown est directeur exécutif de la Sport and Tourism Youth Scholarship Foundation.

En plus de ses activités au TTF, M. Brown est président d'Authentic Outback Experiences Pty Ltd, coentreprise de RM Williams, industriel du vêtement pour le bush, et d'AaCo, société d'élevage de bétail, créée en Australie pour installer et développer des camps de safari à l'intérieur des terres. Il siège au conseil d'administration de la chaîne hôtelière Best Western Australia. En outre, il est directeur de See Australia Ltd, initiative du gouvernement et du secteur privé en faveur du tourisme interne.

M. Brown préside le Groupe consultatif Rugby et Tourisme et le Forum national australien du tourisme et de l'exportation des vins. Il est membre du Conseil fédéral de prévision des tendances du tourisme, du Groupe d'orientation du tourisme indigène, du Groupe stratégique chargé de conseiller le premier ministre en matière d'accessibilité pour les handicapés et de la Table ronde sur le tourisme en tant que secteur exportateur.

M. Brown est actuellement vice-président du Conseil professionnel de l'OMT et représentant régional du prestigieux Conseil mondial du voyage et du tourisme (WTTC).

Thomas J. Wallace

Directeur, Condé Nast Traveler

M. Wallace devient directeur de cette prestigieuse revue américaine de tourisme en 1990. Dès son lancement, cette revue se distingue par la qualité de ses articles. Aux États-Unis, elle a été proposée pour seize prix nationaux décernés aux périodiques, dont six de la catégorie Excellence générale. Elle a gagné cinq prix : en 1998 et en 1999 en raison de son « intérêt spécial » ; en 1991, pour sa « qualité visuelle » et dans la catégorie Excellence générale et en 1999 de nouveau dans cette dernière catégorie. Condé Nast Traveler est la seule publication consacrée aux voyages à avoir remporté de tels prix nationaux.

C'est aussi la seule publication sur le tourisme et la seule revue du groupe Condé Nast à avoir une série d'émissions régulières à la télévision publique, le « Condé Nast Traveler: Insider's Guide », se composant de vingt-six épisodes, qui a été lancée en octobre 2002 à l'occasion du quinzième anniversaire de la revue.

Sous la direction de M. Wallace, la revue Condé Nast Traveler a été, en juin 1995, la première du groupe à paraître en ligne avec un site ambitieux sur la Toile, annonçant le début de relations interactives d'un nouveau genre. Ce site a actuellement pour adresse www.concierge.com.

M. Wallace est un ardent partisan du tourisme conscient de ses responsabilités en matière d'environnement. En 1990, sa revue a créé un prix annuel d'écologie destiné à récompenser les militants indépendants. M. Wallace a fait un pas de plus dans cette direction en créant un prix d'écotourisme qui reconnaît les efforts novateurs du secteur du tourisme.

Avant de rejoindre le groupe Condé Nast, M. Wallace a occupé de hautes fonctions dans les meilleurs journaux des États-Unis, dont le New York Times, le Newsday et le Stamford Advocate, où, en tant que rédacteur en chef pour les nouvelles locales, il a supervisé une série d'articles d'investigation qui a remporté le prix Pulitzer en 1979. Il est diplômé de l'Université de Harvard.

Gary Wardrope

Directeur commercial, Travel Channel

M. Wardrope est chargé, pour le monde entier, de la publicité et des parrainages au Travel Channel et il s'occupe de l'expansion de cette chaîne au Moyen-Orient et dans d'autres régions. À l'heure actuelle, il étudie aussi le lancement de services d'agence de voyages en Scandinavie et en Afrique du Sud. Ancien skieur de compétition, M. Wardrope a travaillé, pendant les années 1980, comme moniteur de ski et comme directeur de station dans son Canada natal, en France, en Suisse et en Autriche, après quoi il a été chef des ventes et du marketing chez Neilson Ski. Dans les années 1990, il a dirigé la division des produits spéciaux d'Airtours qui, avec un chiffre d'affaires de 250 millions de livres sterling, s'occupait de quatre bateaux de croisière, d'un programme pour les jeunes (Escapades) et des sports d'hiver, qui étaient toutes de nouvelles activités de la société.

En 2000, M. Wardrope est engagé comme directeur commercial au Travel Channel où il a supervisé la création de Travel Deals Direct, agence de voyages virtuelle présente dix-heures par jour sur les écrans de télévision de huit millions de foyers et s'occupant de plus de 30 000 voyageurs par an au Royaume-Uni. Il a également été chargé de lancer les premiers services vidéo large bande à la demande avec BT.

Geoffrey Lipman

Conseiller spécial du Secrétaire général de l'OMT chargé du commerce, de la libéralisation à visage humain et de l'initiative ST-EP

M. Lipman est président de Green Globe 21, l'organisation mondiale de certification du tourisme durable, et de GTREX, société de développement de l'Internet de la quatrième génération. Il est aussi administrateur de la Great Canadian Railway Company et d'AIA Communications. De 1990 à 1999, il a été président du Conseil mondial du voyage et du tourisme (WTTC) qu'il a vu passer de dix à cent membres et où il a veillé au positionnement du tourisme comme plus grosse branche d'activité du monde sous l'angle de la croissance.

Pendant vingt ans, M. Lipman a travaillé à l'Association du transport aérien international (IATA), où il a exercé les fonctions de chef du personnel et de chef des relations avec les États. Il a ensuite été nommé directeur général de l'IFAPA, fondation représentant les intérêts des passagers clients des compagnies aériennes. Il a aussi été associé de Global Aviation Associates, cabinet de conseils en stratégie du transport aérien, spécialisé dans les problèmes de réglementation et de concurrence. M. Lipman a écrit des ouvrages et donné des conférences dans le monde entier sur la stratégie du tourisme et la libéralisation du transport aérien. Il a été membre de deux commissions de haut niveau de l'Union européenne, chargées respectivement de la libéralisation du transport aérien et de l'emploi dans le tourisme, de la table ronde britannique sur le développement durable et du conseil consultatif de la compagnie Royal Jordanian Airlines. À l'heure actuelle, il est membre de la Tourism Society et de l'Australian Tourism Research Association, ambassadeur itinérant de l'Organisation du tourisme de l'océan Indien et membre du conseil consultatif en matière économique du président de la Zambie.

Donald E. Hawkins

Professeur titulaire de la chaire Eisenhower de politique touristique, Université George Washington

Parallèlement à ses activités de chercheur et d'enseignant, M. Hawkins facilite une réelle collaboration entre le secteur du tourisme et des institutions internationales comme l'Organisation des Nations Unies, la Banque mondiale, la Banque interaméricaine de développement et l'Organisation mondiale du tourisme. Dans le cadre de ses relations avec l'OMT, il a donné des cours au CICATUR de l'Organisation à Mexico, fait partie de la délégation des États-Unis lors des sessions de Rome et de New Dehli de l'Assemblée générale de cette institution, mené dès le début des travaux de recherche sur TedQual, prononcé des discours en maintes occasions et été membre de comités importants de l'Organisation. En 2003, M. Hawkins a reçu le premier prix Ulysse de l'OMT décerné à titre personnel pour ses travaux de recherche et ses efforts de diffusion du savoir dans le domaine de la politique et de la gestion touristiques. M. Hawkins a à son actif d'avoir assuré le premier cours de tourisme offert en 1970 par l'Université George Washington. Cette université a été, à l'échelon international, parmi les établissements pionniers qui ont proposé une maîtrise d'administration du tourisme et elle a décerné ses premiers diplômes en 1974. Le programme d'études de cette maîtrise a une optique internationale et il est axé sur l'exercice professionnel et sur les travaux de recherche dans le domaine du tourisme et de l'accueil.

Jusqu'en 1999, M. Hawkins a été directeur de l'Institut international d'études de tourisme qui, fondé en 1988, a été le premier établissement d'enseignement créé en collaboration avec l'OMT. En 1994, il est nommé professeur de politique touristique titulaire de la chaire Dwight D. Eisenhower qui bénéficie d'une dotation.

Il est auteur ou éditeur d'une centaine de publications sur les aspects contemporains de la politique et de la stratégie touristiques et il a travaillé comme consultant sur des projets et des études consacrés au tourisme dans plusieurs pays du monde, dont le Honduras, la Jordanie, l'Égypte, les Bermudes, Saint-Kitts-et-Nevis et la Palestine. Plus récemment, il a participé à une étude financée par les Nations Unies sur les relations stratégiques entre, d'une part, le développement du tourisme et, d'autre part, la protection de la biodiversité et l'exploitation durable des ressources en énergie et en eau.

Mariano López
Doyen, Chambre espagnole des journalistes et des communicateurs spécialisés dans le tourisme

M. López est à la tête de la Cámara de Periodistas y Comunicadores de Turismo, association professionnelle espagnole qui rassemble les directeurs des médias spécialisés et les directeurs de la communication des entreprises touristiques. Il est également directeur de la revue Viajar du Grupo Zeta, première revue consacrée aux voyages à être parue en Espagne il y a tout juste vingt-cinq ans.

Richard D. Lewis
Président de Richard Lewis Communications plc

M. Lewis, qui parle dix langues européennes et deux langues asiatiques, est président de Richard Lewis Communications plc, institut international de formation linguistique et transculturelle avec des bureaux dans plus d'une douzaine de pays. En 1989, il fonde la revue trimestrielle Cross Culture. Son livre When Cultures Collide est considéré comme l'ouvrage classique sur les problèmes interculturels. En 1997, il venait en tête de la sélection de printemps du U.S. Book of the Month Club. Actif dans les domaines de la linguistique appliquée et de la linguistique anthropologique depuis plus de trente-cinq ans, M. Lewis a travaillé comme journaliste de radio et de télévision en Allemagne, où il fut aussi scénariste de Konrad Adenauer. En 1961, il lançait en Finlande la première série de cours d'anglais à la télévision du monde. En 1962, il signait le scénario de la série « Walter and Connie » de la BBC.

Il a habité et travaillé dans plusieurs pays européens avec notamment pour clients ABB, Allianz, le Banco de España, la Banque de France, la Deutsche Bank, Ericsson, Fiat, Gillette, IBM, Mercedes Benz, Nestlé, Nokia, Saab et Volvo.

Pendant les cinq ans qu'il a passés au Japon, M. Lewis a été le professeur particulier de l'impératrice Michiko et d'autres membres de la famille impériale. Il y a également travaillé avec des sociétés comme Nomura, Mitsubishi, Hitachi, Sanyo, Mitsui et Nippon Steel.

Plus récemment, il s'est engagé à fond dans le domaine interculturel en créant des entreprises en France, en Allemagne, en Espagne, en Italie et au Brésil et en y enseignant les techniques de communication de même qu'en Finlande, en Suède, au Royaume-Uni et aux États-Unis.

M. Lewis a été choisi en 1999 comme personnalité de l'année par la Pacific Asia Travel Association pour son « travail extraordinairement sérieux dans le domaine de la communication transculturelle grâce à sa compréhension manifeste des cultures de la région Asie-Pacifique et à sa sensibilité incontestable à leur égard ». En 1997, le président finlandais Marti Ahtisaari le faisait chevalier en reconnaissance de ses services dans le domaine transculturel dans le cadre des programmes de formation destinés aux ministères finlandais avant l'adhésion du pays à l'Union européenne.

Rolf Jensen
Chef du service Imagination, Dream Company Ltd

M. Jensen, futurologue et auteur danois, est le chef du service Imagination de la Dream Company Ltd qu'il a fondée en 2001 avec pour objet de persuader la majorité des entreprises mondiales de premier plan d'interpréter les défis actuels et futurs comme la transformation d'une société en une autre en leur offrant les instruments voulus pour faire face à cette profonde mutation.

En 1999, M. Jensen publiait son livre The Dream Society: From Information to Imagination, d'abord aux États-Unis, puis au Danemark. Succès de librairie, ce livre a été traduit depuis en six autres langues. Voyageur enthousiaste, M. Jensen est membre de la Royal Geographic Society de Londres. Un de ses voyages les plus stimulants l'a amené au cœur de l'île de Bornéo où il a pu directement observer la transition d'une société de chasseurs-cueilleurs à une société d'agriculteurs.

M. Jensen a obtenu en 1970 une maîtrise de sciences politiques à l'Université d'Århus, après quoi il est entré au service de l'État aux ministères danois de la Défense, des Pêches et des Affaires étrangères. En 1983, il entrait à l'Institut d'études de l'avenir de Copenhague et cinq ans plus tard, il en devenait directeur.

Scott Wayne

Directeur, SW Associates

En sa qualité de directeur de SW Associates, M. Wayne dirige un large éventail de programmes et de projets de mise en valeur touristique ou il y participe. Ces programmes et projets portent sur le développement économique grâce au tourisme, la promotion des investissements, la stratégie de communication et d'organisation, la gestion des problèmes, la création d'alliances et les relations internationales. Son expérience la plus récente comme consultant comprend une étude de la compétitivité touristique de plusieurs pays pour la Banque mondiale, un système de classement des hôtels et de normes de qualité pour le gouvernement de Bahreïn, une stratégie écologique destinée aux professionnels des croisières pour Conservation International, une étude préalable de faisabilité concernant l'infrastructure touristique du Maroc et une évaluation rapide des conditions d'investissement dans le tourisme en Croatie. Il a en outre à son actif la création d'une association pour les investissements dans le tourisme, la mise sur pied d'organisations du tourisme aux niveaux national et provincial et l'élaboration d'une stratégie de développement d'un produit et de communication. M. Wayne est également professeur vacataire d'aménagement touristique à l'Université George Washington. Par l'intermédiaire de SW Associates, il a dirigé le bureau de Washington, chargé de l'Amérique du Nord, du Conseil mondial du voyage et du tourisme (WTTC) et il s'est occupé à ce titre de projets et de programmes avec des institutions financières multilatérales et plusieurs gouvernements au niveau des nations et des États. Au cours de sa carrière, M. Wayne a aussi été vice-président, chargé du développement international, d'une jeune entreprise s'occupant d'Internet, Vivid Travel Network, filiale de la célèbre société de développement du réseau des réseaux, Vivid Studios.

Il a également exercé la fonction de chef du service Communication de l'Organisation mondiale du tourisme, poste où il était chargé de conseiller le Secrétaire général au sujet des questions stratégiques de communication, de nouer et d'approfondir des alliances avec des groupes gouvernementaux et non gouvernementaux et de développer les programmes de publications, de relations avec les médias et de relations publiques en général de l'OMT.

M. Wayne est l'auteur de sept livres de voyage pour Sierra Club et Lonely Planet consacrés à l'Égypte, au Soudan, aux pays du Maghreb (Algérie, Maroc et Tunisie), au Mexique et à l'État de Basse-Californie, ainsi que de nombreux articles pour des quotidiens et des revues.

Dawid de Villiers

Secrétaire général adjoint, Organisation mondiale du tourisme

M. de Villiers est nommé Secrétaire général adjoint de l'OMT en 1998 après avoir été ministre sud-africain de l'Environnement et du Tourisme sous la présidence de Nelson Mandela. Il est licencié en psychologie, en philosophie et en théologie de l'Université de Stellenbosch, titulaire d'une maîtrise en philosophie de la Rand Afrikaans University et docteur en philosophie diplômé de l'Université de Stellenbosch.

Au cours de sa carrière, il a été professeur de philosophie dans deux universités, pasteur de l'Église réformée hollandaise, député et ambassadeur d'Afrique du Sud à Londres. De retour en Afrique du Sud, M. de Villiers est nommé ministre du Commerce, de l'Industrie et du Tourisme, poste qu'il occupe pendant six ans, puis ministre du Budget et des Affaires sociales, ministre de l'Administration et de la Privatisation, ministre des Mines et de l'Énergie et ministre des Entreprises publiques.

En 1991, M. de Villiers participe très activement aux négociations qui débouchent sur la nouvelle constitution et sur les premières élections démocratiques de l'Afrique du Sud. En 1994, il est président du Conseil exécutif de transition qui oriente et surveille l'action du gouvernement pendant la transition politique du pays vers le régime majoritaire.

M. de Villiers a été gouverneur de la Development Bank of South Africa et il a siégé aux conseils d'administration de sociétés anonymes comme la Bank of Johannesburg, la Santam Bank, Triomf Fertiliser et Landbou-Chemiese Beleggings (investissements agrochimiques).

Passionné de sport, M. de Villiers a fait partie de l'équipe d'Afrique du Sud de rugby lors de matchs internationaux contre l'Angleterre, l'Irlande, le pays de Galles, l'Australie, la Nouvelle-Zélande, la France et l'Argentine. Il a été capitaine de l'équipe d'Afrique du Sud pendant un nombre record de vingt-trois matchs.

Diego Cordovez

Candidat à la présidence du Comité mondial d'éthique du tourisme

M. Cordovez est président du Centro Andino de Estudios Internacionales de l'Universidad Andina Simón Bolivar à Quito, en Équateur, poste qu'il a accepté après avoir travaillé pour les Nations Unies pendant vingt-cinq ans. À l'ONU, il s'est d'abord occupé des questions économiques, puis des questions politiques. Ses premiers postes y ont été directeur du Secrétariat du Conseil économique et social et Sous-Secrétaire général aux affaires économiques et sociales. Il a été le principal conseiller d'une commission spéciale chargée de la restructuration de l'ensemble du système des Nations Unies pour le développement et Secrétaire de la Commission des questions économiques et financières de l'Assemblée générale pendant huit sessions. En 1972 et 1992, M. Cordovez a été conseiller spécial du Secrétaire général pour les conférences des Nations Unies sur l'environnement. En 1981, il est nommé Secrétaire général adjoint aux affaires politiques et, en sa qualité de médiateur dans le conflit afghan, il négocie les accords de Genève en application desquels l'Union soviétique retire ses troupes de l'Afghanistan. La candidature de M. Cordovez a été proposée pour le prix Nobel de la paix 1988, qui fut attribué aux forces de maintien de la paix des Nations Unies. M. Cordovez a été chargé de missions spéciales à Grenade, en Iran (République islamique d'), en Iraq, au Pakistan, en République de Corée, en République dominicaine et en République populaire démocratique de Corée et il a été conseiller principal d'Olof Palme, médiateur des Nations Unies lors de la guerre entre l'Iran et l'Iraq. En 1988, il est nommé ministre des Affaires étrangères de l'Équateur. Quatre ans plus tard, il entre au cabinet juridique international LeBœuf, Lamb, Greene and MacRae, qui a son siège à New York. En 1992, il devient diplomate résident de la faculté d'études internationales de l'Université de Colombie. Aux élections de 1996, il est candidat à la vice-présidence de la République de Colombie. M. Cordovez est licencié de la faculté des sciences juridiques et sociales de l'Université du Chili et il a prêté serment comme avocat devant la Cour suprême. Il a écrit ses mémoires de la guerre d'Afghanistan, Out of Afghanistan, et un autre ouvrage sur le conflit territorial entre l'Équateur et le Pérou. Il est aussi l'auteur de plusieurs essais et articles de presse.

Anil Kumarsingh Gayan

Ministre du Tourisme et des Loisirs, Maurice

M. Anil Kumarsingh Gayan, député, prêtait serment en qualité de ministre des Affaires étrangères et de la Coopération régionale le 16 septembre 2000. Il avait occupé le même poste de 1983 à 1986 alors qu'outre les Affaires étrangères, ce portefeuille comprenait le Tourisme et l'Émigration. Il a été nommé ministre du Tourisme et des Loisirs à compter du 23 décembre 2003. Né à Port-Louis le 22 octobre 1948, M. Gayan fait ses études primaires à Triolet, village de son enfance, et à Port-Louis. Au Royal College of Port Louis, il obtient son diplôme de fin d'études secondaires en 1968. De 1969 à 1972, il fait des études de droit à la London School of Economics et en 1972, il est inscrit au barreau de l'Inner Temple de Londres. En 1973, il passe sa maîtrise de droit international et de droit de la mer à l'Université de Londres. Après une courte période d'exercice dans le privé, il rejoint en 1974 le cabinet du procureur général en qualité d'avocat de la couronne. De 1974 à 1982, il est chargé d'une mission spéciale auprès de la Conférence des Nations Unies sur le droit de la mer et, en tant que délégué de Maurice, il participe à toutes ses sessions et à d'autres conférences sur des thèmes connexes partout dans le monde. En 1982 à Montego Bay, il signe la Convention des Nations Unies sur le droit de la mer. En 1982, M. Gayan se remet à exercer comme avocat dans le privé et il entre en politique. Il est élu au parlement et au conseil municipal de Curepipe. En 1983, il est réélu député et devient ministre des Affaires étrangères, du Tourisme et de l'Émigration. La même année, il devient président du conseil de l'Université de Maurice. En 1986, il exerce de nouveau comme avocat. En 1989 et 1990, il préside le conseil du barreau. En 1995, il est nommé avocat principal. M. Gayan a été consultant auprès du Centre pour les droits de l'homme dont le siège est à Genève et, à ce titre, il a travaillé au Bhoutan, en Mongolie, en Arménie et au Togo.

Jonathan B. Tourtellot

**Directeur du tourisme durable, National Geographic Society,
et Directeur chargé du géotourisme, National Geographic Traveler**

En sa qualité de directeur du tourisme durable de la National Geographic Society et de directeur chargé du géotourisme du National Geographic Traveler, M. Tourtellot rédige la chronique TravelWatch de cette revue, qui traite de la bonne gestion des destinations, et il écrit ou met au point des articles de fond sur des problèmes de tourisme. Il s'occupe actuellement de l'étude intitulée « National Geographic Destination Outlook Survey » sur la durabilité de destinations touristiques renommées, de la préparation d'un livre sur le géotourisme et du développement continu du programme de tourisme durable de la National Geographic Society qui comprend la participation à l'Alliance Mundo Maya, au Forum du tourisme mondial pour la paix et le développement durable et au lancement de l'initiative de protection des sites du patrimoine mondial.

M. Tourtellot rejoint l'équipe de la National Geographic Society en 1979 et il est promu rédacteur en chef un an plus tard. En 2001, il en devient le premier directeur du tourisme durable. Il a inventé la notion et le terme de « géotourisme », dont la définition est « tourisme qui préserve ou met davantage en valeur l'originalité géographique d'un endroit, à savoir son environnement, sa culture, son esthétique, son patrimoine et le bien-être de ses habitants ».

M. Tourtellot est le coauteur de la publication – The Geotourism Study – où ce terme apparaît pour la première fois, ainsi que de la première grande enquête sur le comportement et les attitudes du voyageur des États-Unis à l'égard de la durabilité et de la bonne gestion des destinations, réalisée de 2001 à 2003 par la Travel Association of America. Il est aussi au nombre des fondateurs des nouveaux prix du patrimoine mondial pour le tourisme durable, avec cinq catégories : tourisme de nature, tourisme de découverte du patrimoine, hôtels et stations, et bonne gestion des destinations, présentés pour la première fois en janvier 2003 par la reine Noor de Jordanie au nom du National Geographic Traveler et de Conservation International.

Deborah Luhrman

Consultante en communication auprès de l'OMT

Jusqu'en 2001, Mme Luhrman a été chef de la section Communication de l'Organisation mondiale du tourisme et, à ce titre, elle était chargée des relations avec les médias, des Nouvelles de l'OMT, de la participation aux salons professionnels et du site de l'Organisation sur la Toile. Elle continue à collaborer avec l'OMT dans le cadre de projets liés à la communication et à la gestion des crises et elle est membre du Groupe d'action de l'OMT en cas de crise. Mme Luhrman, citoyenne des États-Unis, a toujours exercé comme journaliste. Elle a travaillé comme journaliste des actualités télévisées en Californie, où elle a gagné un prix Emmy. S'étant installée en Espagne en 1989, elle travaille comme rédactrice à l'agence de presse espagnole EFE et comme réalisatrice pour le réseau de télévision allemand ZDF. Mme Luhrman s'est occupée du secteur touristique espagnol pour plusieurs publications professionnelles, dont la Travel Trade Gazette et Hotel and Motel Management. Elle est coauteur de plusieurs guides de voyage Fodor, notamment sur l'Espagne, la France et le Portugal. Elle a également participé à la réalisation d'émissions de télévision lors des Jeux olympiques d'été de Los Angeles (1984), de Barcelone (1992), d'Atlanta (1996) et de Sydney (2000).

Dexter Koehl

Vice-Président chargé des relations publiques et de la communication, TIA

Depuis sa nomination en mars 1992 au poste de vice-président de la Travel Industry Association of America (TIA), M. Koehl est responsable de la communication devant les 2 100 organisations qui en sont membres et devant les médias nationaux et internationaux avec pour but de soutenir l'Association dans sa mission de promotion et de facilitation des voyages à destination des États-Unis et dans leurs frontières. En matière de communication, il contribue également à faire prendre davantage conscience des effets économiques, sociaux et culturels du tourisme sur le pays et il est chargé de gérer le contenu du site de la TIA sur la Toile.

M. Koehl a une longue expérience des relations publiques, de la communication, du marketing et du développement dans le secteur du tourisme. Avant d'entrer à la TIA, il a été, de 1986 à 1992, directeur des relations publiques du Carlson Travel Group à Minneapolis. Dans ce domaine, il était chargé de toutes les activités de ce détaillant du voyage présent dans le monde entier avec, à l'époque, un chiffre d'affaires de 7 milliards de dollars. M. Koehl a aussi été vice-président chargé du marketing et du développement de la Hershey Entertainment and Resort Company, directeur du développement des marchés de la Sea Pines Company, directeur du marketing de la station Palmas del Mar à Porto Rico et directeur des plans visant les marchés de passagers chez American Airlines.

M. Koehl a une licence d'études extrême-orientales de l'Université de Californie à Berkeley. Après avoir étudié le japonais au Defense Language Institute de Monterrey, en Californie, il a travaillé deux ans comme traducteur de japonais à la National Security Agency.

Sandra Lee

Secrétaire générale chargée du développement économique et du travail, Gouvernement de Hong-Kong (Chine)

Mme Lee a été nommée Secrétaire générale chargée du développement économique et du travail en 2002. Son portefeuille comprend les services aériens, les services portuaires et maritimes, le développement de la logistique, le tourisme, l'énergie, les services postaux, les services météorologiques, la politique de concurrence et la protection du consommateur. Depuis son entrée dans l'Administration de Hong-Kong en 1974 en qualité d'« executive officer », Mme Lee a travaillé dans plusieurs services techniques et politiques à Hong-Kong et à l'étranger, notamment comme conseillère au Bureau économique et commercial de Hong-Kong à Washington de 1985 à 1988 et de 1993 à 1995. Elle a été directrice adjointe du ministère de l'Intérieur de 1995 à 1996, secrétaire adjointe chargée de la fonction publique de 1996 à 1999, directrice générale du Bureau économique et commercial de Hong-Kong à Londres de 1999 à 2000 et secrétaire chargée des services économiques de 2000 à 2002.

Dr. Osmane Aïdi
Président Honoraire, Association internationale de l'hôtellerie et de la restauration (IH&RA)

M. Aïdi, président honoraire de l'IH&RA, a été réélu à ce poste en 2000. Dans l'histoire de cette Association fondée en 1947, il est le seul président à s'être vu confier un deuxième mandat. Il est également président-directeur général d'Irrifrance, un des principaux fabricants européens de matériels d'irrigation. Au cours de sa longue et brillante carrière au service de l'État et du secteur privé, M. Aïdi a été membre de plusieurs comités publics syriens chargés de l'irrigation et de l'énergie et il a occupé des postes dans la banque et dans l'édition. Il est à la tête d'une fondation portant son nom, qui se consacre à la sauvegarde du riche patrimoine culturel de la Syrie.

Depuis de nombreuses années, il siège aux conseils d'administration de plusieurs entreprises des secteurs de l'accueil et du tourisme en Europe, aux États-Unis et au Moyen-Orient. Il a été président de l'Union inter-arabe de l'hôtellerie et du tourisme et de l'Organisation du tourisme euro-méditerranéen. Outre des mentions honorables et des décorations, M. Aïdi s'est vu décerner par les gouvernements français, bulgare et libanais plusieurs prix en reconnaissance de ses réalisations.

Steve Dunne
Directeur exécutif, groupe Brighter

M. Dunne est directeur exécutif du groupe Brighter et président-directeur général de sa filiale Brighter PR qui, au Royaume Uni, est la société de relations publiques en matière de tourisme à la croissance la plus rapide. Spécialiste des relations publiques ayant plus de vingt ans d'expérience dans le domaine de la communication institutionnelle, il a occupé divers postes de cadre supérieur dans des sociétés de premier ordre. M. Dunne était directeur des relations publiques de British Telecom en 1987 à l'époque de la déréglementation (Big Bang) du marché financier du Royaume Uni et il a conduit la campagne de relations publiques de cette entreprise pendant les conflits sociaux de la fin des années 1980. En 1990, il fait partie de l'équipe de professionnels des relations publiques rassemblée pour combattre avec succès la réputation de la Midland Bank qui est d'être, à l'époque, la banque la moins aimée de Grande-Bretagne.

Au milieu des années 1990, M. Dunne, directeur de la communication institutionnelle pour l'Europe de South African Airways, suscite un immense intérêt pour cette compagnie aérienne et il collabore étroitement avec le gouvernement sud-africain pour faire mieux connaître le pays dans toute l'Europe. En 1997, il devient président-directeur général d'Affinity Consulting, un des premiers cabinets de relations publiques en matière de tourisme de Grande-Bretagne, dont, en 2000, il pilote la fusion avec Countrywide Porter Novelli, quatrième cabinet de relations publiques du pays. Directeur de Countrywide, il est à la tête de la division Consommateurs qui a remporté des prix. En 2002, il s'incorpore au conseil d'administration du groupe Brighter.

Christian Nielsen
Réviseur de textes et auteur, European Service Network

M. Nielsen a une vaste expérience universitaire et commerciale dans le domaine du tourisme et des médias et il a publié sur ce sujet un livre et plusieurs articles. Il a obtenu une licence de gestion touristique à l'Université Victoria de Melbourne, en Australie, qui l'a conduit à un mastère de gestion avec pour spécialité l'implantation et le développement des entreprises touristiques, obtenu à l'Université libre de Bruxelles. Maître de conférences dans une université belge, M. Nielsen publie plusieurs articles sur le tourisme et l'aménagement urbain. Titulaire d'un diplôme de journalisme, il fait carrière dans cette profession et il est pendant un certain temps secrétaire de rédaction du Wall Street Journal Europe.

En 2001, M. Nielsen entre en fonction comme réviseur de textes du European Service Network qui publie plusieurs revues et ouvrages pour la Commission européenne à Bruxelles. Il a également écrit pour Europemedia.net et pour plusieurs publications de la Toile d'Internet sur tout un éventail de sujets, dont le tourisme, la technologie de l'information et la recherche dans l'Union européenne. En 2003, il a obtenu un mastère de politique internationale. Il a en projet un nouveau livre sur le thème de la communication dans le domaine du tourisme.

William J. Gaillard

Directeur de la communication institutionnelle, IATA

M. Gaillard est directeur de la communication institutionnelle de l'Association du transport aérien international depuis 1994. Né à Paris en 1950, il a fait ses études supérieures en France (Institut d'études politiques, Paris), en Italie, en Suisse et aux États-Unis (Université de Harvard), où il a commencé sa carrière comme professeur d'université. Avant de rejoindre l'IATA, M. Gaillard avait occupé en seize ans divers postes de direction des relations extérieures et de l'information à la Commission européenne et à l'Organisation des Nations Unies avec des lieux d'affectation en Europe, au Moyen-Orient et aux États-Unis.

Mustapha Elalaoui

Président-directeur général, groupe Strategic Communications

M. Elalaoui est président-directeur général du groupe Strategic Communications, qui a son siège à la Cité des médias de Dubaï dans les Émirats arabes unis. Ce groupe sert de banc d'essai aux institutions des secteurs public et privé et joue le rôle de réservoir à idées pour les responsables politiques et autres décideurs de haut rang. Avant ses fonctions actuelles, il était président-directeur général de la Sunco International Corporation qui a son siège dans l'État du Michigan aux États-Unis et qui s'occupe de promouvoir les investissements, le commerce et le tourisme.

Il a occupé plusieurs postes importants dans le secteur de la défense aux États-Unis et il a été sous-secrétaire au ministère des investissements à l'étranger, du commerce extérieur et du tourisme, président-directeur général de la National Coal Trade Company, directeur de cabinet du ministre de l'Énergie et des Mines et titulaire de diverses fonctions de haut responsable de l'État. M. Elalaoui a également été administrateur de la National Railway Company, de Royal Air Maroc, de la National Airport Authority, de la Société nationale d'aménagement de la baie d'Agadir, de la Capital Time Corporation, de la Talkomatic Corporation et de la Middle East & Mediterranean Tourism and Travel Association. En outre, il est l'auteur de plusieurs ouvrages sur le tourisme, l'administration publique et la gouvernance dans les pays en développement.

Mathieu Hoebrigs

Administrateur principal, unité Tourisme, Commission européenne

Avant de rejoindre la Commission européenne, Mathieu Hoeberigs, juriste et économiste de formation, a été chercheur et chargé de cours à l'Université de Nimègue, aux Pays-Bas. Dans cette ville, il a également été associé d'un cabinet d'avocats, consultant en affaires européennes et conseiller de l'Association des municipalités européennes.

Depuis 1983, M. Hoeberigs travaille à la Commission européenne où il s'est successivement occupé des différents domaines suivants : le service financier à la Direction générale XXV (Institutions financières et droit des sociétés), l'unité Services, services financiers compris, à la Direction générale IV (Concurrence), d'abord à l'unité Politique et gestion des contrats, puis, dans le cadre de la collaboration avec les pays tiers et les organisations internationales, comme membre de la Task Force PECO Copernicus, à la Direction générale XII (Sciences, recherche et développement), la gestion du secteur du sport qui a débouché sur la création de l'unité Sport à la Direction générale X (Information, communication, culture et audiovisuel), les représentations – campagnes d'information, relais et réseaux – à la Direction générale Éducation et culture, la politique de l'information, les représentations, les relais et les réseaux (Team Europe, Groupe Euro, Carrefour, Info.Europe, Urban Forums for sustainable development) à la Direction des relations interinstitutionnelles de la Direction générale Presse, et enfin les relations extérieures de l'unité Tourisme à la Direction générale Entreprises.

Richard Tibbott

Président, Locum Destination Consulting

M. Tibbott est reconnu au Royaume-Uni comme l'un des premiers spécialistes faisant autorité en matière de gestion du tourisme et des destinations. En 1970, il obtient le premier diplôme de maîtrise de loisirs et de tourisme décerné dans ce pays. En mai 2002, dans un article que publie l'Independent on Sunday, ses confrères le désignent comme premier professionnel du tourisme du Royaume-Uni. À l'heure actuelle, il est président de Locum Destination Consulting, qui offre des services de conseil en matière de stratégie, de tactique et de financement aux organismes qui aménagent et gèrent les destinations. Il s'agit de services adaptés aux besoins de divers types de destinations touristiques et à ceux des projets de rénovation de biens immobiliers.

M. Tibbott est spécialiste des conseils économiques et touristiques stratégiques pour les villes, les régions et les pays et pour de grands projets de mise en valeur de destinations du Royaume-Uni et d'Europe concernant des centres d'intérêt, des hôtels, des stations, des musées et des destinations ayant plusieurs atouts. Il a conseillé la Pologne pour l'élaboration d'une stratégie touristique quinquennale et plusieurs autres ministères du Tourisme des pays d'Europe centrale et orientale au fur et à mesure de leur transition vers l'économie de marché. Récemment, M. Tibbott a joué un rôle essentiel dans la définition des stratégies touristiques de l'Angleterre et de la Grande-Bretagne. Ses équipes ont ainsi travaillé au niveau régional pour l'Angleterre, le pays de Galles et l'Écosse et pour des ensembles urbains comme Londres, Manchester, Liverpool, Cardiff et Belfast.

L'activité de conseil de M. Tibbott bénéficie de sa vaste expérience de gérant réputé d'un important portefeuille d'intérêts d'entreprises, dont la société du train-hôtel de luxe Royal Scotsman lauréat du prix de la Reine, Continental Waterways ou Continentale de croisières, une des premières sociétés de croisières en péniche-hôtel de luxe de France, et de la Windsor Royal Arcade (aménagement d'un quartier de boutiques spécialisées).

Stanislava Nikolova Blagoeva

Présidente, European Travel Trade Fairs Association

Mme Blagoeva est présidente de la European Travel Trade Fairs Association et chef d'exploitation de la société britannique ITE Group Plc, organisatrice réputée d'expositions sur les marchés naissants. Elle est titulaire d'une maîtrise de linguistique et de psychologie. Sa carrière professionnelle commence en 1984 à l'Académie des sciences de Bulgarie comme directrice des ventes, du marketing et des expositions de la maison d'édition. En 1994, Mme Blagoeva entre dans l'équipe d'ITE Ltd à son siège de Londres et elle participe au lancement et au maintien de quelques-uns des plus grands salons professionnels actuels de l'Europe centrale et orientale comme l'Exposition internationale du tourisme de Moscou (MITT), le Salon international de l'automobile de Moscou, le Salon international des sports de Moscou, le Salon international du bateau de Moscou, la Semaine russe du bâtiment, l'Exposition internationale du pétrole et du gaz de Moscou, ainsi que de manifestations de premier plan en Ukraine, au Kazakhstan, en Azerbaïdjan, en Turquie, en Bulgarie et en République tchèque. Elle est souvent invitée comme oratrice pour des conférences internationales consacrées aux problèmes du secteur des salons sur les marchés naissants.

Thomas Steinmetz

Président et éditeur, eTurbo News

M. Steinmetz est président et éditeur d'eTurbo News, publication novatrice donnant en ligne des nouvelles aux professionnels du voyage, une des premières à impression numérique à la demande du client. Il supervise l'ensemble des tâches (rédaction, marketing et ventes, diffusion et service clients) pour cette publication qui paraît du lundi au vendredi, exception faite des principaux jours fériés des États-Unis. eTurbo News offre actuellement le service Travel-Telegram pour les messages publicitaires et le service Travel Wire News pour les communiqués de presse. Avec 192 000 abonnés dans le monde entier, eTurbo News est devenue en moins de trois ans la principale publication des professionnels du voyage. En 2003, eTurbo News a été la publication officielle du Sommet mondial sur la paix par le tourisme qui s'est tenu à Genève.

Avant la création d'eTurbo News, M. Steinmetz a été spécialiste de la communication d'une société de marketing, représentant en Amérique du Nord pour le tourisme de la République d'Indonésie, président-directeur général de Unique Destination Asia et copropriétaire de Horizon Travel en Allemagne, où il devient un des premiers et des plus importants groupeurs de vols avant l'installation de la société aux États-Unis.

Rafeeuddin Ahmed

Représentant spécial de l'OMT auprès de l'Organisation des Nations Unies

M. Ahmed est le Représentant spécial de l'Organisation mondiale du tourisme auprès de l'Organisation des Nations Unies à New York. Il est également Conseiller spécial auprès de la Directrice exécutive du Fonds de développement des Nations Unies pour la femme (UNIFEM). De février à juillet 2000, il est Conseiller spécial auprès du Secrétaire général de l'ONU pour l'Iraq. Après ses études à l'Université du Panjab à Lahore, au Pakistan, et à la Fletcher School of Law and Diplomacy aux États-Unis, M. Ahmed entre au service diplomatique du Pakistan et il est affecté à Beijing, au Caire, à Ottawa, à New York et à Islamabad. Au cours de sa longue carrière au sein des Nations Unies, il est Secrétaire du Conseil économique et social de l'ONU et Directeur du Département des affaires économiques et sociales, Assistant exécutif et Chef de cabinet du Secrétaire général de l'ONU, Secrétaire général adjoint aux affaires politiques, à la tutelle et à la décolonisation et Secrétaire général adjoint aux affaires économiques et sociales internationales. Il y a aussi occupé d'autres postes de haut rang.

Martin Brackenbury

Président de la Fédération internationale des tour-opérateurs

M. Brackenbury est président de la Fédération internationale des tour-opérateurs (IFTO), président de la Federation of Tour Operators du Royaume-Uni (après en avoir été vice-président), directeur de Classic Collection Holidays et professeur à l'Université de Nottingham. Il est également associé gérant de Brackenbury & Partners, associé de la société de gestion de l'environnement Travelwatch et membre de la Royal Geographic Society.

M. Brackenbury fait ses études à l'Université de Cambridge. Après une période dans l'industrie, les médias et la banque, il rejoint un cabinet-conseil en gestion dont il devient un des principaux associés. En 1980, il entre chez Thompson Holidays en qualité de directeur et en 1989, il est promu administrateur du Thompson Travel Group, première organisation de voyages du Royaume-Uni. Géant novateur du tourisme émetteur ce groupe finit par intégrer des agents de voyages, des voyagistes, des compagnies aériennes, des hôtels, des bateaux de croisière et des prestataires de services d'escale. M. Brackenbury en reste administrateur jusqu'à l'introduction du groupe en bourse en 1998.

La même année, M. Brackenbury devient président du Panorama Holiday Group vendu par la suite à Airtours Plc, où il est administrateur pendant trois ans. Il préside la société de voyages d'aventure Exodus Holiday. En 1998, il est invité à devenir le premier directeur du Christel De Haan Institute in Travel & Tourism de l'Université de Nottingham, qui s'occupe surtout du poids économique du tourisme.

C'est en 1990 qu'il est nommé président de l'IFTO. Il a été membre du conseil d'administration de l'ABTA pendant six ans et président des Membres affiliés de l'OMT pendant huit ans.

Au cours des vingt-cinq dernières années, M. Brackenbury a été chargé de missions dans plus de quarante pays.

Rok V. Klancnik

Chef du comité organisateur de la conférence TOURCOM

M. en juin 2002. À ce titre, il est chargé des campagnes de communication sur la quinzième session de l'Assemblée générale de l'OMT à Beijing, sur le projet « Le tourisme, source d'enrichissement et sur la transformation de l'OMT en institution spécialisée des Nations Unies. Il a aussi préparé la troisième édition du manuel Shining in the Media Spotlight. Chef du comité organisateur, il a surveillé la préparation et le déroulement de la conférence TOURCOM. Slovène de naissance, M. Klancnik a travaillé avec le Conseil du tourisme de Slovénie dès sa création en 1996. En tant que directeur de la communication de ce Conseil, il s'est occupé de ses campagnes de communication lors des salons professionnels et lors d'importantes manifestations ou événements internationaux comme l'Exposition universelle de Lisbonne en 1998, les Jeux olympiques de Sydney, la Coupe du monde de football en République de Corée et le premier sommet entre le président des États-Unis, George W. Bush, et le président de la Fédération de Russie, Vladimir Poutine, en Slovénie. En qualité d'orateur ou d'organisateur, il est intervenu dans des conférences et des manifestations de promotion dans une quarantaine pays d'Europe, du Moyen-Orient et d'Asie, ainsi qu'aux États-Unis et en Australie.

M. Klancnik, titulaire d'un diplôme universitaire de sciences politiques et de relations internationales, a travaillé comme journaliste au quotidien Delo et à l'agence de presse de Slovénie. Il s'est spécialisé en journalisme et en communication à l'Université du Tennessee et a participé à de nombreux séminaires et stages dans les domaines de la communication, du journalisme, de la gestion et du marketing en Slovénie et dans des institutions internationales comme le Conseil de l'Europe. En qualité de journaliste, il est rédacteur en chef des Nouvelles de l'OMT et il écrit régulièrement des articles pour la presse sur des sujets liés au tourisme international, aux relations publiques, au marketing et à la stratégie de marque.